A G Spelding

**Spalding's official base ball guide**

A G Spelding

**Spalding's official base ball guide**

ISBN/EAN: 9783741176364

Manufactured in Europe, USA, Canada, Australia, Japa

Cover: Foto ©Stingray / pixelio.de

Manufactured and distributed by brebook publishing software (www.brebook.com)

A G Spelding

**Spalding's official base ball guide**

# THE OFFICIAL BALL FOR 1885.

As certain unprincipled manufacturers of *inferior* goods are endeavoring to convey the impression that other than the "Spalding League Ball" has been adopted as the official ball for 1885, we print the following fac-simile letter fr m the Secretary of the National League, which explains itself. At every match game played under League rules, this ball must be used.

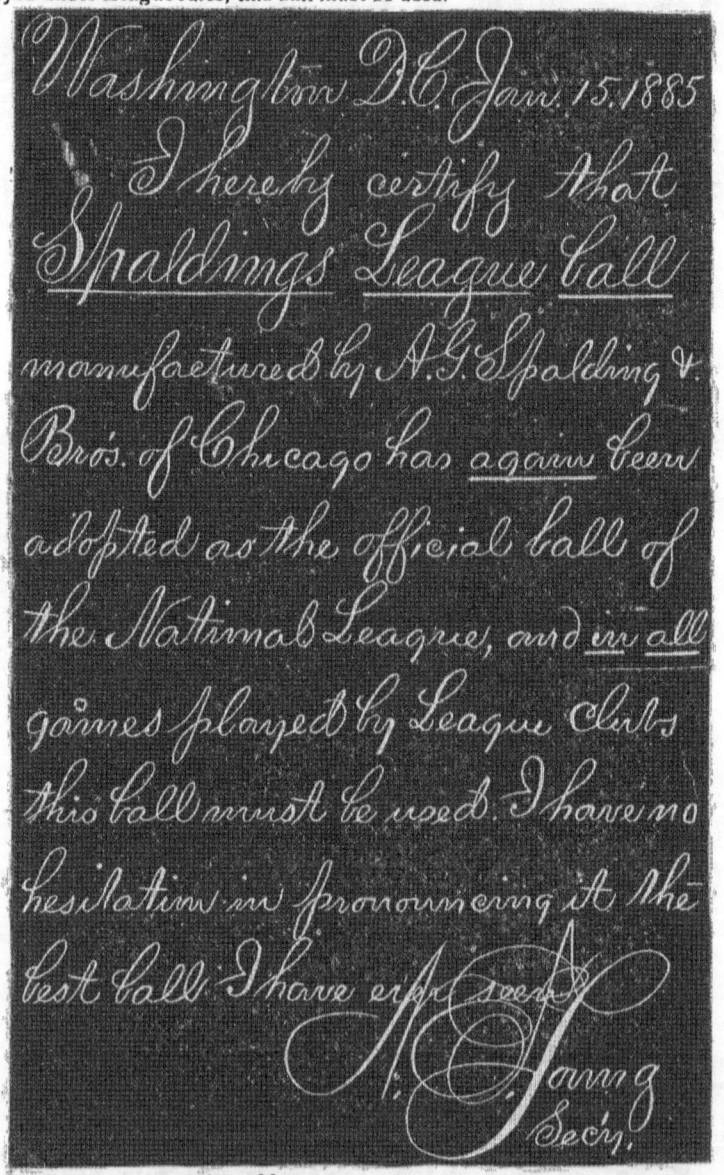

*Washington DC Jan. 15, 1885*

*I hereby certify that Spaldings League ball manufactured by A. G. Spalding & Bros. of Chicago has again been adopted as the official ball of the National League, and in all games played by League Clubs this ball must be used. I have no hesitation in pronouncing it the best ball I have ever seen.*

*N. E. Young, Sec'y.*

For further information address

## A. G. SPALDING & BROS.

108 Madison Street, CHICAGO.      241 Broadway, NEW YORK

THE LARGEST SPORTING GOODS HOUSE IN AMERICA.

# A. G. SPALDING & BROS.,

MANUFACTURERS, IMPORTERS AND DEALERS IN

## General Sporting Goods,

## GUNS & GUN ACCOUTREMENTS,

### FISHING TACKLE,

### Base Ball Supplies,

Lawn Tennis, Cricket, Croquet, Ice and Roller Skates, Foot Balls, Lacrosse, Polo, Cutlery.

Gymnasium, Theatrical and General Sporting Goods.

Send for Illustrated Catalogue, designating kinds of Goods wanted. Address,

### A. G. SPALDING & BROS.,

108 Madison Street, CHICAGO.   241 Broadway, NEW YORK.

# OUR PUBLICATIONS.

The popular encouragement given to the pursuit of Athletic Sports, Recreative Amusements, Gymnastic Exercises, etc., and the comparative scarcity of mediums of instruction on these subjects, suggested the publication of our *Library of Athletic Sports*. The benefits of Athletic and other manly exercises, from an educational as well as from a moral and recreative point of view, are now so generally recognized that the right method of promoting man's physical welfare should be readily accessible.

The aim of the various manuals or hand-books constituting our *Athletic Series* will be to educate the readers in each particular game or sport in which they may be interested. A long experience in sporting matters induces a belief that thorough descriptions accompanied by the necessary illustrations, will enable those who by force of circumstances are deprived of the opportunity of obtaining practical instruction or accurate knowledge, to become proficient without such instruction.

The following list includes those already published as well as those that are under way. Those unfinished will be rapidly completed and placed on sale at all news stands throughout the country.

No. 1. Spalding's Official Base Ball Guide..................Price, 10c
" 2. " " League Book...................... " 10c.
" 3. " Hand Book of Pitching................... " 10c.
" 4. " " " Batting................... " 10c.
" 5. " " " Base Running and Fielding " 10c.
" 6. " Cricket Guide ..................... In Press, " 10c.
" 7. " Lacrosse and Football Rules..... " " 10c.
" 8. " Lawn Tennis Manual............ " " 25c.
" 9. " Manual of Roller Skating........Completed " 25c.
" 10. " " Croquet........................ " 15c.
" 11. " " Manly Sports.................. " 25c.
" 12. " " Bicycling..............In Press, " 25c.
" 13. " Hand Book of Sporting Rules and Training, " 25c.

Any of the above books mailed upon receipt of price. Orders for the books now in press will be received, and the books mailed as soon as issued.

## OUR JOURNALS.

To meet a general want in the sporting world, we have issued a series of JOURNALS, which are replete with information in regard to the various sports; the utensils used, their description, cost, etc., are fully set forth. With the aid of these JOURNALS those interested in any particular line of sporting, games or pastimes, can readily inform themselves in all the particulars of each amusement.

We shall be pleased to mail a sample copy free to any address upon application.

Spalding's Journal of Summer Sports.
" " Field Sports.
" Angler.
" Bicycle Journal.
" Cutlery Journal.

# SPALDING'S
# BASE BALL GUIDE

—AND—

## Official League Book for 1885.

A COMPLETE HAND BOOK OF THE NATIONAL GAME
OF BASE BALL.

CONTAINING REVIEWS OF THE VARIOUS ASSOCIATION SEASONS
—LEAGUE, AMERICAN, NORTHWESTERN AND EASTERN
LEAGUES, WITH SPECIAL ARTICLES ON CLUB MAN-
AGEMENT, ON PITCHING, ON BATTING, ON FIELD-
ING, ON BASE RUNNING AND OTHER
BASE BALL TOPICS OF INTEREST.

TOGETHER WITH THE

### SEASON'S AVERAGES OF THE FOUR PROFESSIONAL ASSOCIATIONS FOR 1884,

AND ALSO

### The College Club Statistics for 1884,

ADDED TO WHICH IS THE

### COMPLETE OFFICIAL LEAGUE RECORD FOR 1884,

Including a Synopsis of the Amended Constitution, the Playing Rules in
their Revised Form; Official Record of all League Games and
Players; and the Official Schedule of League Games for 1885.

As adopted at the Special Meetings of the League, Nov. 18,'84 and March,'85.

PUBLISHED BY
A. G. SPALDING & BROS.,
NEW YORK AND CHICAGO.

Entered according to Act of Congress, in the year of 1885, by A. G. Spalding & Bros., in the
Office of the Librarian of Congress at Washington.

# PUBLISHERS' NOTICE.

"Spalding's Base Ball Guide" again greets the base ball public with the official records of America's national game. First issued in 1877, it has grown in popularity, has been enlarged and improved from year to year, and is now the recognized authority upon base ball matters. The statistics contained in the "Guide" can be relied upon, nearly all of them having been compiled from official records.

The "Guide" has attained such a size—176 pages—as to preclude the possibility of publishing in the same issue the League Constitution in full, and other interesting League matter. We are therefore compelled, in addition, to publish the "Official League Book," which contains only official League matter as furnished by Secretary Young, including the League Constitution in full.

Copies of the "Guide" or "League Book," will be mailed to any address upon receipt of ten cents each. Trade orders supplied through the News Companies, or direct from the publishers.

**A. G. SPALDING & BROS.,**
108 Madison St.,       241 Broadway,
CHICAGO.              NEW YORK.

WASHINGTON, D. C., March 7, 1885.
By the authority vested in me, I do hereby certify that Messrs. A. G. Spalding & Bros., of Chicago, Ill., have been granted the *exclusive* right to publish the Official League Book for 1885.    N. E. YOUNG,
*Secretary National League of Professional Base Ball Clubs.*

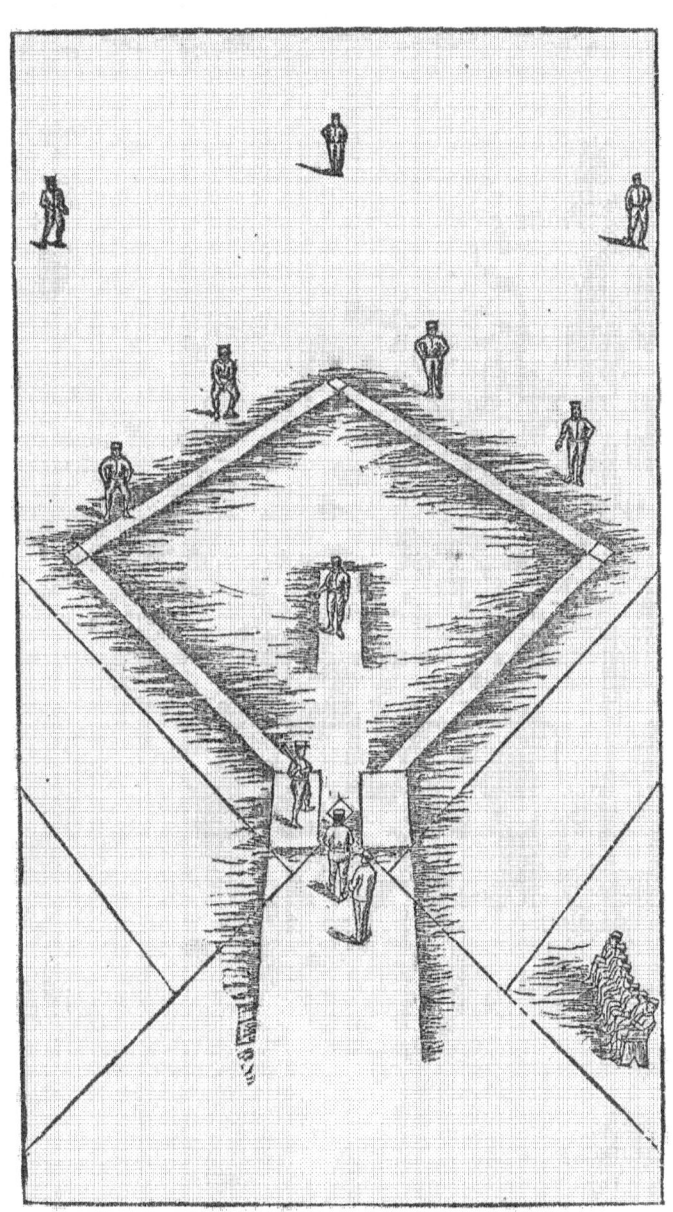

BASE BALL FIELD.

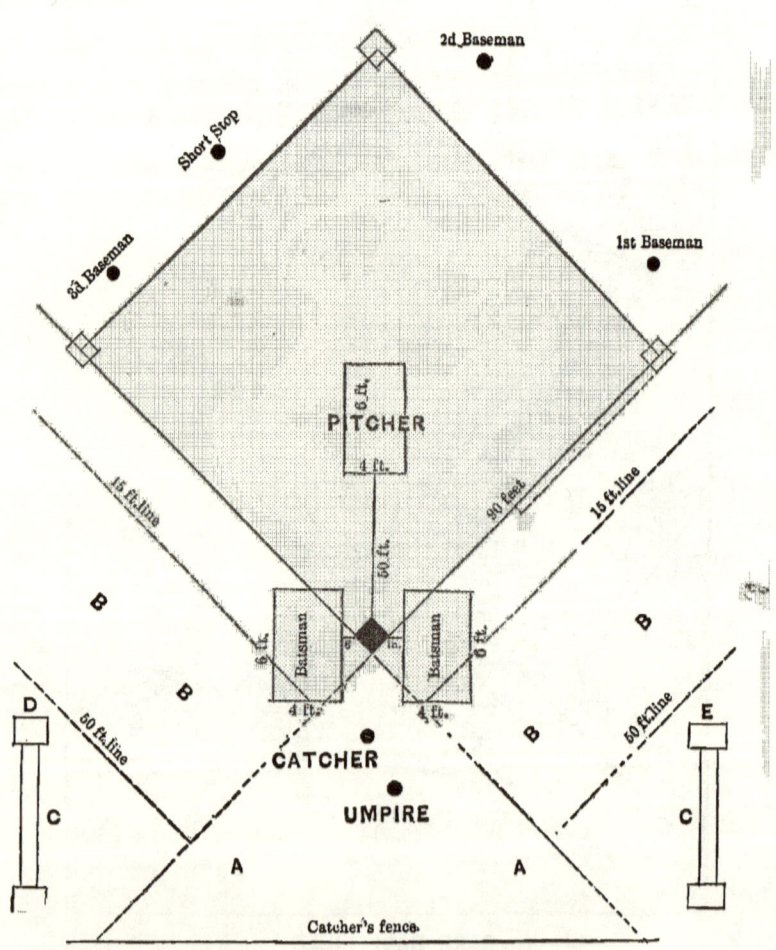

A. A. A.—Ground reserved for Umpire, Batsman and Catcher.
B. B. B.—Ground reserved for Captain and Assistant.
C.—Players' Bench.   D.—Visiting Players' Bat Rack.
E.—Home Players' Bat Rack.

## INTRODUCTION.

It is now over a quarter of a century since the game of base ball became popularized as the game of games for American youth; and within that period it has so extended itself in its sphere of operations that it is now the permanently established national field game of America. Unlike many sports taken up by our people, which have ridden into general favor on the wave of a public furore, base ball has come to stay. Not even the great war of the rebellion could check its progress to any great extent; in fact, in one way—through the national army—it led to its being planted in a Southern clime, and now base ball can be said to "know no North, no South, no East, no West." It has even crossed the border into Canada, and in addition, like cricket, has found its way at times to foreign shores. Within the past fifteen years, too, the national game has burst its youthful bonds, and from the amateur period of its early growth it has entered upon the more advanced condition of its career under the professional system, which system has developed its innate attractions within a single decade to an extent it otherwise could not have reached in thrice the amount of time. In 1871 the first professional association was established, and now, in 1885, we find the professional fraternity, after their passage through the Red Sea of gambling abuses so thoroughly controlled in the interests of honest play by the existing professional organizations, that the evils which attach themselves to professionalism, in sports generally, no longer find space for existence within the arena of professional base ball playing. In fact, our national game now stands alone as a field sport in the one important fact that it is the only public sport in which professional exemplars take part which possesses the power to attract its thousands of spectators without the extrinsic aid of gambling.

At horse races, athletic contests and every other public sport in vogue, if the pool-selling and book-making of the gambling fraternity are prevented, nearly all the attraction which draws most of the public patronage to such sports is removed. This fact was strikingly illustrated in New York during the season of 1882; for at the Jerome Park races that year, when an attempt was made to stop the book-making and public betting, the attendance dwindled down to a few hundred, while, with the betting in operation, the attendance reached five or six thousand a day. It was the same at the last great international pedestrian contest at Madison Square Garden in New York, the prevention of the pool-gambling feature making the meeting a financial failure. At the professional base ball matches for championship honors, however, especially on League Club Grounds, where pool-selling and all forms of open public betting are prohibited—thousands of spectators are attracted to the grounds solely by the excitement of the sport itself. This is a peculiarity of our national game which fully proves, not only the intrinsic merit of the game itself, but what a suitable sport it is for the patronage of the best classes of the community.

Another thing worthy of remark is the eminent fitness of the game of base ball for us Americans. It is very questionable whether there is any public sport in the civilized portion of the world so eminently fitted for the people it was made for as the American national game of base ball. In every respect is it an outdoor sport admirably adapted for our mercurial population. It is full of excitement, is quickly played, and it not only requires vigor of constitution and a healthy physique, but manly courage, steady nerve, plenty of pluck, and considerable powers of judgment to excel in it. Then, too, look at it in the light of its special features as a game for the development of athletic skill.

What can present a more attractive picture to the lover of out door sports than the scene presented at a base ball match between two trained professional teams competing for championship honors, in which every point of play is so well looked after in the field that it is only by some extra display of skill at the bat, or a lucky act of base-running at an opportune moment, that a single run is obtained in a full nine innings game? To watch the progress of a contest in which only one run is required to secure an important lead, and while the game is in such a position to see hit after hit made to the field, either in the form of high fly balls splendidly caught on the run by some active out-fielder, or a sharp ground hit beautifully picked up in the in-field, and swiftly and accurately thrown to the right baseman in time, is to see the perfection of base ball fielding, and that surpasses the fielding of every other known game of ball. Then there is the intense excitement incident to a contest in which one side is endeavoring to escape a " whitewash," while the other side as eagerly strives to retain their lead of a single run; and with the game in such position a three base hit sends the runner to third base before a single hand is out, only to see the hit left unrewarded by the expected run, owing to the telling effect of the strategic pitching, and the splendid field support given it. Add to this the other excitement of a high hit over the out-fielder's head, made while two or three of the bases are occupied, with the result of a tie score or the securing of a lead at a critical point of the game, and a culmination of attractive features is reached, incidental to no other field game in vogue. If it is considered, too, that the pursuit of base ball is that of a healthy, recreative exercise, alike for the mind and body, suitable to all classes of our people, and to the adult as well as the mere boy, there can be no longer room for surprise that such a game should reach the unprecedented popularity that the American game of base ball has attained.

## THE PROFESSIONAL SEASON OF 1884.

The professional season of 1884 was decidedly the most exceptional one, in its general characteristics, since the establishment of the National League. In the first place, it was made specially noteworthy from the fact that the largest number of professional clubs yet organized participated in the championship contests of the season, and as a consequence the greatest number of professional games were played ever yet recorded in a single season. Then, too, it was marked by the peculiar circumstances of the existence of a rival professional association of clubs, which was obnoxious to the interests of honest play in the ranks; inasmuch as the association in question opened its doors to the employment of a class of contract-breakers whom the other association had endeavored to weed out from their midst. In the multiplicity of clubs, however, there proved to be less profit to the stock companies in the professional arena in 1884 than there was when fewer competitors were in the market, and the result was that only a minority of the clubs of the two leading associations of the year had a surplus of funds in their treasuries at the end of the season, while the rival organization above referred to was taught the costly lesson that it does not pay to work in any way against the policy of governing all professional clubs in the interests of thoroughly honest service, in every respect in the club ranks.

Another year's experience of the working of the Arbitration Committee, and the "national agreement" system proved even more than before, the great benefits accruing from both the control of the committee and the rules of the "agreement." In fact, the national agreement has been shown to be the very bulwark of honest play in the ranks, and the only foundation on which professional stock companies can be built up with any hope of pecuniary success.

As in 1883, the season's championship campaigns in the League and American arenas were marked by discreditable disturbances on several club ball fields, which were the result of a failure to strictly enforce those association rules of both organizations, which required each club " to furnish sufficient police force upon its own grounds to preserve order." It goes without saying that the game cannot be played without an Umpire; nor can it be successfully played without the Umpire is one suited for the position; and such a man, if found, will not be likely to accept the position unless fully insured against the insults of a partisan crowd, and against the "kicking" propensities of badly managed teams. It is a conceded fact, too, that integrity of character, sound judgment, and thorough impartiality as essentials in Umpires and umpiring, are vital necessities of the game, and the basis of its very existence. But how are these essentials to be made available unless the position of Umpire is itself properly protected and guarded from the assaults of club "heelers" and betting roughs? These facts have been forcibly presented to the officials of the several professional associations by each season's experience, and yet but little advance had been made toward an improved condition of things up to 1885.

## THE LEAGUE SEASON OF 1884.

The League Club season was opened earlier in the East in 1884 than in the West, the New York team beginning practice as early as March 25, their first game being that with their reserve nine on March 29, which the regular nine won by 6 to 0 The same day the Providence Club opened play in a game with the Brown University nine, which the professionals won by 10 to 9 only. The Boston Club played their opening game on April 1, when they defeated their reserve nine in a five inning game by 31 to 1. The Philadelphia Club, too, opened play the same day with their reserves, whom they defeated by 14 to 1. On April 2 the Cleveland team took the field in a game with their reserve nine, and found difficulty in winning by 10 to 9. The Buffalo team opened play at Baltimore on April 7 and the contest proved to be exceptionally fine, the League team winning by 1 to 0 only. The same day the Detroit team opened at Richmond, in a match with the Virginia nine, which the League team won by 6 to 5 only. It was not until April 17 that the Chicago team took the field, and then they defeated their reserves by 10 to 3. During April all the League Clubs had the reserve team fever badly, and they calculated on deriving considerable benefit from the plan of keeping a reserve nine in the field, pecuniarily as well as in other respects. But the scheme was not worked up well and it failed to meet the high expectations formed of it. The idea is a good one, but it wants to be better developed than it was last spring.

The championship season was preceded by the customary series of exhibition games between the League and American Association Clubs, and the close of the championship season was followed by more such games; but during the summer campaign not half a dozen were played. The Clubs of the two associations played eighty-six exhibition games together during 1884, of which the League Clubs won fifty-eight and the American Clubs twenty-six, two being drawn. The record of these exhibition games is as follows:

LEAGUE VS. AMERICAN.

| | | |
|---|---|---|
| April | 5, New York vs Metropolitan, New York...................... | 7—3 |
| " | 7, Athletic vs. Philadelphia, Athletic ground................ | 9—8 |
| " | 7, Cleveland vs. Metropolitan, New York.............. .. | 7—0 |
| " | 7, Buffalo vs. Baltimore, Baltimore........................ | 1—0 |
| " | 7, Providence vs. Washington, Washington............... | 10—3 |
| " | 8, Metropolitan vs. Cleveland, New York (8 innings)........ | 4—3 |
| " | 10, Philadelphia vs. Athletic, Philadelphia ground............ | 7—1 |
| " | 10, Providence vs. Baltimore, Baltimore... ............... | 13—4 |
| " | 10, Washington vs. Detroit, Washington.................... | 6—0 |
| " | 11, Detroit vs. Washington, Washington... ............... | 6—0 |
| " | 11, Providence vs. Baltimore, Baltimore..................... | 5—2 |
| " | 12, Providence vs. Baltimore, Baltimore..................... | 7—1 |
| " | 12, Cleveland vs. Brooklyn, Brooklyn....................... | 5—2 |
| " | 12, Detroit vs. Washington, Washington..................... | 5—1 |
| " | 12, Athletic vs. Philadelphia, Athletic ground.............. | 5—4 |
| " | 12, New York vs. Metropolitan, New York.................. | 2—1 |
| " | 14, Brooklyn vs. Cleveland, Brooklyn...................... | 10—4 |
| " | 14, Metropolitan vs. New York, New York................. | 9—7 |
| " | 14, Baltimore vs. Detroit, Baltimore....................... | 10—3 |
| " | 14, Philadelphia vs. Athletic, Philadelphia ground........... | 17—6 |
| " | 15, Baltimore vs. Detroit, Baltimore (5 innings)............. | 6—4 |
| " | 16, New York vs. Brooklyn, New York.................... | 10—2 |
| " | 16, Athletic vs. Philadelphia, Athletic ground............... | 5—3 |
| " | 17, Philadelphia vs. Brooklyn, Brooklyn.................... | 8—1 |
| " | 17, Metropolitan vs. New York, New York................. | 4—1 |
| " | 17, Buffalo vs. Washington, Washington.................... | 4—8 |
| " | 17, Detroit vs. Pittsburg, Pittsburg......................... | 3—2 |
| " | 18, Pittsburg vs. Detroit, Pittsburg.. ...................... | 12—7 |
| " | 18, New York vs. Brooklyn, Brooklyn..................... | 8—0 |
| " | 18, Boston vs. Metropolitan, New York.................... | 6—0 |
| " | 18, Cleveland vs. Baltimore, Baltimore..................... | 10—1 |
| " | 19, Metropolitan vs. New York............................ | 6—4 |
| " | 19, Providence vs. Brooklyn, Brooklyn..................... | 15—0 |
| " | 19, Detroit vs. Pittsburg, Pittsburg......................... | 7—4 |
| " | 19, Athletic vs. Philadelphia, Philadelphia ground........... | 2—1 |
| " | 19, Baltimore vs. Cleveland, Baltimore...................... | 8—5 |
| " | 21, Brooklyn vs. Providence, Brooklyn (7 innings) (f-9-0)..... | 10—8 |
| " | 21, Philadelphia vs. Athletic, Athletic ground............... | 18—11 |
| " | 21, Baltimore vs. Cleveland, Baltimore..................... | 5—3 |
| " | 21, Detroit vs. Indianapolis, Indianapolis.................... | 12—8 |
| " | 21, Boston vs. Metropolitan, New York .................... | 5—2 |
| " | 22, Metropolitan vs. Boston, New York ................ | 5—2 |
| " | 22, Buffalo vs. Baltimore, Baltimore........................ | 12—8 |
| " | 23, Boston vs. Brooklyn, W. P............................ | 15—4 |
| " | 23, Providence vs. Metropolitan, New York................. | 7—2 |
| " | 23, Buffalo vs. Baltimore, Baltimore....................... | 9—5 |
| " | 23, Philadelphia vs. Athletic, Philadelphia ground .......... | 10—1 |
| " | 24, Philadelphia vs. Baltimore, Philadelphia................ | 4—3 |
| " | 24, Boston vs. Brooklyn, W. P............................ | 11—5 |
| " | 24, Providence vs. Metropolitan, New York................. | 13—6 |
| " | 24, Cleveland vs. Washington, Washington.................. | 9—5 |
| " | 25, Buffalo vs. Brooklyn, W. P............................ | 13—3 |
| " | 25, Providence vs. Metropolitan, New York................. | 14—2 |
| " | 26, Buffalo vs. Brooklyn, W. P............................ | 3—2 |

April 26, New York vs. Metropolitan, New York................. 8—4
" 26, Athletic vs. Philadelphia, Athletic ground.............. 9—5
" 26, Cleveland vs. Washington, Washington................. 9—6
" 28, Boston vs. Metropolitan, Boston (10 innings)........... 4—3
" 28, Philadelphia vs. Athletic, Philadelphia ground......... 12—6
" 28, Chicago vs. Indianapolis, Indianapolis................. 8—4
" 28, Baltimore vs. New York, Baltimore.................... 8—3
" 28, Cleveland vs. Pittsburg, Pittsburg..................... 19—6
" 29, Detroit vs. Brooklyn, Brooklyn........................ 19—1
" 29, Metropolitan vs. New York, New York................. 14—6
" 29, Pittsburg vs. Cleveland, Pittsburg..................... 6—4
" 30, Brooklyn vs. Detroit, Brooklyn........................ 14—6
" 30, New York vs. Metropolitan, New York................. 13—0
" 30, Philadelphia vs. Athletic, Athletic ground.............. 9—4
July 25, Chicago vs. Toledo, Toledo.......................... 10—8
Sept. 15, "     "  Louisville, Louisville................... 11—7
" 15, Cincinnati vs. Boston, Cincinnati..................... 10—3
" 22, Indianapolis vs. Boston, Indianapolis.................. 8—7
Oct. 13, Providence vs. Allegheny, Pittsburg.................. 9—0
" 14, Philadelphia vs. Athletic, Athletic ground.............. 6—4
" 16,     "     "     " Athletic ground.............. 12—9
" 16, Boston vs. Cincinnati, Boston......................... 10—0
" 16, Metropolitan vs. New York, New York (5 innings)...... 5—5
" 17,   "     "     "     "     " (6 innings)...... 9—8
" 17, Cincinnati vs. Boston, Boston......................... 5—2
" 18, New York vs. Metropolitan, New York.................. 9—7
" 18, Providence vs. Cincinnati, Providence.................. 4—1
" 18, Philadelphia vs. Athletic, Philadelphia ground.......... 13—5
" 20, Cincinnati vs. Providence, Providence.................. 2—2
" 23, Providence vs. Metropolitan, New York................. 6—0
" 24,   "     "     "     "     " (7 innings)...... 3—1
" 25,   "     "     "     "     " (6 innings)...... 12—2

The summary of the above record is as follows:

### LEAGUE VICTORIES.

|  | Louisville. | Toledo. | Cincinnati. | Indianapolis. | Allegheny. | Washington. | Baltimore. | Athletic. | Brooklyn. | Metropolitan. | Games Won. |
|---|---|---|---|---|---|---|---|---|---|---|---|
| Providence........... | 0 | 0 | 1 | 0 | 1 | 1 | 3 | 0 | 1 | 6 | 13 |
| Philadelphia.......... | 0 | 0 | 0 | 0 | 0 | 0 | 1 | 9 | 1 | 0 | 11 |
| New York............ | 0 | 0 | 0 | 0 | 0 | 0 | 0 | 0 | 2 | 5 | 7 |
| Buffalo .............. | 0 | 0 | 0 | 0 | 0 | 1 | 3 | 2 | 0 | 0 | 6 |
| Boston............... | 0 | 0 | 1 | 0 | 0 | 0 | 0 | 0 | 2 | 3 | 6 |
| Cleveland............ | 0 | 0 | 0 | 2 | 1 | 0 | 1 | 1 | 0 | 1 | 6 |
| Detroit............... | 0 | 0 | 0 | 1 | 2 | 2 | 0 | 0 | 1 | 0 | 6 |
| Chicago.............. | 1 | 1 | 0 | 1 | 0 | 0 | 0 | 0 | 0 | 0 | 3 |
| Games Lost ......... | 1 | 1 | 2 | 2 | 4 | 6 | 8 | 9 | 10 | 15 | 58 |

## AMERICAN VICTORIES.

|              | Providence | Boston | Philadelphia | Cleveland | Detroit | New York | Games Won |
|--------------|------------|--------|--------------|-----------|---------|----------|-----------|
| Metropolitan | 0          | 1      | 0            | 1         | 0       | 5        | 7         |
| Baltimore    | 0          | 0      | 0            | 2         | 2       | 1        | 5         |
| Athletic     | 0          | 0      | 5            | 0         | 0       | 0        | 5         |
| Brooklyn     | 1          | 0      | 0            | 1         | 1       | 0        | 3         |
| Cincinnati   | 0          | 2      | 0            | 0         | 0       | 0        | 2         |
| Allegheny    | 0          | 0      | 0            | 1         | 1       | 0        | 2         |
| Indianapolis | 0          | 1      | 0            | 0         | 0       | 0        | 1         |
| Washington   | 0          | 0      | 0            | 0         | 1       | 0        | 1         |
| Games Lost   | 1          | 4      | 5            | 5         | 5       | 6        | 26        |

To show the difference between the records of 1883 and 1884 in these League and American exhibition games, we append the record of the victories scored by the Clubs of each Association over the other in 1883.

## LEAGUE VICTORIES.

|              | Columbus | Louisville | Allegheny | St. Louis | Cincinnati | Athletic | Baltimore | Metropolitan | Games Won |
|--------------|----------|------------|-----------|-----------|------------|----------|-----------|--------------|-----------|
| Cleveland    | 0        | 0          | 3         | 2         | 3          | 1        | 4         | 3            | 16        |
| New York     | 0        | 0          | 0         | 1         | 1          | 0        | 1         | 9            | 12        |
| Boston       | 0        | 0          | 0         | 0         | 0          | 0        | 4         | 5            | 9         |
| Providence   | 0        | 0          | 1         | 3         | 3          | 1        | 0         | 0            | 8         |
| Buffalo      | 0        | 0          | 3         | 0         | 0          | 3        | 1         | 0            | 7         |
| Philadelphia | 0        | 0          | 0         | 0         | 0          | 5        | 2         | 0            | 7         |
| Chicago      | 1        | 0          | 0         | 2         | 1          | 0        | 0         | 0            | 4         |
| Detroit      | 0        | 2          | 0         | 1         | 0          | 0        | 0         | 0            | 3         |
| Games Lost   | 1        | 2          | 7         | 9         | 8          | 10       | 12        | 17           | 66        |

## AMERICAN VICTORIES.

|              | Boston | Chicago | Detroit | Buffalo | Providence | Cleveland | Philadelphia | New York | Games Won |
|--------------|--------|---------|---------|---------|------------|-----------|--------------|----------|-----------|
| St. Louis    | 0      | 0       | 1       | 0       | 1          | 3         | 0            | 2        | 7         |
| Metropolitan | 1      | 0       | 0       | 0       | 2          | 0         | 0            | 3        | 6         |
| Athletic     | 0      | 0       | 0       | 0       | 0          | 0         | 4            | 0        | 4         |
| Cincinnati   | 0      | 2       | 0       | 1       | 0          | 0         | 0            | 0        | 3         |
| Baltimore    | 0      | 0       | 1       | 1       | 0          | 1         | 0            | 0        | 3         |
| Games Lost   | 1      | 2       | 2       | 2       | 3          | 4         | 4            | 5        | 23        |

## THE CHAMPIONSHIP GAMES.

The feature of the series of games between the Clubs of the two organizations, was the marked success of the League champion team of Providence over the American champion Metropolitans, in their October games. In April the Providence team defeated the "Mets" by 7 to 2, 13 to 6 and 14 to 2 in three successive games. In October, when both were champion teams, the Providence defeated the "Mets" by 6 to 0, 3 to 1 and 12 to 2, thus winning six successive games during the season by a total of 55 runs to 13. The only American team that won a game from Providence in 1884 was the Brooklyn team. The Cincinnatis got a drawn game—2 to 2—but that was the nearest they could get to a victory. The Cincinnatis in their series with the Boston team, however, won two out of three. In the series between the Philadelphia and Athletic Clubs, the former won nine games to the latter's five, the total runs being 128 to 74 in favor of the League team, a worse defeat than the Athletics sustained in 1883, when they won the American Association championship. In the series between the New York League team and the Metropolitans, each won five games, one being drawn, New York leading in total runs by 70 to 62.

The League championship season of 1884 began on May 1, when the New York team defeated the Chicagos at the Polo Grounds by 15 to 3; Philadelphia whipped Detroit at Philadelphia by 13 to 2; Boston beat Buffalo at Boston by 5 to 3 only, and Cleveland defeated Providence by 2 to 1 at Providence. The month of May opened most promisingly for New York, but it proved to be only a dash for the lead at the start, the team not proving to be harmonious or united enough to hold their lead. Up to May 17 they had not lost a game out of a dozen played, but the close of the month saw them third in the race, Boston being first and Providence second. The progress of the championship campaign can best be seen by studying the monthly records which we present below.

### THE MONTHLY RECORDS.

The most interesting chapter of the championship campaigns of each year, is that relating to the progress made each month, by each competing team, toward the goal of the season's championship. The monthly record shows when each team "spurted" in the race, or fell off in the running, and when they showed the most strength or displayed their weakness most. A great deal of important information, too, can be derived from a careful comparison of the monthly record; especially in regard to the strength a team possesses in rallying for the lead toward the close of the season. Experience has plainly shown that it is not the club which makes a brilliant dash at the start which is the most likely to come in first at the finish.

This fact was strikingly illustrated during the League season of 1884 in the case of the New York club team, which won twelve out of the first thirteen games they played; they defeating the Detroit, Cleveland, Chicago and Buffalo teams in every game played up to the 17th of May, when they lost their thirteenth game to the Buffalo team by a score of 4 to 1. At the end of the month, however, the Boston and Providence teams had taken the lead from the New Yorkers, the Providence team giving them a bad set back by defeating them in five games out of the six they played together in May. During May the four Eastern teams took a decided lead in the pennant race over the Western teams, the former scoring 66 victories in May to the latter's 31, Buffalo alone getting double figures in the record. Boston leading with 21 victories out of 24 games, Providence winning 20 out of 24, and New York 17 out of 25, Buffalo being next with 11 victories out of 25 games. Philadelphia was the lowest of the Eastern teams and Detroit of the Western. More championship games were played during May than in any other of the six months comprising the League season. Boston found the Philadelphia team their easiest victims in May, and Providence gave the New Yorkers the next worst whipping of the month. Detroit failed to win a single game from an Eastern team in May; while not a single Western team escaped losing at least one game to an Eastern rival. The full record of the month of May in the League arena is as follows, the names of the clubs being given in the order of their victories during the month.

MAY.

|  | Boston. | Providence. | New York. | Buffalo. | Chicago. | Cleveland. | Philadelphia. | Detroit. | Won. |
|---|---|---|---|---|---|---|---|---|---|
| Boston | .... | 0 | 2 | 3 | 4 | 3 | 6 | 3 | 21 |
| Providence | 0 | .... | 5 | 3 | 3 | 1 | 4 | 4 | 20 |
| New York | 3 | 1 | .... | 3 | 2 | 4 | 0 | 4 | 17 |
| Buffalo | 1 | 0 | 1 | .... | 2 | 2 | 2 | 3 | 11 |
| Chicago | 0 | 1 | 0 | 1 | .... | 1 | 3 | 3 | 9 |
| Cleveland | 0 | 1 | 0 | 2 | 2 | .... | 2 | 1 | 8 |
| Philadelphia | 0 | 1 | 0 | 2 | 1 | 2 | .... | 2 | 8 |
| Detroit | 0 | 0 | 0 | 0 | 1 | 2 | 0 | .... | 3 |
| Lost | 4 | 4 | 8 | 14 | 15 | 15 | 17 | 20 | 97 |

During June the monthly record shows that while Boston still held the lead for the month, Buffalo had pulled up to an even record, the only advantage the champions had over Buffalo being that they defeated Providence in four out of their six games together that month. Providence was a close third, Buffalo leading them by having one defeat less charged to them. New York this month had to be content with fourth place, Chicago being next, and the others in the same relative positions as in May, though Cleveland showed a better record. No club escaped defeat or failed to win a victory in June, all but Philadelphia and Detroit scoring double figures in victories, while all but Boston, Buffalo and Providence led in defeats. All except Buffalo, Chicago, Cleveland, and Detroit, fell off from their May record of victories during June, Boston and Providence especially, this result being mainly due to improved play by the other teams. The record for June is as follows:

JUNE.

|  | Boston. | Buffalo. | Providence. | New York. | Chicago. | Cleveland. | Philadelphia. | Detroit. | Won. |
|---|---|---|---|---|---|---|---|---|---|
| Boston |  | 0 | 4 | 2 | 1 | 0 | 3 | 4 | 14 |
| Buffalo | 0 |  | 0 | 1 | 4 | 3 | 3 | 3 | 14 |
| Providence | 2 | 0 |  | 3 | 2 | 0 | 3 | 4 | 14 |
| New York | 2 | 2 | 1 |  | 0 | 2 | 5 | 0 | 12 |
| Chicago | 2 | 2 | 2 | 0 |  | 3 | 0 | 2 | 11 |
| Cleveland | 0 | 0 | 0 | 2 | 2 |  | 3 | 4 | 11 |
| Philadelphia | 1 | 1 | 1 | 3 | 0 | 1 |  | 0 | 7 |
| Detroit | 0 | 2 | 0 | 0 | 2 | 2 | 0 |  | 6 |
| Lost | 7 | 7 | 8 | 11 | 11 | 11 | 17 | 17 | 8 |

In July Buffalo and Chicago did the best running in the pennant race, Providence and Boston being third and fourth in the month's record, New York declining to fifth place, their May "spurt" having apparently exhausted them. A feature of the July campaign was the marked falling off in Cleveland's running, Buffalo defeating them during June in nine successive games, the worst month's record of the season, they losing 18 out of 22 games. Philadelphia, too, lost ground this month, they losing 15 out of 20. The month's record is:

JULY.

|  | Buffalo. | Chicago. | Providence. | Boston. | New York. | Detroit. | Philadelphia. | Cleveland. | Won. |
|---|---|---|---|---|---|---|---|---|---|
| Buffalo |  | 1 | 2 | 0 | 0 | 2 | 0 | 9 | 14 |
| Chicago | 1 |  | 0 | 0 | 3 | 5 | 3 | 2 | 14 |
| Providence | 2 | 0 |  | 3 | 3 | 0 | 3 | 2 | 13 |
| Boston | 2 | 0 | 3 |  | 2 | 0 | 3 | 3 | 13 |
| New York | 0 | 1 | 0 | 3 |  | 3 | 4 | 0 | 11 |
| Detroit | 1 | 2 | 0 | 0 | 0 |  | 2 | 2 | 7 |
| Philadelphia | 0 | 1 | 1 | 1 | 0 | 2 |  | 0 | 5 |
| Cleveland | 0 | 1 | 1 | 1 | 0 | 1 | 0 |  | 4 |
| Lost | 6 | 6 | 7 | 8 | 8 | 13 | 15 | 18 | 81 |

BASE BALL GUIDE. 17

The month of August was marked by the phenomenal record made by the Providence club team, they winning no less than 17 out of the 18 games they played during the July campaign. It was in this month that Radbourne began to put in his prettiest work in the box. The solitary defeat the Providence team sustained in August, was that of their eleven innings game of Aug. 6, with the New York team at the Polo grounds, when the home nine won by 2 to 1 only. Their seventeen victories comprised four each over Boston, Chicago and Detroit; two each over New York and Philadelphia, and one over Cleveland, they not playing Buffalo in August. Buffalo had the next best record in August, Boston and New York being third and fourth in the month's table, while Cleveland pulled up to fifth place, and Chicago took a decided "tumble" they winning but 7 out of 20 games, the worst month's record of their season. Detroit was again last on the monthly list, they winning but two games out of their eighteen in August. The record is as follows:

AUGUST.

| | Providence. | Buffalo. | Boston. | New York. | Cleveland. | Philadelphia. | Chicago. | Detroit. | Won. |
|---|---|---|---|---|---|---|---|---|---|
| Providence | | 0 | 4 | 2 | 1 | 2 | 4 | 4 | 17 |
| Buffalo | 0 | | 0 | 1 | 0 | 3 | 3 | 4 | 11 |
| Boston | 0 | 0 | | 2 | 1 | 1 | 2 | 4 | 10 |
| New York | 1 | 3 | 0 | | 3 | 2 | 1 | 0 | 10 |
| Cleveland | 0 | 0 | 0 | 1 | | 1 | 3 | 3 | 8 |
| Philadelphia | 0 | 1 | 1 | 2 | 3 | | 0 | 0 | 7 |
| Chicago | 0 | 2 | 1 | 1 | 2 | 0 | | 1 | 7 |
| Detroit | 0 | 1 | 0 | 0 | 1 | 0 | 0 | | 2 |
| Lost | 1 | 7 | 6 | 9 | 11 | 9 | 13 | 16 | 72 |

In September Providence kept the lead despite of a strong rally made by Chicago, while Boston fell off in their running, they losing nine games out of nineteen this month. Philadelphia also rallied well this month, they doing better than New York, while Buffalo did their least effective work in August. In fact, Buffalo, Detroit and Cleveland combined only won a total of 17 games to 15 by Providence alone, while the three Western teams lost no less than 39 games out of the total of 56 they played this month. Providence again won every game they played with Cleveland in September, as they had done in August, the "coming champions" winning 15 out of the 16 games they were scheduled to play Cleveland during the season. The record for the month is as follows:

SEPTEMBER.

| | Providence. | Chicago. | Boston. | Philadelphia. | New York. | Buffalo. | Detroit. | Cleveland. | Won. |
|---|---|---|---|---|---|---|---|---|---|
| Providence | .... | 2 | 0 | 0 | 0 | 4 | 3 | 6 | 15 |
| Chicago | 2 | .... | 3 | 4 | 5 | 0 | 0 | 0 | 14 |
| Boston | 0 | 3 | .... | 0 | 0 | 2 | 1 | 4 | 10 |
| Philadelphia | 0 | 0 | 0 | .... | 0 | 1 | 5 | 4 | 10 |
| New York | 0 | 0 | 0 | 0 | .... | 3 | 4 | 2 | 9 |
| Buffalo | 1 | 0 | 2 | 3 | 2 | .... | 0 | 0 | 8 |
| Detroit | 1 | 0 | 3 | 2 | 0 | 0 | .... | 0 | 6 |
| Cleveland | 0 | 0 | 1 | 0 | 2 | 0 | 0 | .... | 3 |
| Lost | 4 | 5 | 9 | 9 | 9 | 10 | 13 | 16 | 75 |

Now comes the last month of the season, and this time we find the "Chicago rally" telling its tale, they making the closing month decidedly interesting. They won every game they played this month, they scoring their victories in New York and Philadelphia. The Providence team having "passed the Rubicon," and being virtually in possession of the championship, gave Radbourne a rest, and in consequence they only won five out of the nine games they played in October. The Bostons, too, made sure of second place, and Chicago and New York were left to fight it out for fourth place, Buffalo having won third before the season closed. It proved to be "nip and tuck" between New York and Chicago, and finally they came out a tie for fourth place, each winning 62 games and losing 50. Cleveland only won a single game in October, but singularly enough that was with the champion team of Providence. The record in full is as follows:

OCTOBER.

| | Chicago. | Buffalo. | Boston. | Providence. | Detroit. | New York. | Philadelphia. | Cleveland. | Won. |
|---|---|---|---|---|---|---|---|---|---|
| Chicago | .... | 0 | 0 | 0 | 0 | 3 | 4 | 0 | 7 |
| Buffalo | 0 | .... | 3 | 3 | 0 | 0 | 0 | 0 | 6 |
| Boston | 0 | 2 | .... | 0 | 0 | 0 | 0 | 3 | 5 |
| Providence | 0 | 1 | 0 | .... | 0 | 0 | 1 | 3 | 5 |
| Detroit | 0 | 0 | 1 | 0 | .... | 2 | 1 | 0 | 4 |
| New York | 0 | 0 | 0 | 0 | 3 | .... | 0 | 0 | 3 |
| Philadelphia | 0 | 0 | 0 | 0 | 2 | 0 | .... | 0 | 2 |
| Cleveland | 0 | 0 | 0 | 1 | 0 | 0 | 0 | .... | 1 |
| Lost | 0 | 3 | 4 | 4 | 5 | 5 | 6 | 6 | 33 |

The summary of the six months' games in the League, showing the victories scored each month in the championship arena for 1884, is as follows:

SUMMARY:

|  | May. | June. | July. | Aug | Sept. | Oct. | Total. |
|---|---|---|---|---|---|---|---|
| Providence | 20 | 14 | 13 | 17 | 15 | 5 | 84 |
| Boston | 21 | 14 | 13 | 10 | 10 | 5 | 73 |
| Buffalo | 11 | 14 | 14 | 11 | 8 | 6 | 64 |
| New York | 17 | 12 | 11 | 10 | 9 | 3 | 62 |
| Chicago | 9 | 11 | 14 | 7 | 14 | 7 | 62 |
| Philadelphia | 8 | 7 | 5 | 7 | 10 | 2 | 39 |
| Cleveland | 8 | 11 | 4 | 8 | 3 | 1 | 35 |
| Detroit | 3 | 6 | 7 | 2 | 6 | 4 | 28 |
| Total | 97 | 89 | 81 | 72 | 75 | 33 | 447 |

The summary of the monthly defeats is as follows:

|  | May. | June. | July. | Aug. | Sept. | Oct. | Total. |
|---|---|---|---|---|---|---|---|
| Providence | 4 | 8 | 7 | 1 | 4 | 4 | 28 |
| Boston | 4 | 7 | 8 | 6 | 9 | 4 | 38 |
| Buffalo | 14 | 7 | 6 | 7 | 10 | 3 | 47 |
| New York | 8 | 11 | 8 | 9 | 9 | 5 | 50 |
| Chicago | 15 | 11 | 6 | 13 | 5 | 0 | 50 |
| Philadelphia | 17 | 17 | 15 | 9 | 9 | 6 | 73 |
| Cleveland | 15 | 11 | 18 | 11 | 16 | 6 | 77 |
| Detroit | 20 | 17 | 13 | 16 | 13 | 5 | 84 |
| Total | 97 | 89 | 81 | 72 | 75 | 33 | 447 |

The extra innings games in the championship arena in 1884 were not as numerous as in preceding seasons, as the record below shows:

```
June  16, Boston vs. Providence, at Providence (16 innings).........  1—1
  "   14, Providence vs. Boston, at Boston (15 innings)............  4—3
  "   24, Providence vs. Detroit, at Detroit (14 innings)..........  1—0
Aug.   8, Detroit vs. Buffalo, at Detroit (12 innings)..............  1—0
June  17, New York vs. Boston, at Boston, 12 innings..............   7—6
*July 29, Buffalo vs. Cleveland, at Buffalo (11 innings)............  1—0
Aug.   9, Providence vs. Boston, at Boston (11 innings).............  1—0
  "    6, New York vs. Providence, at New York (11 innings)......  2—1
July  25, Buffalo vs. Cleveland, at Buffalo (11 innings)............  4—2
Oct.   4, Philadelphia vs. Detroit, at Detroit (11 innings).........  4—3
Aug.  30, Philadelphia vs. Buffalo, at Buffalo (11 innings).........  5—3
  "   18, Cleveland vs. Philadelphia, at Philadelphia (11 innings)...  5—4
  "   30, Providence vs. Detroit, at Detroit (11 innings)...........  6—5
May   17, Boston vs. Chicago, at Boston (11 innings)...............  9—7
July   3, Philadelphia vs. Chicago, at Chicago (11 innings).........  15—13
Oct.  13, Boston vs. Buffalo, at Buffalo (10 innings)...............  2—2
*May  22, Cleveland vs. Chicago, Cleveland, 10 innings............  3—0
Aug.  23, Philadelphia vs. Cleveland, at Cleveland (10 innings).....  5—4
```

May 31, Providence vs. Philadelphia, at Providence (10 innings)... 6—5
June 13, Detroit vs. Chicago, at Detroit (10 innings).............. 6—5
Aug. 30, Chicago vs. Boston, at Chicago (10 innings)............. 6—5
Sept. 25, Providence vs. Chicago, at Chicago (10 innings)......... 6—5
July 5, Chicago vs. New York, at Chicago (10 innings)............ 7—6
June 17, Buffalo vs. Chicago, at Buffalo (10 innings)............. 8—7
Aug. 20, Cleveland vs. Philadelphia, at Philadelphia (10 innings)... 9—9

*The two games marked by asterisks were made noteworthy from the fact that in the Buffalo-Cleveland game 11 innings were played without a run being scored, and in the Cleveland-Chicago game ten were thus played.

The championship season was marked by no less than seventy "Chicago" games, or games in which the losing side failed to score a single run. Providence led in victories of this character, and Detroit sustained the most "Chicago" defeats, as will be seen by the appended record:

|  | Providence. | Boston. | Buffalo. | Chicago. | Cleveland. | New York. | Philadelphia. | Detroit. | Won. |
|---|---|---|---|---|---|---|---|---|---|
| Providence.......... |  .... | 4 | 2 | 0 | 1 | 3 | 3 | 3 | 16 |
| Boston ............. | 2 | .... | 2 | 0 | 3 | 0 | 3 | 4 | 14 |
| Buffalo............. | 2 | 1 | .... | 1 | 2 | 1 | 3 | 4 | 14 |
| Chicago............ | 2 | 1 | 0 | .... | 2 | 1 | 2 | 1 | 9 |
| Cleveland........... | 0 | 1 | 1 | 1 | .... | 0 | 1 | 3 | 7 |
| New York........... | 0 | 1 | 1 | 0 | 1 | .... | 0 | 1 | 4 |
| Philadelphia......... | 0 | 0 | 1 | 0 | 0 | 1 | .... | 1 | 3 |
| Detroit.............. | 0 | 0 | 1 | 1 | 0 | 0 | 1 | .... | 3 |
| Lost................ | 6 | 8 | 8 | 3 | 9 | 6 | 13 | 17 | 70 |

The bulk of the campaign work was done in May, June and July, when a total of no less than 267 games were played, 97 of which took place in May. During August, September and October only 200 games were played, only 33 taking place in October. Providence opened play for the season very spiritedly, doing their best work in May. They then fell off until August, when sundry divisions in their ranks were healed by the retirement of Sweeny, their change pitcher, and then it was that Radbourne settled down to carry out his intention of "pitching the Providence team into the championship," and he did it splendidly, his work in the "box" never before having been equaled. It was in August that the Providence club made its unprecedented record of 17 championship victories out of 18 games played that month. Boston led the season's record of most victories in a single month in May, when they scored 21 victories out of 25 games, Providence being second with 20 the same month. Chicago began the season very inauspiciously, but they improved up to August as much as the other leaders fell off. Then their turn to "disappear" came, and August lost them the chance for a successful rally at an important period of the campaign. They "bobbed up serenely" in September, but in the interim both Providence and Boston had got too far in the van to be overtaken. They led New York early in September, but lost the lead later, but only by their failure to win as many series of games as New York did. Buffalo, also, lost their grip in September and fell back, but not far enough to lose third place in the race. Philadelphia rallied well in September, after being low down in the record before, and Harry Wright managed to place his team ahead of both Cleveland and Detroit. The full record of the season is given below:

|  | Providence. | Boston. | Buffalo. | New York. | Chicago. | Philadelphia. | Cleveland. | Detroit. | Games won. | Games played. | Games tied. | Unplayed. | Per cent. of victories. |
|---|---|---|---|---|---|---|---|---|---|---|---|---|---|
| Providence... | .... | 9 | 10 | 13 | 11 | 13 | 13 | 15 | 84 | 112 | 2 | 0 | .750 |
| Boston........ | 7 | .... | 9 | 8 | 10 | 13 | 14 | 12 | 73 | 111 | 5 | 1 | .650 |
| Buffalo....... | 6 | 6 | .... | 5 | 10 | 11 | 14 | 12 | 64 | 111 | 4 | 1 | .570 |
| New York... | 3 | 8 | 11 | .... | 4 | 11 | 11 | 14 | 62 | 112 | 4 | 0 | .550 |
| Chicago...... | 5 | 6 | 6 | 12 | .... | 14 | 8 | 11 | 62 | 112 | 1 | 0 | .550 |
| Philadelphia. | 3 | 3 | 5 | 5 | 2 | .... | 10 | 11 | 39 | 112 | 1 | 0 | .340 |
| Cleveland.... | 3 | 2 | 2 | 5 | 8 | 6 | .... | 9 | 35 | 112 | 1 | 0 | .310 |
| Detroit....... | 1 | 4 | 4 | 2 | 5 | 5 | 7 | .... | 28 | 112 | 2 | 0 | .250 |
| Games Lost.. | 28 | 38 | 47 | 50 | 50 | 73 | 77 | 84 | 447 | | | | |

A summary of the above records shows the appended result:

| CLUBS | Won. | Lost. | Played. | To play. | Tied. | Series won. | Series lost. | Series tied. |
|---|---|---|---|---|---|---|---|---|
| Providence........................ | 84 | 28 | 112 | 0 | 2 | 7 | 0 | 0 |
| Boston............................. | 73 | 38 | 111 | 1 | 5 | 5 | 1 | 1 |
| Buffalo............................ | 64 | 47 | 111 | 1 | 4 | 4 | 3 | 0 |
| New York......................... | 62 | 50 | 112 | 0 | 4 | 4 | 2 | 1 |
| Chicago........................... | 62 | 50 | 112 | 0 | 1 | 3 | 3 | 1 |
| Philadelphia...................... | 39 | 73 | 112 | 0 | 1 | 2 | 5 | 0 |
| Cleveland......................... | 35 | 77 | 112 | 0 | 1 | 1 | 5 | 1 |
| Detroit............................ | 28 | 84 | 112 | 0 | 2 | 0 | 7 | 0 |
| | 447 | 447 | | | | | | |

LEAGUE "CHICAGO" GAMES.

The record of games played in the League arena in 1884, in

which one side or other failed to score a single run, is as follows:

|  | Providence. | Boston. | Buffalo. | Chicago. | Cleveland. | New York. | Philadelphia. | Detroit. | Games won. |
|---|---|---|---|---|---|---|---|---|---|
| Providence......... | .... | 4 | 2 | 0 | 1 | 3 | 3 | 3 | 16 |
| Boston............ | 2 | .... | 2 | 0 | 3 | 0 | 3 | 4 | 14 |
| Buffalo........... | 2 | 1 | .... | 1 | 2 | 1 | 3 | 4 | 14 |
| Chicago........... | 2 | 1 | 0 | .... | 2 | 1 | 2 | 1 | 9 |
| Cleveland......... | 0 | 1 | 1 | 1 | .... | 0 | 1 | 3 | 7 |
| New York.......... | 0 | 1 | 1 | 0 | 1 | .... | 0 | 1 | 4 |
| Philadelphia...... | 0 | 0 | 1 | 0 | 0 | 1 | .... | 1 | 3 |
| Detroit........... | 0 | 0 | 1 | 1 | 0 | 0 | 1 | .. | 3 |
| Games Lost........ | 6 | 8 | 8 | 3 | 9 | 6 | 13 | 17 | 70 |

Providence bore off the palm in this respect, Detroit sustaining the most '"Chicago" defeats.

The record showing how each series of games was won in the League championship arena in 1884, is as follows. The names are given in the order of series won and lost.

|  | Providence. | Boston. | New York. | Buffalo. | Chicago. | Philadelphia. | Cleveland. | Detroit. | Series won. | Series tied. |
|---|---|---|---|---|---|---|---|---|---|---|
| Providence........ | .... | 9-7 | 13-3 | 10-6 | 11-5 | 13-3 | 13-3 | 15-1 | 7 | 0 |
| Boston............ | 7-9 | .... | 8-8 | 9-6 | 10-6 | 13-3 | 14-2 | 12-4 | 5 | 1 |
| New York.......... | 3-13 | 8-8 | .... | 11-5 | 4-12 | 11-5 | 11-5 | 14-2 | 4 | 1 |
| Buffalo........... | 6-10 | 6-9 | 5-11 | .... | 10-6 | 11-5 | 14-2 | 12-4 | 4 | 0 |
| Chicago........... | 5-11 | 6-10 | 12-4 | 6-10 | .... | 14-2 | 8-8 | 11-5 | 3 | 1 |
| Philadelphia...... | 3-13 | 3-13 | 5-11 | 5-11 | 2-14 | .... | 10-6 | 11-5 | 2 | 0 |
| Cleveland......... | 3-13 | 2-14 | 5-11 | 2-14 | 8-8 | 6-10 | .... | 9-7 | 1 | 1 |
| Detroit........... | 1-15 | 4-12 | 2-14 | 4-12 | 5-11 | 5-11 | 7-9 | .... | 0 | 0 |
| Series Lost....... | 0 | 1 | 2 | 3 | 3 | 5 | 5 | 7 | 26 | 4 |

## THE EAST VS. WEST.

The annual contest between the League representative teams of the East and the West, resulted, this season, in the marked success of the four Eastern teams, as will be seen by the appended record:

BASE BALL GUIDE. 23

| EASTERN vs. WESTERN. | Chicago. | Buffalo. | Cleveland. | Detroit. | Games won. | WESTERN vs. EASTERN. | Providence. | Boston. | New York. | Philadelphia. | Games won. |
|---|---|---|---|---|---|---|---|---|---|---|---|
| Providence..... | 11 | 10 | 13 | 15 | 49 | Chicago........ | 5 | 6 | 12 | 14 | 37 |
| Boston ......... | 10 | 9 | 14 | 12 | 45 | Buffalo......... | 6 | 6 | 5 | 11 | 28 |
| New York..... | 4 | 11 | 11 | 14 | 40 | C eveland .. | 3 | 2 | 5 | 6 | 16 |
| Philadelphia... | 2 | 5 | 10 | 11 | 28 | Detroit......... | 1 | 4 | 2 | 5 | 12 |
| Games lost..... | 27 | 35 | 48 | 52 | 162 | Games lost..... | 15 | 18 | 24 | 36 | 93 |

Providence took the lead in defeating Western teams, and Chicago in winning games from Eastern rivals. The very reverse was the case in the American arena in 1884.

### THE HOME AND HOME SERIES.

In the home and home series of games of the Eastern and Western League Clubs in their championship matches together in 1884, the record stands as fellows:

| EASTERN CLUBS. | Providence.. | Boston. | New York. | Philadelphia | Games won. | WESTERN CLUBS. | Buffalo. | Chicago. | Cleveland. | Detroit. | Games won. |
|---|---|---|---|---|---|---|---|---|---|---|---|
| Providence... | .... | 9 | 13 | 13 | 35 | Buffalo. ...... | .... | 10 | 14 | 12 | 36 |
| Boston....... | 7 | .... | 8 | 13 | 28 | Chicago...... | 6 | .... | 8 | 11 | 25 |
| New York... | 3 | 8 | .... | 11 | 22 | Cleveland.... | 2 | 8 | .... | 9 | 19 |
| Philadelphia. | 3 | 3 | 5 | .... | 11 | Detroit ..... | 4 | 5 | 7 | .... | 16 |
| Games lost... | 13 | 20 | 26 | 37 | 96 | Games lost... | 12 | 23 | 29 | 32 | 96 |

It will be seen that Buffalo had the best record in the West and Providence in the East.

## BATTING AVERAGES OF PLAYERS WHO HAVE TAKEN PART IN LEAGUE CHAMPIONSHIP GAMES FOR FOUR OR MORE SEASONS.

### 1876 to 1884, Both Inclusive.

| Rank. | NAME. | Number of Seasons Played. | Number of Games Played. | Times at Bat. | First Bases. | Percentage of Base Hits per Times at Bat. |
|---|---|---|---|---|---|---|
| 1 | Adrian C. Anson | 9 | 680 | 2889 | 1019 | .352 |
| 2 | Dennis Brouthers | 5 | 375 | 1590 | 541 | .340 |
| 3 | Rodger Connor | 5 | 454 | 1903 | 619 | .325 |
| 4 | Geo. F. Gore | 6 | 484 | 2050 | 654 | .319 |
| 5 | James L. White | 9 | 648 | 2714 | 860 | .317 |
| 6 | James H. O'Rourke | 9 | 707 | 3103 | 879 | .315 |
| 7 | A. Dalrymple | 7 | 566 | 2592 | 815 | .314 |
| 8 | P. A. Hines | 9 | 710 | 3175 | 989 | .311 |
| 9 | Roscoe C. Barnes | 4 | 228 | 1082 | 319 | .309 |
| 10 | M. J. Kelly | 7 | 586 | 2516 | 773 | .307 |
| 11 | Joseph Start | 9 | 648 | 2870 | 865 | .301 |
| 11 | Fred Dunlap | 4 | 334 | 1450 | 437 | .301 |
| 12 | C. W. Jones | 4 | 271 | 1163 | 347 | .298 |
| 13 | L. P. Dickerson | 4 | 248 | 1085 | 318 | .293 |
| 14 | E. M. Gross | 4 | 221 | 874 | 252 | .288 |
| 15 | J. C. Rowe | 5 | 390 | 1633 | 469 | .287 |
| 16 | E. B. Sutton | 9 | 681 | 2803 | 803 | .286 |
| 17 | H. Richardson | 6 | 512 | 2171 | 620 | .285 |
| 18 | C. J. Foley | 5 | 303 | 1296 | 368 | .284 |
| 19 | Geo. Shaffer | 7 | 521 | 2137 | 602 | .281 |
| 20 | J. E. Whitney | 4 | 292 | 1188 | 333 | .280 |
| 21 | Chas. W. Bennett | 6 | 431 | 1688 | 473 | .280 |
| 22 | Wm. Ewing | 4 | 310 | 1328 | 369 | .277 |
| 23 | John F. Morrill | 9 | 708 | 2857 | 787 | .275 |
| 23 | John E. Clapp | 7 | 398 | 1688 | 465 | .275 |
| 24 | John A. Peters | 6 | 384 | 1700 | 468 | .275 |
| 25 | Thos. Burns | 5 | 429 | 1764 | 485 | .274 |
| 25 | P. Gillespie | 5 | 429 | 1784 | 489 | .274 |
| 26 | E. N. Williamson | 7 | 579 | 2362 | 640 | .271 |
| 27 | G. A. Wood | 5 | 448 | 1905 | 515 | .270 |
| 27 | Joseph Hornung | 6 | 585 | 2291 | 619 | .270 |
| 28 | Robt. Ferguson | 8 | 538 | 2209 | 596 | .269 |
| 28 | Wm. M. Crowley | 5 | 364 | 1452 | 391 | .269 |
| 28 | Thos. York | 8 | 566 | 2291 | 617 | .269 |
| 29 | W. A. Purcell | 6 | 479 | 2049 | 540 | .263 |
| 29 | W. B. Phillips | 6 | 529 | 2203 | 581 | .263 |
| 30 | M. C. Dorgan | 6 | 383 | 1622 | 426 | .261 |
| 30 | John Farrell | 6 | 511 | 2201 | 576 | .261 |
| 30 | P. J. Hotaling | 6 | 514 | 2185 | 572 | .261 |
| 31 | John J. Burdock | 9 | 682 | 2856 | 744 | .260 |

## BATTING AVERAGES OF PLAYERS—CONTINUED.

| Rank. | NAME. | Number of Seasons Played. | Number of Games Played. | Times at Bat. | First Bases. | Percentage of Base Hits per Times at Bat. |
|---|---|---|---|---|---|---|
| 32 | Lewis J. Brown............ | 5 | 252 | 1042 | 270 | .259 |
| 33 | J. E. Manning............. | 5 | 378 | 1569 | 405 | .258 |
|  | A. J. Leonard............. | 4 | 203 | 917 | 247 | .258 |
| 34 | John W. Glasscock......... | 6 | 487 | 1949 | 504 | .258 |
|  | J. Lee Richmond........... | 4 | 238 | 968 | 248 | .256 |
| 35 | Edward Hanlon............ | 5 | 435 | 1752 | 448 | .255 |
|  | J. J. Gerhardt............. | 5 | 330 | 1357 | 346 | .255 |
|  | A. A. Irwin............... | 5 | 413 | 1679 | 429 | .255 |
| 36 | Jeremiah Denny........... | 4 | 374 | 1468 | 373 | .254 |
| 37 | Geo. Wright............... | 5 | 307 | 1415 | 358 | .253 |
| 38 | S. P. Houck............... | 4 | 312 | 1289 | 325 | .252 |
| 39 | J. P. Cassidy.............. | 7 | 416 | 1718 | 433 | .252 |
| 40 | M. Welch................. | 5 | 290 | 1082 | 272 | .251 |
|  | Thos. Carey............... | 4 | 257 | 1097 | 276 | .251 |
| 41 | John M. Ward............. | 7 | 562 | 2382 | 593 | .249 |
| 42 | F. S. Flint................ | 6 | 522 | 2069 | 514 | .248 |
| 43 | Chas. Radbourn........... | 4 | 327 | 1326 | 327 | .246 |
| 44 | James McCormick......... | 7 | 392 | 1526 | 361 | .243 |
| 45 | M. H. McGeary............ | 5 | 271 | 1155 | 279 | .241 |
|  | John J. Remsen............ | 5 | 240 | 965 | 233 | .241 |
| 46 | Alonzo Knight............. | 4 | 269 | 1113 | 268 | .240 |
|  | Jacob Evans............... | 6 | 447 | 1737 | 413 | .237 |
| 47 | Wm. L. Hague............. | 4 | 225 | 962 | 228 | .237 |
|  | E. J. Caskins.............. | 5 | 401 | 1585 | 377 | .237 |
| 48 | W. A. Harbidge........... | 5 | 224 | 895 | 212 | .236 |
| 49 | Geo. W. Bradley........... | 6 | 336 | 1319 | 311 | .225 |
| 50 | David Eggler.............. | 5 | 236 | 964 | 222 | .230 |
| 51 | Joseph L. Quest........... | 6 | 372 | 1459 | 333 | .228 |
|  | Thos. H. Bond............. | 5 | 292 | 1150 | 263 | .228 |
| 52 | F. E. Goldsmith........... | 5 | 201 | 799 | 180 | .225 |
| 53 | W. H. McClellan........... | 4 | 299 | 1224 | 275 | .224 |
| 54 | Frank Hankinson.......... | 6 | 442 | 1671 | 369 | .220 |
|  | Chas. N. Snyder........... | 5 | 306 | 1196 | 264 | .220 |
|  | John Richmond............ | 4 | 158 | 618 | 136 | .220 |
| 55 | Lawrence Corcoran........ | 5 | 287 | 1146 | 250 | .218 |
| 56 | James F. Galvin........... | 6 | 393 | 1508 | 326 | .216 |
| 57 | George Creamer........... | 5 | 308 | 1139 | 242 | .213 |
| 58 | B. Gilligan................ | 6 | 332 | 1228 | 258 | .210 |
| 59 | D. W. Force............... | 8 | 607 | 2378 | 497 | .209 |
| 60 | W. H. Holbert............. | 6 | 286 | 1066 | 221 | .207 |
| 61 | Robt. Matthews........... | 4 | 177 | 688 | 135 | .196 |
| 62 | A. J. Bushong............. | 5 | 302 | 1063 | 207 | .194 |
| 63 | Geo. E. Wiedman.......... | 4 | 223 | 855 | 149 | .174 |

## JAMES O'ROURKE.

James O'Rourke is a native of Bridgeport, Conn., and he first played ball as one of the nine of the Osceola Club of that city in 1871, he being their catcher. In 1872 he played with the once well-known Mansfield Club of Middletown, Ct., and occupied the positions of catcher, short-stop and third base. About this time Harry Wright, having thoroughly satisfied himself that O'Rourke possessed every requisite for a first-class professional player, secured his services for the Bostons. He commenced the season of 1873 by playing right-field and change-catcher for the Bostons, but was afterward transferred to first base, filling that position admirably. He remained with the Bostons six years, and during that time played in almost every position. He accompanied that club on their trip to England in 1874, and distinguished himself in the cricket matches there played by his fine fielding, hard hitting and excellent defense. The Providence Club succeeded in securing his services for 1879, and he played right field for them in that year, and materially helped to lift them into the championship that year under George Wright's able management. In 1880 O'Rourke returned to the Boston Club, and in 1881 was offered the management of the Buffalo Club, and from that year to 1885, when he accepted a high salary from the New York Club, he acted as manager of the Buffalo Club, and brought the team into third place in the pennant race of 1884. He ranks among the highest for integrity of character, faithful service in the field, and for his marked ability, not only as a fielder, but as a batsman, he leading in the averages of the League for 1884.

"He has made a brilliant record for himself as an outfielder, being an excellent judge of a ball, a swift runner, and making the most difficult running-catches with the utmost ease and certainty. His average each season has proved him to be in the front rank in handling the bat, and shows that his usefulness is not merely confined to his fielding abilities. He has always enjoyed the reputation of being a thoroughly reliable and honest player, and one who works hard for the best interests of his club. His gentlemanly conduct, both on and off the ball field, has won for him a host of friends."

**JAMES O'ROURKE,**
CHAMPION BATTER OF 1884.

## THE LEADING BATSMEN AND FIELDERS.

The nine leading players at the bat and in the field in the League championship arena during 1884, based upon the estimates of their taking part in the majority of the games of their respective clubs are as follows:

### BATSMEN.

| Players. | Clubs. | Games Played in. | Average. |
|---|---|---|---|
| O'Rourke | Buffalo | 104 | 350 |
| Sutton | Boston | 106 | 349 |
| Kelly | Chicago | 107 | 341 |
| Anson | Chicago | 111 | 337 |
| White | Buffalo | 106 | 325 |
| Brouthers | Buffalo | 90 | 325 |
| Condon | New York | 112 | 316 |
| Gore | Chicago | 101 | 316 |
| Pfeffer | Chicago | 111 | 310 |

### FIELDERS.

| Players. | Position. | Clubs. | Games Played in. | Average. |
|---|---|---|---|---|
| Hines | Catcher | Boston | 103 | 879 |
| Galvin | Pitcher | Buffalo | 68 | 843 |
| Start | First Baseman | Providence | 90 | 979 |
| Burdock | Second Baseman | Boston | 84 | 925 |
| Sutton | Third Baseman | Boston | 106 | 906 |
| Force | Shortstop | Buffalo | 101 | 901 |
| Hornung | Left Fielder | Boston | 106 | 913 |
| Hines | Center Fielder | Providence | 107 | 895 |
| Evans | Right Fielder | Cleveland | 76 | 911 |

## THE LEAGUE PITCHING OF 1884.

There was a decided improvement shown in the pitching of 1884 compared with that of 1883, far more attention having been paid to strategic pitching, as a primary element of success in the game, last season than ever before. In fact, the general class of batsmen have now become so familiar with the overhand throwing in the delivery of the ball to the bat, that pitchers have had to resort to strategy as a strong point in their attack, in order to overcome the advantage the better class of batsmen would frequently obtain in facing the merely swift delivery of the ball. In 1883 the pitchers rushed the swift-throwing business to quite an extent, and it had the effect of producing a high record of assistance on strikes; but last year not half as many batsmen were intimidated by the speed as in 1883. The best exhibition of pitching of the season of 1884, was that of Radbourne of the Providence club, who pitched in 74 games out of the 112 played by that club, and out of the 74 he pitched in, 62 were victories. The average of runs charged to him as being earned off his pitching, was but a fraction over one run to each game, and the average of base hits scored from his delivery, a trifle over seven to a game, while the average of his assistances on strikes was nearly six to a game. He undoubtedly led every pitcher of the League, in 1884, in strategic skill, and this it was, in fact, which gave him his supremacy in the position. In the record we give below of the work done by the League pitchers of 1884, we have rated those as first on the list whose averages rank high while they played in the largest number of games. In the averages of those who pitched in from fifty to seventy games, Radbourne, Welch, Buffinton, Galvin and Corcoran take the lead. In the averages of those who pitched in from thirty to fifty games, Whitney, McCormick, Begley, Mienke, Ferguson and Harkins have the best record; while those who pitched in from twenty to thirty games the leaders are Sweeny, Vinton, Shaw, Moffatt, Weidman and Goldsmith. Of those who pitched in from ten to twenty games, Dorgan, Clarkson, Getzien, McElroy, Coleman and Brill stand in the order named. Of those who had but an average of one earned run and over charged against their pitching, irrespective of the number of games they pitched in, the order of their average places them as follows: Dorgnn, Radbourne, Sweeny, Whitney, Clarkson, Getzien, Welch, Buffinton, Galvin, Vinton, McCormick and Begley. The poorest record made by a League pitcher in 1884 was that of Brill of Detroit, who had an average of over four earned runs to a game charged against him. Next to him was Coleman of Philadelphia, whose average was 3-62; Goldsmith of Chicago, being third from last with an average of 3-05. These were all the pitchers whose average of earned runs against them reached three runs to a game.

The record of the League pitchers who played in fifty games and over during 1884, showing the runs earned and the base-hits made off their pitching, as also the number of games won in which they pitched, together with the number of assistances on strikes credited to them, is as follows:

| Pitcher. | Club. | Games Played. | Average Runs Earned. | Average Base-hits. | Games Won. | Average Assists on Strikes. |
|---|---|---|---|---|---|---|
| Radbourne | Providence | 74 | 1·09 | 7·09 | 62 | 5·90 |
| Welde | New York | 62 | 1-66 | 8-27 | 38 | 5-35 |
| Buffinton | Boston | 67 | 1-68 | 7-50 | 48 | 6-29 |
| Galvin | Buffalo | 72 | 1-70 | 7-80 | 46 | 4·97 |
| Corcoran | Chicago | 57 | 2-07 | 7·93 | 35 | 4·50 |

Of those who pitched in thirty games and over, and in less than fifty, a similar class of figures show the appended result.

| Pitcher. | Club. | Games Played. | Average Runs Earned. | Average Base-hits. | Games Won. | Average Assists on Strikes. |
|---|---|---|---|---|---|---|
| Whitney | Boston | 37 | 1-45 | 7-05 | 23 | 7·21 |
| McCormick | Cleveland | 39 | 1-89 | 8-82 | 19 | 4-56 |
| Begley | New York | 30 | 1·90 | 9-66 | 12 | 3-56 |
| Mienke | Detroit | 31 | 2-35 | 9-83 | 8 | 3-58 |
| Ferguson | Philadelphia | 47 | 2-36 | 9-46 | 20 | 4·14 |
| Harkins | Cleveland | 44 | 2-36 | 9·00 | 12 | 4·15 |

Of those who played in twenty games and over and in less than thirty, the record of the same class of figures is as follows:

| Pitcher. | Club. | Games Played. | Average Runs Earned. | Average Base-hits. | Games Won. | Average Assists on Strikes. |
|---|---|---|---|---|---|---|
| Sweeny | Providence | 24 | 1-20 | 6-50 | 16 | 6-04 |
| Vinton | Philadelphia | 20 | 1-85 | 7-80 | 10 | 4-75 |
| Shaw | Detroit | 26 | 2-19 | 8-30 | 9 | 5-40 |
| Moffatt | Cleveland | 21 | 2-43 | 10-05 | 3 | 3-90 |
| Weidman | Detroit | 24 | 2-50 | 10-00 | 4 | 3-79 |
| Goldsmith | Chicago | 20 | 3-05 | 11-70 | 9 | 1-90 |

Of those who played in ten games and less than twenty, the record is as follows:

| Pitcher. | Club. | Games Played. | Average Runs Earned. | Average Base-hits. | Games Won. | Average Assists on Strikes. |
|---|---|---|---|---|---|---|
| Dorgan | New York | 12 | 1-00 | 6-58 | 8 | 6-91 |
| Clarkson | Chicago | 12 | 1-50 | 6-50 | 10 | 7-41 |
| Getzein | Detroit | 17 | 1-64 | 6-94 | 5 | 6-29 |
| McElroy | Philadelphia | 13 | 2-30 | 8-92 | 1 | 3-38 |
| Coleman | Philadelphia | 16 | 3-62 | 11-06 | 4 | 2-25 |
| Brill | Detroit | 12 | 4-59 | 12-41 | 2 | 1-50 |

The only criterion of effective pitching is the record of earned runs scored off the pitching. It should be remembered in this connection, that there is quite a difference between runs earned off the pitching and runs earned off the fielding. If the first, second, and third strikers at the bat each make a base-hit, and the fourth striker hits the ball so as to oblige the fielder to throw him out at first base, one run being scored off the hitting alone, then one run is clean earned off the pitching. But if the first striker makes a single base hit, steals to second, is given his third on another base hit, and goes home by a steal in on a throw to second to cut off the runner from first, then a run is earned off the fielding, inasmuch as from the base hits made alone two men would have been on bases, and no run scored. It is necessary, therefore, for a correct record of earned runs off the pitching, that scorers should see to it that a proper distinction should be made between runs distinctly earned off the pitching and those earned off the fielding. Of course, direct fielding errors are not to be included in runs earned off the fielding, but only runs earned by effective base-running, as no runs can be earned at all from fielding errors.

In regard to the averages of base hits made off the pitching, they are necessarily of secondary consideration, as base hits may be made to a large extent off the pitching after the pitcher has given the field three chances for outs which have not been accepted.

## STRATEGY VS. SPEED IN PITCHING.

Now that each season's campaign lessens the value of mere speed in pitching in comparison with the effectiveness of skilful strategy, it is worth while to comment a little on what constitutes effective strategic work in the delivery of the ball to the bat. In reply to the question as to what constitutes strategic pitching, the answer is that it is the art of out-manœuvering the batsman, by puzzling his judgment and deceiving his eyesight; in plain words it is the skill which leads him to think that the very ball he likes to hit is coming from the pitcher, when in reality it is a ball he cannot hit successfully. The essentials of strategic pitching are, *First*, thorough command of the ball in delivery; *second*, the skill to disguise a marked change of pace; *third*, to try and get the batsman out of form for hitting, and when he is so to send the ball in "over the plate" and at the height called for. These points of play, combined with a judicious use of the "curves," and of a swift delivery—the latter according to the ability of the catcher only—constitute the elements of strategic pitching, and it is this style of pitching, and this only, which will eventually supersede all others as the game approaches the point of perfect play. There was a great deal of intentional intimidation of the batsmen indulged in by the "pacers" of the pitching arena last season, the ball being sent in time and again purposely so close to the batsman's person as to render it difficult for him to avoid being struck by the ball. This is a vile, cowardly practice, which no manly pitcher will ever indulge in. It should be put a stop to by proper League enactments, as it is an obstacle to progress in the game. The rule in legislating for a perfect code of playing rules affecting the power of attack and defence in the game—viz: Rules governing the pitching and batting—should be to equalize them as much as possible. With the growth of the game has come almost perfect fielding, and hence the excellent field support the pitching now has in every first-class team gives the attacking force in the game a very powerful advantage. The new rule governing the delivery of the ball to the bat which is in force this season, will have the effect of forcing pitchers to depend more than ever upon strategic skill for a successful delivery of the ball. The new position of the pitcher will oblige him to be more accurate in his pitching and thereby give him more command of the ball than was possible under the jumping step of the method of delivery which prevailed in 1884.

## THE AMERICAN SEASON OF 1884.

The American Association entered upon the third year of its history in 1884, and during that year its clubs played more championship games than were ever before played by any professional association in a single season. Financially, however, the result of the campaign was not as satisfactory to the majority of the clubs as was the season previous. The fact was there were altogether too many clubs in the arena in 1884, nearly fifty Association clubs of one kind or another participating in the campaign of 1884, not counting the clubs of State Associations. Of these twelve entered for the American Association championship, and the experience of the season showed that the number was too large for financial success. The paying rule in professional association campaigns is "Few clubs but strong ones," and the American Association, like the League, has found six clubs to be the minimum number and eight the maximum.

In the inaugural season of the American Association in 1882, the Western clubs took the lead over those of the Eastern section by a record of eighty-six victories for the West to fifty-eight for the East. This was with six clubs in the campaign of that year. In 1883 the West improved upon this record by scoring 186 victories to only 96 by the East. Then they had eight clubs in the arena. In 1884 with twelve clubs the West took the lead by a record of 200 victories to 150 by the Eastern clubs. This gives a total of 472 victories for the West to 304 for the East, in three years' campaigns. So marked a record of superior play by the Western clubs is noteworthy, especially in view of the fact that in older times the Eastern clubs almost invariably bore off the honors. As an interesting record for reference we give below the official figures of the victories and defeats scored by the clubs of the two sections during the three seasons of the existence of the American Association.

### RECORD OF 1882.

| WESTERN CLUB VICTORIES. | Athletic. | Allegheny. | Baltimore. | Games Won. | EASTERN CLUB VICTORIES. | Cincinnati. | Louisville. | St. Louis. | Games Won. |
|---|---|---|---|---|---|---|---|---|---|
| Cincinnati | 10 | 10 | 14 | 34 | Athletic | 6 | 11 | 11 | 28 |
| Louisville | 5 | 10 | 13 | 28 | Allegheny | 6 | 6 | 10 | 22 |
| St. Louis | 5 | 6 | 13 | 24 | Baltimore | 2 | 3 | 3 | 8 |
| Games Lost | 20 | 26 | 40 | 86 | Games Lost | 14 | 20 | 24 | 58 |

### RECORD OF 1883.

| WESTERN CLUB VICTORIES | Athletic. | Metropolitan. | Baltimore. | Allegheny. | Games won. | EASTERN CLUB VICTORIES | St. Louis. | Louisville. | Cincinnati. | Columbus. | Games won. |
|---|---|---|---|---|---|---|---|---|---|---|---|
| St. Louis | 5 | 11 | 12 | 12 | 40 | Athletic | 9 | 7 | 5 | 13 | 34 |
| Louisville | 9 | 4 | 11 | 8 | 33 | Metropolitan | 3 | 6 | 10 | 11 | 30 |
| Cincinnati | 7 | 7 | 8 | 11 | 32 | Baltimore | 2 | 6 | 3 | 6 | 17 |
| Columbus | 1 | 3 | 7 | 10 | 21 | Allegheny | 2 | 3 | 6 | 4 | 15 |
| Games lost | 22 | 25 | 38 | 41 | 186 | Games lost | 16 | 22 | 24 | 34 | 96 |

## BASE BALL GUIDE. 33

### RECORD OF 1884.

| | Metropolitan. | Baltimore. | Athletic. | Brooklyn. | Allegheny. | Virginia. | Games won. | | St. Louis. | Cincinnati. | Columbus. | Louisville. | Toledo. | Indianapolis. | Games Won. |
|---|---|---|---|---|---|---|---|---|---|---|---|---|---|---|---|
| St. Louis..... | 4 | 5 | 7 | 7 | 9 | 8 | 40 | Metropolitan. | 5 | 6 | 5 | 7 | 5 | 8 | 36 |
| Cincinnati ... | 4 | 6 | 4 | 8 | 8 | 10 | 40 | Baltimore.... | 5 | 6 | 6 | 6 | 5 | 9 | 35 |
| Columbus.... | 4 | 4 | 5 | 7 | 9 | 7 | 36 | Athletic...... | 3 | 6 | 5 | 3 | 6 | 6 | 29 |
| Louisville.... | 3 | 4 | 6 | 6 | 7 | 8 | 34 | Brooklyn..... | 3 | 2 | 3 | 3 | 4 | 7 | 22 |
| Toledo...... | 4 | 5 | 3 | 5 | 5 | 9 | 31 | Allegheny·.. | 1 | 1 | 1 | 2 | 5 | 6 | 16 |
| Indianapolis.. | 2 | 1 | 4 | 3 | 4 | 5 | 19 | Virginia..... | 2 | 0 | 3 | 2 | 1 | 4 | 12 |
| Games Lost | 21 | 25 | 29 | 36 | 42 | 47 | 200 | Games Lost.. | 19 | 19 | 23 | 23 | 26 | 40 | 150 |

A noteworthy fact in the above statistics is the gradual, but sure, improvement shown by the St. Louis Club in the West, and the Baltimore in the East, over their first season's campaign.

A feature of the campaign work of 1884, in the American arena, was the brilliant play shown by the Louisville and Columbus Clubs. In fact, up to the last month of the season, it looked as if one or the other would bear off the honors; whereas, in '83 they were both way down in the season's record. In the home and home games of the clubs of each section during 1884, it was a nip and tuck race between Columbus and Louisville, the former having the lead by a slightly better percentage of victories; Cincinnati having the best of St. Louis in their games, while Toledo did better than Indianapolis. In the same class of games among the Eastern clubs, the Metropolitans held the honors with the Baltimore Club occupying second place and the Athletics third, Brooklyn, Allegheny and Virginia bringing up the rear. The record of these home and home games is as follows:

| WEST. | Columbus. | Louisville. | Cincinnati. | St. Louis. | Toledo. | Indianapolis. | Won. | EAST. | Metropolitan. | Athletic. | Baltimore. | Brooklyn. | Allegheny. | Virginia. | Won. |
|---|---|---|---|---|---|---|---|---|---|---|---|---|---|---|---|
| Columbus.... | .. | 5 | 7 | 5 | 8 | 8 | 33 | Metropolitan. | .. | 8 | 5 | 9 | 9 | 8 | 39 |
| Louisville.... | 5 | .. | 5 | 5 | 9 | 9 | 33 | Athletic...... | 2 | ... | 7 | 6 | 8 | 9 | 32 |
| Cincinnati.... | 3 | 5 | .. | 4 | 7 | 9 | 28 | Baltimore.... | 5 | 3 | ... | 5 | 9 | 6 | 28 |
| St. Louis..... | 5 | 5 | 6 | .. | .. | 5 | 27 | Brooklyn..... | 1 | 3 | 5 | ... | 4 | 6 | 19 |
| Toledo....... | 1 | 1 | 3 | 5 | ... | 6 | 16 | Allegheny. .. | 1 | 2 | 1 | 6 | ... | 5 | 15 |
| Indianapolis . | 2 | 1 | 1 | 3 | 3 | ... | 10 | Virginia..... | 2 | 1 | 1 | 3 | 5 | ... | 12 |
| Lost......... | 16 | 17 | 22 | 22 | 32 | 38 | 147 | Lost.......... | 11 | 17 | 19 | 29 | 36 | 34 | 145 |

In fact, as regards the playing strength of a majority of the

American Club teams in 1884, there was very little choice to be made taking each team as a whole, for where one would excel in its "battery" strength another would lead in its general field support. But there were two damaging drawbacks to success in the American clubs in 1884 which, in three or four prominent cases, offset all the advantages derived from effective "batteries" and excellent field support; and these were drunkenness in the ranks and the giving out of pitchers' arms and catchers' hands in critical periods of the campaign. Of course, a sufficient reserve force in the line of "battery" players will obviate one of these difficulties; but, in regard to drunkenness, there is no remedy but the severe one of expulsion from service, or the strict observance in the very beginning of the season, of total abstinence from liquor drinking for the entire championship campaign.

In reviewing the American campaign of 1884, the best story can be told through the medium of the records of each month's work in the championship arena, a study of the figures of these records showing very plainly where each club gained in the race or fell off in their running. Only one club of the twelve which entered the lists in May, failed to go through the work of the entire season, and that one was the Washington Club; and when the club disbanded on August 2, the Virginia Club took its place on August 4, and of the 105 games played by these two clubs, the Washington won 12 and lost 51, and the Virginia won 12 and lost but 30, thereby showing far superior play, the figures of their respective percentage of victories being 285 to 190 in favor of the Virginia Club.

### THE MONTHLY RECORDS.

The American Association's season of 1884 opened with the Athletic Club of Philadelphia in possession of the pennant won in 1883. In the place of the eight competitors of 1883 there were now twelve, the four new members comprising the Brooklyn Club—which had won the championship of the Interstate Association in '83—the Toledo—which had won the championship of the N. W. League in 1883—Indianapolis and Washington Clubs. The first week of the May campaign saw the Louisville Club go to the front, while the champion Athletics, the ex-champion Cincinnatis and the "coming champions," the Metropolitans, had to occupy rear positions. By the end of May Louisville had secured the lead in the race by first class play, the "Mets" being second, and the champion Athletics third. During the month all but the Pittsburg, Toledo, Washington and Indianapolis Clubs had scored double figures in victories, and, except Brooklyn, all save the four above named had won more games than they had lost, the May record ending as follows:

## MAY RECORD.

| | Louisville. | Metropolitan. | Athletic. | Columbus. | St. Louis. | Cincinnati. | Baltimore. | Brooklyn. | Allegheny. | Toledo. | Washington. | Indianapolis. | Games won. |
|---|---|---|---|---|---|---|---|---|---|---|---|---|---|
| Louisville.... | .... | 0 | 2 | 3 | 0 | 0 | 0 | 0 | 0 | 6 | 2 | 5 | 18 |
| Metropolitan. | 0 | .... | 0 | 0 | 1 | 0 | 3 | 0 | 6 | 0 | 5 | 2 | 17 |
| Athletic...... | 1 | 0 | .... | 0 | 0 | 0 | 2 | 0 | 5 | 2 | 5 | 0 | 15 |
| Columbus.... | 3 | 0 | 0 | .... | 4 | 4 | 1 | 0 | 2 | 0 | 0 | 0 | 14 |
| St. Louis..... | 0 | 1 | 0 | 2 | .... | 0 | 0 | 1 | 0 | 4 | 0 | 5 | 13 |
| Cincinnati.... | 0 | 0 | 0 | 2 | 0 | .... | 1 | 0 | 0 | 3 | 2 | 4 | 12 |
| Baltimore.... | 0 | 3 | 3 | 1 | 0 | 2 | .... | 3 | 0 | 0 | 0 | 0 | 12 |
| Brooklyn..... | 0 | 0 | 0 | 0 | 2 | 0 | 3 | .... | 1 | 0 | 3 | 1 | 10 |
| Allegheny ... | 0 | 0 | 1 | 0 | 0 | 0 | 0 | 5 | .... | 2 | 0 | 0 | 8 |
| Toledo....... | 0 | 0 | 1 | 0 | 2 | 2 | 0 | 0 | 1 | .... | 0 | 0 | 6 |
| Washington.. | 0 | 1 | 1 | 1 | 0 | 0 | 0 | 1 | 0 | 0 | .... | 0 | 4 |
| Indianapolis.. | 1 | 1 | 0 | 0 | 0 | 0 | 0 | 1 | 0 | 0 | 0 | .... | 3 |
| Games lost... | 5 | 6 | 8 | 9 | 9 | 8 | 10 | 11 | 15 | 17 | 17 | 17 | 132 |

In June St. Louis stepped to the front, the schedule giving them chances for scoring against the new teams in a majority of their games, besides which they rattled the champion Athletics pretty badly this month, they winning five of the six games they played together during June. Cincinnati also loomed up well, as did Baltimore; the latter winning ten games during June from the Indianapolis and Toledo Clubs, Cincinnati at the same time taking the starch out of the "Mets," while Columbus gave the Brooklyns a set back in the latter's efforts to win a good place in the American Club ranks. This month, too, saw the Athletics lose valuable ground, they losing eleven out of their nineteen games in June. Pittsburg, too, made a bad tumble, the dissipation in their ranks proving costly again. The record for the month was as follows:

## JUNE RECORD.

| | St. Louis. | Cincinnati. | Baltimore. | Columbus. | Metropolitan. | Louisvil'e. | Athletic. | Brooklyn. | Indianapolis. | Toledo. | Washington. | Allegheny. | Games Won. |
|---|---|---|---|---|---|---|---|---|---|---|---|---|---|
| St. Louis..... | .... | 0 | 2 | 0 | 0 | 0 | 5 | 0 | 0 | 0 | 5 | 3 | 15 |
| Cincinnati.... | 0 | .... | 0 | 0 | 4 | 0 | 1 | 2 | 0 | 0 | 2 | 5 | 14 |
| Baltimore.... | 2 | 0 | .... | 1 | 0 | 0 | 0 | 0 | 6 | 4 | 0 | 0 | 13 |
| Columbus.... | 0 | 0 | 0 | .... | 1 | 0 | 1 | 5 | 0 | 0 | 2 | 4 | 13 |
| Metropolitan. | 0 | 2 | 0 | 3 | .... | 4 | 0 | 0 | 0 | 3 | 0 | 0 | 12 |
| Louisville.... | 0 | 0 | 0 | 0 | 2 | .... | 1 | 2 | 0 | 0 | 2 | 2 | 9 |
| Athletic...... | 1 | 2 | 0 | 2 | 0 | 0 | .... | 0 | 3 | 0 | 0 | 0 | 8 |
| Brooklyn..... | 0 | 1 | 0 | 1 | 0 | 1 | 0 | .... | 1 | 4 | 0 | 0 | 8 |
| Indianapolis . | 0 | 0 | 0 | 0 | 0 | 0 | 3 | 1 | .... | 0 | 1 | 2 | 7 |
| Toledo....... | 0 | 0 | 2 | 0 | 0 | 0 | 2 | 0 | 1 | .... | 2 | 0 | 6 |
| Washington . | 1 | 0 | 0 | 0 | 0 | 1 | 0 | 0 | 2 | 1 | .... | 0 | 5 |
| Allegheny... | 0 | 1 | 0 | 0 | 0 | 1 | 0 | 0 | 1 | 1 | 0 | .... | 4 |
| Games Lost. | 4 | 6 | 4 | 7 | 7 | 7 | 11 | 12 | 13 | 13 | 14 | 16 | 114 |

In July the Metropolitans made a successful rally, and
aided by their easy victories over the champion Athletics, and
their success against Brooklyn, they went to the front for July,
being closely followed by Columbus, Cincinnati and Louisville,
while the champions had to be content with fifth place on the
month's record. Brooklyn and Baltimore this month showed
up very weak, Brooklyn only winning 6 out of 25 games, and
Baltimore but 5 out of 18. By this time the Washington
Club's team had been distanced in the race, they only winning
2 out of 21 games during July. Already the Western teams
of Louisville, Columbus and St. Louis had loomed up stronger
than ever before, especially the two former; and it was seen
that the season's race bid fair to be exciting as far as at least
six clubs were concerned. The Athletics improved on their
June record in July, but it was already evident that their
chances for retaining the pennant in '84 were getting to be
rather slim. The record for July is as follows:

### JULY RECORD.

|  | Metropolitan. | Columbus. | Cincinnati. | Louisville. | Athletic. | St. Louis. | Toledo. | Allegheny. | Indianapolis. | Brooklyn. | Baltimore. | Washington. | Games Won. |
|---|---|---|---|---|---|---|---|---|---|---|---|---|---|
| Metropolitan............ | ... | 0 | 0 | 0 | 5 | 3 | 1 | 2 | 3 | 4 | 0 | 0 | 18 |
| Columbus............... | 2 | ... | 0 | 0 | 2 | 1 | 1 | 0 | 1 | 4 | 2 | 3 | 16 |
| Cincinnati.............. | 0 | 0 | ... | 3 | 1 | 2 | 0 | 0 | 2 | 2 | 3 | 2 | 15 |
| Louisville.............. | 0 | 0 | 0 | ... | 1 | 1 | 5 | 2 | 1 | 2 | 3 | 0 | 15 |
| Athletic................ | 1 | 1 | 2 | 1 | ... | 0 | 3 | 0 | 2 | 2 | 2 | 0 | 14 |
| St. Louis............... | 0 | 1 | 3 | 2 | 0 | ... | 0 | 3 | 0 | 3 | 1 | 0 | 13 |
| Toledo.................. | 2 | 0 | 0 | 0 | 0 | 0 | ... | 1 | 3 | 0 | 0 | 3 | 9 |
| Allegheny.............. | 0 | 0 | 0 | 1 | 0 | 0 | 1 | ... | 1 | 1 | 0 | 4 | 8 |
| Indianapolis........... | 0 | 1 | 0 | 0 | 0 | 0 | 0 | 2 | ... | 0 | 0 | 3 | 6 |
| Brooklyn............... | 0 | 0 | 1 | 1 | 0 | 0 | 0 | 1 | 2 | ... | 1 | 0 | 6 |
| Baltimore.............. | 0 | 0 | 0 | 0 | 1 | 0 | 1 | 0 | 1 | 1 | ... | 2 | 5 |
| Washington............ | 0 | 0 | 0 | 0 | 0 | 0 | 0 | 1 | 0 | 0 | 1 | ... | 2 |
| Games Lost......... | 5 | 3 | 6 | 8 | 9 | 8 | 11 | 13 | 13 | 19 | 13 | 19 | 127 |

In August the Baltimore team made their best month's
record of the season, and secured the lead in the August
record, Columbus being a close second. The Athletics, too,
rallied well, and got up to third place on the monthly table,
while Cincinnati and St. Louis fell off in the running. In this
month the Washingtons gave up the ghost, they having up
to Aug. 2 won but 12 games out of 63 played. The Virginia
Club of Richmond, of the Eastern League, entered the American Association in their place, and the new comers made a
very good record for the balance of the season. The record
for the month of August is as follows:

## AUGUST RECORD.

| | Baltimore. | Columbus. | Athletic. | Louisville. | Metropolitan. | Brooklyn. | Toledo. | Cincinnati. | St. Louis. | Indianapolis. | Allegheny. | Virginia. | Washington. | Games Won. |
|---|---|---|---|---|---|---|---|---|---|---|---|---|---|---|
| Baltimore........... | ... | 0 | 0 | 0 | 2 | 1 | 0 | 0 | 0 | 0 | 7 | 4 | 0 | 14 |
| Columbus........... | 0 | ... | 0 | 1 | 0 | 0 | 3 | 3 | 0 | 7 | 0 | 0 | 0 | 14 |
| Athletic............ | 2 | 0 | ... | 0 | 1 | 4 | 0 | 0 | 0 | 0 | 3 | 2 | 0 | 12 |
| Louisville.......... | 0 | 1 | 0 | ... | 0 | 0 | 1 | 3 | 4 | 2 | 0 | 0 | 0 | 11 |
| Metropolitan........ | 2 | 0 | 2 | 0 | ... | 2 | 0 | 0 | 0 | 1 | 0 | 2 | 1 | 10 |
| Brooklyn............ | 1 | 0 | 3 | 0 | 0 | ... | 0 | 0 | 0 | 0 | 2 | 3 | 0 | 9 |
| Toledo.............. | 0 | 1 | 0 | 1 | 0 | 0 | ... | 1 | 3 | 3 | 0 | 0 | 0 | 9 |
| Cincinnati.......... | 0 | 1 | 0 | 2 | 0 | 0 | 2 | ... | 2 | 2 | 0 | 0 | 0 | 9 |
| St. Louis........... | 0 | 2 | 0 | 3 | 0 | 0 | 1 | 3 | ... | 0 | 0 | 0 | 0 | 9 |
| Indianapolis........ | 0 | 1 | 0 | 0 | 0 | 0 | 3 | 1 | 2 | ... | 0 | 0 | 0 | 7 |
| Allegheny........... | 1 | 0 | 1 | 0 | 1 | 0 | 0 | 0 | 0 | 0 | ... | 1 | 0 | 4 |
| Virginia............ | 0 | 0 | 0 | 0 | 0 | 2 | 0 | 0 | 0 | 0 | 1 | ... | 0 | 3 |
| Washington.......... | 0 | 0 | 0 | 0 | 1 | 0 | 0 | 0 | 0 | 0 | 0 | 0 | ... | 1 |
| Games Lost......... | 6 | 6 | 6 | 7 | 5 | 9 | 10 | 11 | 11 | 14 | 14 | 12 | 1 | 112 |

In September the Cincinnati and St. Louis Clubs did the best work that month, the former leading by having one less defeat charged to them. The "Mets," too, were well up in the front, and they were now regarded as the coming champions, the Athletics, by this time, having lost their chance of success in 1884. The Toledo team, in September, did their best work of the month, they whipping the Metropolitans handsomely. Louisville and Baltimore fell off in their running, and Brooklyn had to take the last seat in the September class, as the record for the month below shows:

## SEPTEMBER RECORD.

| | Cincinnati. | Metropolitan. | St. Louis. | Toledo. | Louisville. | Baltimore. | Athletic. | Columbus. | Virginia. | Allegheny. | Indianapolis. | Brooklyn. | Games Won |
|---|---|---|---|---|---|---|---|---|---|---|---|---|---|
| Cincinnati.... | .... | 0 | 0 | 2 | 0 | 2 | 2 | 0 | 2 | 2 | 0 | 2 | 12 |
| Metropolitan. | 2 | .... | 1 | 0 | 3 | 0 | 1 | 1 | 0 | 0 | 1 | 3 | 12 |
| St. Louis..... | 0 | 1 | .... | 0 | 0 | 1 | 1 | 0 | 3 | 2 | 1 | 2 | 11 |
| Toledo........ | 0 | 2 | 0 | .... | 0 | 3 | 1 | 0 | 2 | 1 | 0 | 2 | 11 |
| Louisville.... | 0 | 1 | 0 | 0 | .... | 1 | 2 | 1 | 2 | 2 | 0 | 1 | 10 |
| Baltimore.... | 0 | 0 | 1 | 1 | 3 | .... | 0 | 3 | 0 | 1 | 1 | 0 | 10 |
| Athletic...... | 2 | 0 | 1 | 1 | 0 | 1 | .... | 1 | 0 | 0 | 1 | 0 | 7 |
| Columbus .... | 0 | 1 | 0 | 0 | 1 | 0 | 1 | .... | 1 | 1 | 0 | 2 | 7 |
| Virginia.. .... | 0 | 0 | 1 | 0 | 0 | 0 | 0 | 1 | .... | 3 | 1 | 0 | 6 |
| Allegheny.... | 0 | 0 | 0 | 1 | 0 | 0 | 0 | 1 | 0 | .... | 4 | 0 | 6 |
| Indianapolis.. | 0 | 1 | 1 | 0 | 0 | 1 | 1 | 0 | 0 | 0 | .... | 1 | 5 |
| Brooklyn..... | 0 | 1 | 0 | 0 | 1 | 0 | 0 | 2 | 0 | 0 | 1 | .... | 5 |
| Games Lost. | 4 | 7 | 5 | 5 | 8 | 9 | 9 | 10 | 10 | 12 | 10 | 13 | 102 |

In October Baltimore made a good spurt, and excelled all their opponents for the month, they winning 9 out of 11 games in October. The contest for the lead toward the last was quite exciting, the Columbus and Louisville dying hard. The St. Louis Club, however, was the only one which won games from the Mets this month. The final result was the success of the Mets, leaving the Columbus team second and the Louisville third. The monthly record was as follows:

OCTOBER RECORD.

|  | Baltimore. | Metropolitan. | St. Louis. | Cincinnati. | Toledo. | Athletic. | Columbus. | Louisville. | Virginia. | Brooklyn. | Allegheny. | Indianapolis. | Games Won. |
|---|---|---|---|---|---|---|---|---|---|---|---|---|---|
| Baltimore..... | .... | 0 | 1 | 2 | 0 | 0 | 1 | 3 | 0 | 0 | 0 | 2 | 9 |
| Metropolitan. | 0 | .. | 0 | 2 | 1 | 0 | 1 | 0 | 0 | 0 | 0 | 2 | 6 |
| St. Louis..... | 1 | 2 | .. | 0 | 0 | 1 | 0 | 0 | 0 | 1 | 1 | 0 | 6 |
| Cincinnati.... | 0 | 0 | 0 | .... | 0 | 0 | 0 | 0 | 2 | 2 | 1 | 1 | 6 |
| Toledo........ | 0 | 0 | 0 | 0 | .... | 1 | 0 | 0 | 2 | 0 | 2 | 0 | 5 |
| Athletic...... | 0 | 0 | 1 | 0 | 0 | .... | 1 | 1 | 0 | 0 | 0 | 2 | 5 |
| Columbus.... | 1 | 0 | 0 | 0 | 0 | 1 | .... | 0 | 1 | 0 | 2 | 0 | 5 |
| Louisville.... | 0 | 0 | 0 | 0 | 0 | 0 | 0 | .... | 2 | 1 | 2 | 0 | 5 |
| Virginia...... | 0 | 0 | 0 | 0 | 0 | 0 | 1 | 1 | .... | 0 | 0 | 1 | 3 |
| Brooklyn..... | 0 | 0 | 0 | 0 | 0 | 0 | 0 | 0 | 0 | .... | 0 | 2 | 2 |
| Allegheny.... | 0 | 0 | 1 | 0 | 0 | 0 | 0 | 0 | 0 | 0 | .... | 0 | 1 |
| Indianapolis.. | 0 | 0 | 0 | 0 | 0 | 0 | 0 | 0 | 1 | 0 | 0 | .. | 1 |
| Games Lost. | 2 | 2 | 3 | 4 | 1 | 3 | 4 | 5 | 8 | 4 | 8 | 10 | 54 |

The summary of the monthly victories for 1884 is appended:

|  | May. | June. | July. | August. | September. | October. | Total. |
|---|---|---|---|---|---|---|---|
| Metropolitan............................. | 17 | 12 | 18 | 10 | 12 | 6 | 75 |
| Columbus................................. | 14 | 13 | 16 | 14 | 7 | 5 | 69 |
| Louisville................................. | 18 | 9 | 15 | 11 | 10 | 5 | 68 |
| Cincinnati................................ | 12 | 14 | 15 | 9 | 12 | 6 | 68 |
| St. Louis................................. | 13 | 15 | 13 | 9 | 11 | 6 | 67 |
| Baltimore................................. | 12 | 13 | 5 | 14 | 10 | 9 | 63 |
| Athletic................................... | 15 | 8 | 14 | 12 | 7 | 5 | 61 |
| Toledo.................................... | 6 | 6 | 9 | 9 | 11 | 5 | 46 |
| Brooklyn.................................. | 10 | 8 | 6 | 9 | 5 | 2 | 40 |
| Pittsburg................................. | 8 | 4 | 8 | 4 | 6 | 1 | 31 |
| Indianapolis.............................. | 3 | 7 | 6 | 7 | 5 | 1 | 29 |
| Washington.............................. | 4 | 5 | 2 | 1 | 0 | 0 | 12 |
| Virginia................................... | 0 | 0 | 0 | 0 | 6 | 3 | 12 |
| Total............................ | 132 | 114 | 127 | 112 | 102 | 54 | 641 |

The summary of the monthly defeats for 1884 is as follows:

| | May. | June. | July. | August. | September. | October. | Total. |
|---|---|---|---|---|---|---|---|
| Metropolitan | 6 | 7 | 5 | 5 | 7 | 2 | 32 |
| Columbus | 9 | 7 | 3 | 6 | 10 | 4 | 39 |
| Louisville | 5 | 7 | 8 | 7 | 8 | 5 | 40 |
| Cincinnati | 8 | 6 | 6 | 11 | 4 | 4 | 41 |
| St. Louis | 9 | 4 | 8 | 11 | 5 | 3 | 40 |
| Baltimore | 10 | 4 | 13 | 6 | 9 | 2 | 44 |
| Athletic | 8 | 11 | 9 | 6 | 9 | 3 | 46 |
| Toledo | 17 | 13 | 11 | 10 | 5 | 1 | 58 |
| Brooklyn | 11 | 12 | 19 | 9 | 13 | 4 | 64 |
| Allegheny | 15 | 16 | 13 | 14 | 12 | 8 | 78 |
| Indianapolis | 17 | 13 | 13 | 14 | 10 | 10 | 78 |
| Washington | 17 | 14 | 19 | 1 | 0 | 0 | 51 |
| Virginia | 0 | 0 | 0 | 12 | 10 | 8 | 30 |
| Total | 132 | 114 | 127 | 112 | 102 | 54 | 641 |

The full official record of championship matches given in the order of the percentage of victories for 1884 is appended:

| | Metropolitan. | Columbus. | Louisville. | St. Louis. | Cincinnati. | Baltimore. | Athletic. | Toledo. | Brooklyn. | Allegheny. | Indianapolis. | Washington. | Virginia. | Games Won. | Per cent. of Victories. | Games Played. |
|---|---|---|---|---|---|---|---|---|---|---|---|---|---|---|---|---|
| Metropolitan | .. | 5 | 7 | 5 | 6 | 5 | 8 | 5 | 8 | 9 | 9 | 8 | 6 | 2 | 75 | .700 | 107 |
| Columbus | 4 | .. | 5 | 5 | 7 | 4 | 5 | 8 | 7 | 9 | 8 | 8 | 5 | 2 | 69 | .638 | 108 |
| Louisville | 3 | 5 | .. | 5 | 5 | 4 | 6 | 9 | 6 | 8 | 9 | 4 | 4 | 68 | .629 | 108 |
| St. Louis | 4 | 5 | 5 | .. | 6 | 5 | 7 | 5 | 7 | 9 | 6 | 5 | 3 | 67 | .626 | 107 |
| Cincinnati | 4 | 3 | 5 | 4 | .. | 6 | 4 | 7 | 8 | 8 | 9 | 6 | 4 | 68 | .623 | 109 |
| Baltimore | 5 | 6 | 6 | 5 | 4 | .. | 3 | 5 | 5 | 9 | 9 | 2 | 4 | 63 | .594 | 106 |
| Athletic | 2 | 5 | 3 | 3 | 6 | 7 | .. | 6 | 6 | 8 | 6 | 7 | 2 | 61 | .564 | 108 |
| Toledo | 4 | 1 | 1 | 5 | 3 | 5 | 3 | .. | 4 | 5 | 6 | 5 | 4 | 46 | .442 | 104 |
| Brooklyn | 1 | 3 | 3 | 2 | 2 | 5 | 3 | 4 | .. | 4 | 7 | 3 | 3 | 40 | .384 | 104 |
| Allegheny | 1 | 1 | 2 | 1 | 1 | 1 | 2 | 5 | 6 | .. | 6 | 4 | 1 | 31 | .284 | 109 |
| Indianapolis | 2 | 2 | 1 | 3 | 1 | 1 | 4 | 3 | 3 | 4 | .. | 4 | 1 | 29 | .271 | 107 |
| Washington | 2 | 1 | 1 | 1 | 0 | 1 | 1 | 1 | .. | 1 | 3 | .. | 0 | 12 | .190 | 63 |
| Virginia | 0 | 2 | 1 | 1 | 0 | 0 | 0 | 2 | 4 | 2 | 0 | .. | .. | 12 | .285 | 42 |
| Games Lost | 32 | 39 | 40 | 40 | 41 | 44 | 46 | 58 | 64 | 78 | 78 | 51 | 30 | 641 | | |

A summary of the work of the American championship campaign of 1884 shows the appended figures:

| CLUBS. | Won. | Lost. | Played. | To Play. | Tied. | Series Won. | Series Lost. | Series Tied. |
|---|---|---|---|---|---|---|---|---|
| Metropolitan | 75 | 32 | 107 | 3 | 4 | 7 | 0 | 4 |
| Columbus | 69 | 39 | 108 | 2 | 2 | 6 | 2 | 3 |
| Louisville | 68 | 40 | 108 | 2 | 2 | 6 | 2 | 3 |
| Cincinnati | 68 | 41 | 109 | 1 | 3 | 6 | 3 | 1 |
| St. Louis | 67 | 41 | 107 | 3 | 3 | 6 | 1 | 2 |
| Baltimore | 63 | 44 | 107 | 3 | 2 | 5 | 2 | 4 |
| Athletic | 61 | 46 | 107 | 3 | 2 | 7 | 3 | 1 |
| Toledo | 46 | 58 | 104 | 6 | 5 | 2 | 6 | 3 |
| Brooklyn | 41 | 64 | 105 | 5 | 4 | 2 | 8 | 1 |
| Allegheny | 31 | 78 | 109 | 1 | 2 | 1 | 7 | 2 |
| Indianapolis | 29 | 78 | 107 | 3 | 3 | 0 | 10 | 1 |
| Virginia | 12 | 30 | 42 | 1 | 4 | 0 | 4 | 1 |
| Washington | 12 | 51 | 63 | 4 | 0 | 0 | 5 | 0 |

The record of the championship series won and lost by each club during the season of 1884 is as follows:

| | Metropolitan. | Athletic. | St. Louis. | Columbus. | Louisville. | Cincinnati. | Baltimore. | Allegheny. | Toledo. | Brooklyn. | Indianapolis. | Virginia. | Series Won. | Series Tied. |
|---|---|---|---|---|---|---|---|---|---|---|---|---|---|---|
| Metropolitan | ... | 8-2 | 5-4 | 5-4 | 7-3 | 6-4 | 5-5 | 9-1 | 5-4 | 9-1 | 8-2 | 8-2 | 7 | 4 |
| Athletic | 2-8 | ... | 3-7 | 5-5 | 3-6 | 6-4 | 7-3 | 8-2 | 6-3 | 6-3 | 6-4 | | 9-1 | 7 | 1 |
| St. Louis | 4-5 | 7-3 | ... | 5-5 | 5-5 | 6-4 | 5-5 | 9-1 | 5-5 | 7-3 | 6-3 | 8-2 | 6 | 4 |
| Columbus | 4-5 | 5-5 | 5-5 | ... | 5-5 | 7-3 | 4-6 | 9-1 | 8 | 1 | 7-3 | 8-2 | 7-3 | 6 | 3 |
| Louisville | 3-7 | 6-4 | 5-5 | 5-5 | ... | 5-5 | 4-6 | 7-2 | 9-1 | 6-3 | 9-1 | 8-2 | 6 | 3 |
| Cincinnati | 4-6 | 4-6 | 4-6 | 3-7 | 5-5 | ... | 6-6 | 8-1 | 6-3 | 8-2 | 9-1 | 10-0 | 6 | 1 |
| Baltimore | 5-5 | 3-7 | 5-5 | 6-4 | 6-4 | 4-6 | ... | 9-1 | 5-5 | 5-5 | 9-1 | 6-1 | 5 | 4 |
| Allegheny | 1-9 | 2-8 | 1-9 | 1-9 | 2-7 | 1-8 | 1-9 | ... | 5-5 | 6-4 | 6-4 | 5-5 | 2 | 2 |
| Toledo | 4-5 | 3-6 | 5-5 | 1-8 | 1-9 | 3-7 | 5-5 | 5-5 | ... | 5-4 | 6-3 | 9-1 | 2 | 3 |
| Brooklyn | 1-9 | 3-6 | 3-7 | 3-7 | 3-6 | 2-8 | 5-5 | 4-6 | 4-5 | ... | 7-3 | 6-3 | 1 | |
| Indianapolis | 2-8 | 4-6 | 3-6 | 2-8 | 1-9 | 1-9 | 1-9 | 4-6 | 3-6 | 3-7 | ... | 5-4 | 0 | 1 |
| Virginia | 2-8 | 1-9 | 2-8 | 3-7 | 2-8 | 0-10 | 1-6 | 5-5 | 1-9 | 3-6 | 4-5 | ... | 0 | 1 |
| Series Lost | 0 | 3 | 0 | 1 | 2 | 4 | 2 | 7 | 4 | 7 | 10 | 9 | 49 | |

## AMERICAN CLUBS VS. LEAGUE CLUBS.

The spring season of the American campaign was marked by the playing of sixty-eight games between American and League Clubs. During the summer, however, but one of these exhibition games was played, and that was the contest between the Chicago and Toledo Clubs at Toledo, which the League team won by 10 to 8 only. The fall season was marked by the playing of seventeen of these games, making a total of 85 games for the entire season. Of these the League Clubs won 58 and the American 26, two being drawn. The full record of these games will be found in the chapter on the League season of 1884. A summary showing the victories of American clubs over League teams is appended.

LEAGUE VICTORIES.

|  | Columbus. | Louisville. | Allegheny. | St. Louis. | Cincinnati. | Athletic. | Baltimore. | Metropolitan. | Games Won. |
|---|---|---|---|---|---|---|---|---|---|
| Cleveland | 0 | 0 | 3 | 2 | 3 | 1 | 4 | 3 | 16 |
| New York | 0 | 0 | 0 | 1 | 1 | 0 | 1 | 9 | 12 |
| Boston | 0 | 0 | 0 | 0 | 0 | 0 | 4 | 5 | 9 |
| Providence | 0 | 0 | 1 | 3 | 3 | 1 | 0 | 0 | 8 |
| Buffalo | 0 | 0 | 3 | 0 | 0 | 3 | 1 | 0 | 7 |
| Philadelphia | 0 | 0 | 0 | 0 | 0 | 5 | 2 | 0 | 7 |
| Chicago | 1 | 0 | 0 | 2 | 0 | 0 | 0 | 0 | 4 |
| Detroit | 0 | 2 | 0 | 1 | 0 | 0 | 0 | 0 | 3 |
| Games Lost | 1 | 2 | 7 | 9 | 8 | 10 | 12 | 17 | 66 |

EAST VS. WEST.

The records of the games played by the six Eastern clubs together on their home grounds, and those of the Western clubs on their own fields, together with the records of the games East vs. West for 1884, are as follows:

HOME AND HOME GAMES.

|  | Columbus. | Louisville. | Cincinnati. | St. Louis. | Toledo. | Indianapolis. | Won. |  | Metropolitan. | Athletic. | Baltimore. | Brooklyn. | Allegheny. | Virginia. | Won. |
|---|---|---|---|---|---|---|---|---|---|---|---|---|---|---|---|
| Columbus |  | 5 | 7 | 5 | 8 | 8 | 33 | Metropolitan |  | 8 | 5 | 9 | 9 | 8 | 39 |
| Louisville | 5 |  | 5 | 5 | 9 | 9 | 33 | Athletic | 5 |  | 7 | 5 | 6 | 6 | 32 |
| Cincinnati | 3 | 5 |  | 4 | 7 | 9 | 28 | Baltimore | 2 | 3 |  | 6 | 8 | 9 | 28 |
| St. Louis | 5 | 5 | 6 |  | 5 | 6 | 27 | Brooklyn | 1 | 3 | 5 |  | 4 | 6 | 19 |
| Toledo | 1 | 1 | 3 | 5 |  | 6 | 16 | Allegheny | 1 | 2 | 1 | 6 |  | 5 | 15 |
| Indianapolis | 2 | 1 | 1 | 3 | 3 |  | 10 | Virginia | 2 | 1 | 1 | 3 | 5 |  | 12 |
| Lost | 16 | 17 | 22 | 22 | 32 | 38 | 147 | Lost | 11 | 17 | 19 | 29 | 35 | 34 | 145 |

## EAST VS. WEST.

| | Metropolitan. | Baltimore. | Athletic. | Brooklyn. | Allegheny. | Virginia. | Won. | | Cincinnati. | St. Louis. | Columbus. | Louisville. | Toledo. | Indianapolis. | Won. |
|---|---|---|---|---|---|---|---|---|---|---|---|---|---|---|---|
| Cincinnati.... | 4 | 6 | 4 | 8 | 8 | 10 | 40 | Metropolitan. | 6 | 5 | 5 | 7 | 5 | 8 | 36 |
| St. Louis..... | 4 | 5 | 7 | 7 | 9 | 8 | 40 | Baltimore ... | 4 | 5 | 6 | 6 | 5 | 9 | 35 |
| Columbus ... | 4 | 4 | 5 | 7 | 9 | 7 | 36 | Athletic ..... | 6 | 3 | 5 | 3 | 6 | 6 | 29 |
| Louisville.... | 3 | 4 | 6 | 6 | 7 | 8 | 34 | Brooklyn ... | 2 | 3 | 3 | 3 | 4 | 7 | 22 |
| Toledo....... | 4 | 5 | 3 | 5 | 5 | 9 | 31 | Allegheny... | 1 | 1 | 1 | 2 | 5 | 6 | 16 |
| Indianapolis . | 2 | 1 | 4 | 3 | 4 | 5 | 19 | Virginia.... | 0 | 2 | 3 | 2 | 1 | 4 | 12 |
| Lost. ... | 21 | 25 | 29 | 36 | 42 | 47 | 200 | Lost. .... | 19 | 19 | 23 | 23 | 26 | 40 | 150 |

## THE AMERICAN AVERAGES.

We append the official averages of the American Association Clubs for 1884, simply as a record of the players of the club teams who have taken part in the season's games, for the figures of the statistics given by the club scorers are, generally speaking, of far too unreliable data to be taken as any correct criterion of the relative skill of the players in their several positions. Especially is this the case in regard to the batting averages in general, and the fielding averages of pitchers in particular. So much partiality on the one hand, and prejudice on the other, interferes with the work of the majority of the official scorers, that it is not fair to hold up these averages as a record by which to judge a player's skill either at the bat or in the field. As regards the pitcher's fielding figures, those representing his actual work as a mere fielder in the position, and those which show his work as a "battery" player outside of actual fielding, are so mixed up in the record, that it is impossible to decide what his skill as a fielder is by the figures of the fielding averages. For instance—Dundon of the Columbus Club, who played in ten games as a pitcher, is given a record clear of a single fielding error in the ten games he played in, something next to an impossibility under the existing method of pitching. McCauley, too, a pitcher of the Indianapolis Club, is given a similar record, though he too played in nine games, and these two players head the list as having the best fielding averages of the season, while such splendid fielders in the position, as Fautz, Hecker, Keefe, Emslie, Terry, Mathews and others who each played in from fifty to sixty games, are way down in the list.

In the batting averages, Murphy of the Washington Club is given first place, though he played in only five games, and against comparatively weak teams, while Esterbrook of the

BASE BALL GUIDE.    43

Metropolitans is given second place though he played in over a hundred games. In proof of the inaccuracy of the figures furnished the American Secretary, the instance of the figures of Esterbrook's record are presented as a striking illustration. The official statement of Oct. 1 gives Esterbrook's average as follows: Games, 101; base-hits, 162; average of hits to times at bat 389. From Oct. 1 to 15, he played in eleven games, and only made 12 base-hits in the eleven games as reported in the New York *Clipper*, and yet the figures given him at the close of the season are 112 games, 185 hits, with an average of .404. Here is a discrepancy showing a gain of 23 base-hits between Oct. 1, and Oct. 15, though the reports only show a dozen hits. This gain is out of all proportion to the rates of each month throughout the season. This is only one case out of twenty which might be quoted to show the utter unreliability of the figures furnished the Secretary by alleged "official" scorers. We append the record as it is with all its inaccuracies, simply as a record giving the names of the players who took part in the American campaign of 1884.

### AMERICAN BATTING AVERAGES FOR 1884.

| Rank. | NAME. | CLUB. | No. Games. | No. B. H. | Av. B. H. |
|---|---|---|---|---|---|
| 1 | Murphy | Washington | 5 | 10 | .500 |
| 2 | Esterbroook | Metropolitan | 112 | 185 | .408 |
| 3 | Stovey | Athletic | 106 | 179 | .404 |
| 4 | Orr | Metropolitan | 110 | 162 | .352 |
| 5 | Browning | Louisville | 105 | 155 | .341 |
| 6 | Reilly | Cincinnati | 106 | 155 | .339 |
| 7 | Swartwood | Allegheny | 102 | 131 | .330 |
| 8 | Fennelly | Wash. and Cin | 90 | 124 | .326 |
| 9 | Jones | Cincinnati | 113 | 153 | .322 |
| 9 | Lewis | St. Louis | 72 | 99 | .322 |
| 10 | Eden | Allegheny | 32 | 37 | .305 |
| 10 | Olin | Wash. and Toledo | 47 | 52 | .305 |
| 10 | Keenan | Indianapolis | 68 | 76 | .305 |
| 11 | Wolf | Louisville | 112 | 151 | .303 |
| 11 | Burns, T. P | Baltimore | 36 | 41 | .303 |
| 12 | Houck | Athletic | 110 | 143 | .302 |
| 13 | O'Brien | Athletic | 38 | 43 | .300 |
| 13 | Barkley | Toledo | 104 | 130 | .300 |
| 14 | Whitney | Allegheny | 22 | 27 | .299 |
| 15 | Dorgan | Ind. and Brooklyn | 38 | 45 | .298 |
| 16 | Hecker | Louisville | 79 | 95 | .296 |
| 16 | Larkin | Athletic | 87 | 97 | .296 |
| 17 | Roseman | Metropolitan | 107 | 129 | .295 |
| 17 | Milligan | Athletic | 66 | 78 | .295 |
| 18 | West | Cincinnati | 33 | 34 | .292 |
| 18 | McPhee | Cincinnati | 113 | 135 | .292 |
| 19 | Cline | Louisville | 94 | 114 | .287 |
| 20 | Troy | Indianapolis | 6 | 6 | .285 |

## Batting Averages—Continued.

| Rank. | NAME. | CLUB. | No. Games. | No. B.H. | Av. B.H. |
|---|---|---|---|---|---|
| 21 | Snyder | Cincinnati | 68 | 72 | .284 |
|    | Johnston | Virginia | 39 | 42 | .284 |
| 22 | Carroll | Columbus | 69 | 72 | .283 |
|    | Robinson | Indianapolis | 20 | 23 | .283 |
| 23 | Clinton | Baltimore | 105 | 122 | .281 |
|    | Mann | Columbus | 99 | 102 | .276 |
| 24 | Corkhill | Cincinnati | 111 | 127 | .276 |
|    | Mullane | Toledo | 95 | 98 | .276 |
|    | Latham, W | St. Louis | 110 | 131 | .276 |
| 25 | Brown | Columbus | 107 | 123 | .275 |
| 26 | Knight | Athletic | 110 | 134 | .275 |
| 27 | Casey | Baltimore | 38 | 42 | .274 |
|    | Corey | Athletic | 106 | 124 | .273 |
| 28 | O'Neill | St. Louis | 77 | 82 | .272 |
|    | Sommer | Baltimore | 107 | 129 | .272 |
| 29 | Taylor | Athletic | 32 | 31 | .271 |
| 30 | Nicol | St. Louis | 110 | 119 | .270 |
| 31 | Gleason | St. Louis | 110 | 128 | .269 |
|    | Brady | Metropolitan | 112 | 121 | .269 |
| 32 | Walker | Brooklyn | 95 | 103 | .268 |
| 33 | Phillips | Indianapolis | 97 | 110 | .266 |
| 34 | Carpenter | Cincinnati | 109 | 128 | .265 |
| 35 | Troy | Metropolitan | 107 | 112 | .264 |
|    | Miller | Cincinnati | 6 | 5 | .263 |
|    | Callahan | Indianapolis | 61 | 68 | .263 |
| 36 | Cassidy | Brooklyn | 106 | 113 | .263 |
|    | Smith, E | Allegheny | 10 | 10 | .263 |
|    | Dolan | St. Louis | 35 | 36 | .263 |
|    | Wheeler | St. Louis | 5 | 5 | .263 |
|    | Caruthers | St. Louis | 23 | 22 | .262 |
| 37 | Doyle | Allegheny | 15 | 16 | .262 |
|    | Birchal | Athletic | 53 | 56 | .262 |
| 38 | Weihe | Indianapolis | 64 | 68 | .261 |
| 39 | Nelson | Metropolitan | 111 | 112 | .259 |
| 40 | Yewell | Washington | 35 | 24 | .258 |
| 41 | Krehmeyer | St. Louis | 20 | 17 | .257 |
| 42 | Hawkes | Washington | 38 | 40 | .256 |
|    | Morrison | Indianapolis | 43 | 47 | .256 |
| 43 | Trott | Baltimore | 72 | 73 | .254 |
| 44 | Keefe | Metropolitan | 62 | 52 | .252 |
| 45 | Walker | Toledo | 46 | 42 | .251 |
|    | Moriarty | Indianapolis | 10 | 7 | .250 |
|    | Blakiston | Athletic and Indianapolis | 38 | 37 | .250 |
|    | Powell | Virginia | 41 | 38 | .250 |
| 46 | Miller, L | Toledo | 9 | 7 | .250 |
|    | Fox | Allegheny | 8 | 6 | .250 |
|    | Pearce | Metropolitan | 5 | 5 | .250 |
|    | Hilsey | Athletic | 6 | 6 | .250 |
|    | Reccius | Louisville | 75 | 67 | .249 |
| 47 | McSorley | Toledo | 21 | 17 | .249 |
|    | Donnelly | Indianapolis | 40 | 33 | .249 |
| 48 | Maskrey | Louisville | 107 | 105 | .247 |
|    | Goldsby | St. Louis, Wash and Va | 23 | 22 | .247 |
| 49 | Reed | Allegheny | 19 | 17 | .246 |

BASE BALL GUIDE.                    45

BATTING AVERAGES—*Continued.*

| Rank. | NAME. | CLUB. | No. Games. | No. B. H. | Av. B. H. |
|---|---|---|---|---|---|
| 50 | Sullivan.. | Louisville | 64 | 61 | .245 |
| 51 | Householder | Brooklyn | 76 | 66 | .243 |
| 52 | Stearns | Baltimore | 101 | 97 | .241 |
|    | Comiskey | St. Louis | 108 | 11 | .241 |
|    | Glenn | Virginia | 43 | 143 | .241 |
|    | Smith | Columbus | 108 | 08 | .240 |
| 53 | Berkelback | Cincinnati | 6 | 1 6 | .240 |
|    | Kuehne | Columbus | 110 | 00 | .238 |
| 54 | Remsen | Brooklyn | 81 | 171 | .238 |
|    | Mountain | Columbus | 58 | 50 | .237 |
| 55 | Richmond | Columbus | 105 | 94 | .237 |
|    | Miller, J | Toledo | 105 | 00 | .236 |
| 56 | Stricker | Athletic | 109 | 196 | .236 |
|    | Reipschlager | Metropolitan | 59 | 55 | .236 |
| 57 | Terry | Brooklyn | 67 | 55 | .235 |
| 58 | McGinnis | St. Louis | 40 | 34 | .234 |
|    | Foutz | St. Louis | 32 | 28 | .233 |
| 59 | Locke | Indianapolis | 7 | 7 | .233 |
|    | Mansell | Cincinnati and Columbus | 89 | 81 | .233 |
|    | Knowles | Allegheny and Brooklyn | 87 | 79 | .231 |
| 60 | Lane | Toledo | 56 | 49 | .231 |
|    | Quinton | Virginia | 26 | 22 | .231 |
| 61 | Burns, P | Baltimore | 6 | 6 | .230 |
|    | Faatz | Allegheny | 29 | 24 | .230 |
| 62 | Fields | Columbus | 105 | 96 | .229 |
|    | Collins | Indianapolis | 38 | 31 | .229 |
| 63 | York | Baltimore | 84 | 72 | .228 |
| 64 | McLaughlin | Baltimore | 5 | 5 | .227 |
|    | Hayes | Allegheny and Brooklyn | 48 | 40 | .227 |
| 65 | Geer | Brooklyn | 107 | 86 | .226 |
| 66 | Butler | Indianapolis | 9 | 7 | .225 |
| 67 | Welch | Toledo | 109 | 96 | .224 |
|    | Poorman | Toledo | 93 | 85 | .224 |
| 68 | Miller | Allegheny | 88 | 78 | .222 |
|    | Henderson | Baltimore | 54 | 45 | .222 |
|    | Gerhardt | Louisville | 108 | 91 | .220 |
| 69 | Whiting | Louisville | 42 | 35 | .220 |
|    | Greenwood | Brooklyn | 92 | 84 | .220 |
| 70 | White | Allegheny | 74 | 64 | .219 |
| 71 | Mansell, M | Allegheny, Ath. and Va | 76 | 62 | .217 |
| 72 | McKeon | Indianapolis | 70 | 54 | .215 |
|    | Corcoran | Brooklyn | 52 | 41 | .215 |
| 73 | Wilson | Brooklyn | 24 | 18 | .214 |
| 74 | Peltz | Indianapolis | 106 | 84 | .213 |
|    | Warner | Brooklyn | 85 | 78 | .212 |
| 75 | Forster | Allegheny | 35 | 27 | .212 |
|    | Watkins | Indianapolis | 34 | 26 | .211 |
| 76 | Prince | Washington | 43 | 35 | .211 |
|    | Kerins | Indianapolis | 93 | 76 | .210 |
| 77 | Cahill | Columbus | 59 | 44 | .210 |
| 78 | O'Day | Toledo | 65 | 52 | .209 |
|    | Benners | Brooklyn | 49 | 39 | .209 |
| 79 | Holbert | Metropolitan | 65 | 53 | .208 |

## Batting Averages—*Continued*.

| Rank. | NAME. | CLUB. | No. Games. | Ch's off. | Pr'ct acc. |
|---|---|---|---|---|---|
| 80 | Manning....... | Baltimore....... | 91 | 70 | .207 |
|    | Moffitt........ | Toledo......... | 56 | 42 | .207 |
| 81 | Kiley.......... | Washington..... | 12 | 12 | .206 |
| 82 | Thompson...... | Indianapolis.... | 24 | 20 | .204 |
|    | Lavin......... | St. Louis....... | 16 | 11 | .204 |
| 83 | Gardner....... | Baltimore....... | 41 | 35 | .203 |
|    | Quest......... | St. Louis and Allegheny.... | 93 | 72 | .203 |
|    | Deasley....... | St. Louis....... | 73 | 52 | .202 |
|    | Atkinson...... | Athletic........ | 22 | 17 | .202 |
| 84 | Taylor........ | Allegheny...... | 41 | 31 | .202 |
|    | Kemmler...... | Columbus...... | 61 | 43 | .202 |
|    | Schenck....... | Virginia........ | 42 | 31 | .202 |
| 85 | White......... | Cincinnati...... | 54 | 38 | .200 |
|    | Nash.......... | Virginia........ | 45 | 33 | .200 |
| 86 | Emslie........ | Baltimore....... | 51 | 39 | .199 |
|    | Meister....... | Toledo......... | 34 | 24 | .199 |
| 87 | Coleman....... | Athletic........ | 30 | 22 | .196 |
| 88 | Strief.......... | St. Louis....... | 47 | 35 | .193 |
|    | Macullar...... | Baltimore...... | 108 | 70 | .193 |
| 89 | McLaughlin.... | Louisville...... | 100 | 65 | .191 |
| 90 | Farrow........ | Brooklyn....... | 16 | 11 | .190 |
|    | Larkin......... | Virginia........ | 40 | 27 | .190 |
| 91 | Morton........ | Toledo......... | 31 | 19 | .189 |
|    | McCauley..... | Indianapolis.... | 17 | 10 | .189 |
| 92 | Farley......... | Washington..... | 14 | 10 | .188 |
|    | Jones......... | Brooklyn....... | 24 | 16 | .188 |
| 93 | Traffley........ | Baltimore....... | 54 | 40 | .186 |
| 94 | Creamer....... | Allegheny...... | 100 | 65 | .185 |
|    | Andrews....... | Louisville...... | 15 | 10 | .185 |
| 95 | Kennedy....... | Metropolitan.... | 103 | 71 | .184 |
|    | McGuire....... | Toledo......... | 45 | 28 | .184 |
| 96 | Merrill........ | Indianapolis.... | 54 | 37 | .183 |
| 97 | Tilley......... | Toledo......... | 17 | 10 | .182 |
| 98 | Morris......... | Columbus...... | 57 | 37 | .181 |
| 99 | Peoples........ | Cincinnati...... | 70 | 49 | .180 |
| 100 | Battin......... | Allegheny...... | 43 | 29 | .178 |
|     | Humphries..... | Washington..... | 48 | 34 | .178 |
| 101 | Fulmer........ | Cincinnati and St. Louis.... | 30 | 20 | .177 |
|     | Matthews...... | Athletic........ | 49 | 33 | .177 |
| 102 | Houtz.......... | Allegheny...... | 7 | 6 | .176 |
| 103 | Siffel.......... | Athletic........ | 7 | 3 | .175 |
| 104 | Barr........... | Washington and Ind.... | 56 | 11 | .174 |
|     | Brown......... | Toledo......... | 42 | 27 | .174 |
| 105 | Gorman........ | Allegheny...... | 8 | 5 | .172 |
|     | Ake........... | Baltimore....... | 13 | 9 | .172 |
| 106 | Mountjoy...... | Cincinnati...... | 34 | 20 | .171 |
| 107 | Davis.......... | St. Louis....... | 26 | 15 | .168 |
| 108 | Morgan........ | Wash. and Virginia.... | 51 | 30 | .167 |
|     | Driscoll........ | Louisville...... | 13 | 8 | .167 |
| 109 | King.......... | Washington..... | 12 | 7 | .166 |
|     | Colgan........ | Allegheny...... | 48 | 27 | .166 |
| 110 | Hanna......... | Wash. and Virginia.... | 47 | 25 | .162 |
| 111 | Latham........ | Louisville...... | 78 | 50 | .161 |

BATTING AVERAGES—*Continued.*

| Rank | NAME | CLUB | No. Games | Ch's off | Pr'ct acc. |
|---|---|---|---|---|---|
| 112 | Meegan | Virginia | 23 | 12 | .160 |
| 113 | Powers | Cincinnati | 35 | 21 | .158 |
| 113 | Gladman | Washington | 56 | 35 | .158 |
| 114 | McDonald | Allegheny | 38 | 22 | .151 |
| 114 | Sullivan | Allegheny | 54 | 29 | .151 |
| 115 | Ferguson | Allegheny | 10 | 6 | .150 |
| 116 | Neagle | Allegheny | 41 | 21 | .148 |
| 117 | Lynch | Metropolitan | 54 | 28 | .144 |
| 118 | Foster | Athletic | 5 | 2 | .143 |
| 119 | Swan | Washington | 5 | 3 | .142 |
| 119 | Conway | Brooklyn | 14 | 7 | .142 |
| 120 | Mullin | Washington | 34 | 17 | .139 |
| 120 | Dundon | Columbus | 26 | 12 | .139 |
| 121 | Kimber | Brooklyn | 41 | 19 | .137 |
| 122 | Bond | Indianapolis | 7 | 3 | .130 |
| 122 | Lauer | Allegheny | 12 | 6 | .130 |
| 123 | Woulffe | Cincinnati and Allegheny | 24 | 7 | .125 |
| 123 | Dee | Allegheny | 12 | 5 | .125 |
| 124 | Deagle | Cincinnati and L'ville | 16 | 6 | .122 |
| 125 | Dugan, E | Virginia | 22 | 8 | .114 |
| 126 | Aydelotte | Indianapolis | 12 | 5 | .111 |
| 127 | Trumbull | Washington | 24 | 9 | .109 |
| 128 | Sneed | Indianapolis | 27 | 22 | .105 |
| 128 | Dickerson | Baltimore and L'ville | 21 | 17 | .105 |
| 128 | Holdsworth | Indianapolis | 5 | 2 | .105 |
| 129 | Hamill | Washington | 21 | 7 | .101 |
| 130 | McArthur | Indianapolis | 6 | 2 | .100 |
| 131 | Beach | Washington | 8 | 3 | .093 |
| 132 | Arundel | Toledo | 14 | 4 | .088 |
| 133 | Dugan, W | Virginia | 9 | 2 | .071 |
| 134 | Smith | Washington | 14 | 4 | .070 |
| 135 | Bullis | Toledo | 13 | 3 | .067 |
| 136 | Shallix | Cincinnati | 23 | 4 | .049 |
| 137 | Barrett | Indianapolis | 5 | 0 | .000 |

## THE AMERICAN FIELDING AVERAGES FOR 1884.

The fielding averages giving the catchers' records, place Miller of Cincinnati at the head of the list, though he only played in six games, while Milligan of the Athletes, who played in 65 games, has to be content with third place. The fact is, the record of the latter is far superior to that of the former. Here are the official averages as published by Secretary Wikoff:

## CATCHERS.

| Rank. | NAME. | CLUB. | No. Games. | Ch's off. | Pr'ct'nce. |
|---|---|---|---|---|---|
| 1 | Miller | Cincinnati | 6 | 41 | .976 |
| 2 | Robinson | Indianapolis | 17 | 126 | .969 |
| 3 | Milligan | Athletic | 65 | 602 | .959 |
| 4 | Peoples | Cincinnati | 13 | 95 | .958 |
| 5 | Arundel | Toledo | 14 | 146 | .946 |
| 6 | Carroll | Columbus | 54 | 502 | .945 |
| 7 | Householder | Brooklyn | 30 | 300 | .937 |
| 8 | Trott | Baltimore | 63 | 648 | .936 |
| 9 | Dorgan | Ind. and Brooklyn | 8 | 60 | .934 |
| 10 | Sullivan | Louisville | 63 | 441 | .930 |
| 11 | Traffley | Baltimore | 47 | 416 | .928 |
| 11 | Snyder | Cincinnati | 66 | 528 | .928 |
| 12 | Deasley | St. Louis | 73 | 605 | .925 |
| 13 | Reipschlager | Metropolitan | 52 | 521 | .924 |
| 14 | Hayes | Allegheny and Brooklyn | 38 | 293 | .919 |
| 15 | O'Brien | Athletic | 32 | 246 | .912 |
| 16 | Holbert | Metropolitan | 59 | 473 | .910 |
| 16 | McGuire | Toledo | 40 | 302 | .910 |
| 17 | Bullis | Toledo | 12 | 77 | .909 |
| 18 | Kemmler | Columbus | 58 | 400 | .908 |
| 19 | Hanna | Washington and Virginia | 40 | 302 | .904 |
| 20 | Powers | Cincinnati | 31 | 235 | .903 |
| 21 | Foster | Athletic |  | 30 | .900 |
| 21 | Miller | Allegheny | 36 | 249 | .900 |
| 22 | Whiting | Louisville | 40 | 290 | .897 |
| 23 | Smith, E | Allegheny | 7 | 48 | .896 |
| 24 | Krehmeyer | St. Louis | 6 | 38 | .895 |
| 25 | Farrow | Brooklyn | 16 | 120 | .892 |
| 26 | Walker | Toledo | 41 | 328 | .888 |
| 27 | Humphries | Washington | 34 | 282 | .887 |
| 28 | Colgan | Allegheny | 44 | 337 | .885 |
| 28 | Wilson | Brooklyn | 9 | 52 | .885 |
| 29 | Thompson | Indianapolis | 12 | 85 | .883 |
| 30 | Keenan | Indianapolis | 59 | 212 | .882 |
| 31 | Dougan, W | Virginia | 9 | 67 | .881 |
| 32 | Quinton | Virginia | 14 | 79 | .874 |
| 33 | Dolan | St. Louis | 33 | 269 | .870 |
| 33 | Morgan | Washington and Virginia | 14 | 100 | .870 |
| 33 | Corcoran | Brooklyn | 3 | 284 | .870 |
| 34 | Wolf | Louisville | 11 | 77 | .869 |
| 35 | Siffel | Athletic | 7 | 33 | .849 |

## PITCHERS.

| Rank. | NAME. | CLUB. | No. Games. | Ch's off. | Pr'ct'nce. |
|---|---|---|---|---|---|
| 1 | Dundon | Columbus | 10 | 25 | 1.000 |
| 1 | McCauley | Indianapolis | 9 | 26 | 1.000 |
| 2 | Foutz | St. Louis | 23 | 82 | .964 |
| 3 | Reccius | Louisville | 18 | 64 | .954 |
| 3 | Mountjoy | Cincinnati | 32 | 89 | .954 |
| 4 | Hecker | Louisville | 76 | 274 | .953 |
| 5 | Meegan | Virginia | 22 | 121 | .943 |
| 6 | Shallix | Cincinnati | 23 | 76 | .935 |
| 7 | Henderson | Baltimore | 51 | 329 | .934 |
| 8 | Emslie | Baltimore | 50 | 312 | .927 |
| 9 | Keefe | Metropolitan | 57 | 324 | .926 |
| 10 | Mullane | Toledo | 66 | 262 | .912 |
| 11 | Caruthers | St. Louis | 13 | 33 | .910 |
| 12 | Lynch | Metropolitan | 54 | 283 | .906 |

## BASE BALL GUIDE.

### PITCHERS—Concluded.

| Rank. | NAME. | CLUB. | No. Games. | Ch's off. | Pr'ct acc. |
|---|---|---|---|---|---|
| 13 | Deagle............ | Louisville and Cincinnati.. | 15 | 30 | .900 |
| 14 | O'Day............ | Toledo............ | 40 | 139 | .885 |
| 15 | McGinnis........ | St. Louis......... | 40 | 104 | .875 |
| 16 | Sullivan.......... | Allegheny........ | 51 | 171 | .866 |
| 17 | Mountain........ | Columbus........ | 43 | 125 | .856 |
| 18 | Dugan, E........ | Virginia.......... | 20 | 82 | .854 |
| 19 | Morris............ | Columbus........ | 49 | 172 | .849 |
| 20 | Neagle........... | Allegheny........ | 37 | 111 | .847 |
| 21 | Taylor............ | Athletic.......... | 32 | 133 | .843 |
| 22 | { Atkisson | Athletic.......... | 22 | 86 | .838 |
|    | { McArthur | Indianapolis..... | 6 | 37 | .838 |
| 23 | Kimber........... | Brooklyn......... | 41 | 171 | .837 |
| 24 | Driscoll.......... | Louisville........ | 13 | 53 | .831 |
| 25 | White............. | Cincinnati........ | 54 | 108 | .824 |
| 26 | Barr.............. | Indianapolis and Wash.... | 46 | 124 | .823 |
| 27 | Terry............. | Brooklyn......... | 55 | 182 | .819 |
| 28 | Conway.......... | Brooklyn......... | 13 | 47 | .811 |
| 29 | McKeon......... | Indianapolis..... | 61 | 208 | .809 |
| 30 | Matthews........ | Athletic.......... | 49 | 135 | .801 |
| 31 | Fox.............. | Allegheny........ | 7 | 20 | .800 |
| 32 | Trumbull......... | Washington...... | 10 | 42 | .786 |
| 33 | O'Neill........... | St. Louis......... | 17 | 46 | .783 |
| 34 | Hamill........... | Washington...... | 18 | 59 | .782 |
| 35 | Davis............. | St. Louis......... | 23 | 49 | .756 |
| 36 | Aydelotte........ | Indianapolis..... | 12 | 29 | .725 |
| 37 | Bond............. | Indianapolis..... | 5 | 10 | .700 |

### FIRST BASEMEN.

| Rank. | NAME. | CLUB. | No. Games. | Ch's off. | Pr'ct acc. |
|---|---|---|---|---|---|
| 1 | Keenan........... | Indianapolis..... | 6 | 68 | .986 |
| 2 | Houtz............ | Allegheny........ | 5 | 52 | .982 |
| 3 | { McSorley | Toledo........... | 16 | 168 | .977 |
|   | { Orr | Metropolitan..... | 110 | 1216 | .977 |
| 4 | { Reilly | Cincinnati....... | 103 | 1056 | .975 |
|   | { Kerins | Indianapolis..... | 86 | 957 | .975 |
| 5 | Corkhill.......... | Cincinnati....... | 6 | 71 | .973 |
| 6 | Stovey............ | Athletic.......... | 106 | 1148 | .972 |
| 7 | Comiskey........ | St. Louis......... | 108 | 1255 | .971 |
| 8 | Walker........... | Brooklyn......... | 36 | 411 | .962 |
| 9 | Moffett........... | Toledo........... | 39 | 432 | .961 |
| 10 | Faatz............. | Allegheny........ | 29 | 295 | .960 |
| 11 | Field............. | Columbus........ | 105 | 1223 | .959 |
| 12 | { Hayes | Allegheny and Brooklyn... | 5 | 47 | .958 |
|    | { Latham | Louisville........ | 78 | 857 | .958 |
| 13 | Knowles.......... | Brooklyn and Allegheny.. | 85 | 906 | .957 |
| 14 | Browning........ | Louisville........ | 24 | 289 | .956 |
| 15 | { Householder | Brooklyn......... | 41 | 472 | .954 |
|    | { P. Burns | Baltimore........ | 6 | 64 | .954 |
| 16 | Lane.............. | Toledo........... | 44 | 521 | .952 |
| 17 | Andrews.......... | Louisville........ | 9 | 101 | .951 |
| 18 | Stearns........... | Baltimore........ | 100 | 1053 | .949 |
| 19 | McCauley........ | Indianapolis..... | 5 | 38 | .948 |
| 20 | Powell............ | Virginia.......... | 41 | 419 | .943 |
| 21 | Prince............ | Washington...... | 43 | 453 | .940 |
| 22 | McKeon.......... | Indianapolis..... | 5 | 48 | .938 |
| 23 | King.............. | Washington...... | 12 | 132 | .933 |
| 24 | Mullane.......... | Toledo........... | 6 | 67 | .926 |
| 25 | Blakiston......... | Athletic and Ind.......... | 5 | 41 | .903 |
| 26 | Swartwood....... | Allegheny........ | 22 | 121 | .835 |

## SECOND BASEMEN.

| Rank. | NAME. | CLUB. | No. Games. | Ch's off. | Pr'ct ac. |
|---|---|---|---|---|---|
| 1 | Creamer | Allegheny | 98 | 671 | .944 |
| 2 | Barkley | Toledo | 102 | 717 | .934 |
| 3 | McPhee | Cincinnati | 113 | 851 | .925 |
| 4 | Gerhardt | Louisville | 108 | 819 | .924 |
| 5 | Watkins | Indianapolis | 11 | 67 | .911 |
| 6 | Smith | Columbus | 108 | 793 | .910 |
| 7 | { Manning | Baltimore | 91 | 542 | .908 |
|   | { Hawkes | Washington | 35 | 248 | .908 |
| 8 | Greenwood | Brooklyn | 92 | 593 | .899 |
| 9 | Larkin | Virginia | 40 | 244 | .898 |
| 10 | Merrill | Indianapolis | 54 | 336 | .896 |
| 11 | Quest | St. Louis and Allegheny | 89 | 595 | .895 |
| 12 | T. P. Burns | Baltimore | 9 | 66 | .894 |
| 13 | Nicol | St. Louis | 23 | 157 | .892 |
| 14 | Yewell | Washington | 10 | 73 | .891 |
| 15 | { Stricker | Athletic | 109 | 623 | .880 |
|    | { Troy | Metropolitan | 107 | 614 | .880 |
| 16 | Collins | Indianapolis | 38 | 227 | .873 |
| 17 | Jones | Brooklyn | 13 | 72 | .862 |
| 18 | Olin | Washington and Toledo | 11 | 69 | .783 |

## THIRD BASEMEN.

| 1 | Battin | Allegheny | 43 | 170 | .924 |
|---|---|---|---|---|---|
| 2 | Whitney | Allegheny | 22 | 89 | .911 |
| 3 | Esterbrook | Metropolitan | 112 | 375 | .904 |
| 4 | Corey | Athletic | 106 | 379 | .900 |
| 5 | Kuehne | Columbus | 110 | 387 | .889 |
| 6 | Carpenter | Cincinnati | 109 | 369 | .884 |
| 7 | Latham | St. Louis | 110 | 495 | .869 |
| 8 | Yewell | Washington | 6 | 15 | .867 |
| 9 | Reccius | Louisville | 48 | 145 | .856 |
| 10 | Morton | Toledo | 14 | 33 | .849 |
| 11 | Sommer | Baltimore | 98 | 341 | .833 |
| 12 | Watkins | Indianapolis | 21 | 47 | .830 |
| 13 | Nash | Virginia | 45 | 198 | .829 |
| 14 | Donnelly | Indianapolis | 26 | 69 | .827 |
| 15 | McDonald | Allegheny | 22 | 76 | .816 |
| 16 | White | Allegheny | 10 | 42 | .810 |
| 17 | Warner | Brooklyn | 85 | 303 | .806 |
| 18 | Callahan | Indianapolis | 61 | 199 | .805 |
| 19 | Brown | Toledo | 40 | 111 | .802 |
| 20 | Meister | Toledo | 34 | 79 | .798 |
| 21 | Browning | Louisville | 52 | 184 | .789 |
| 22 | Gladman | Washington | 54 | 185 | .784 |
| 23 | Ake | Baltimore | 9 | 23 | .783 |
| 24 | Jones | Brooklyn | 10 | 27 | .778 |
| 25 | Foster | Allegheny | 5 | 17 | .765 |
| 26 | Moffitt | Toledo | 11 | 43 | .721 |

## SHORT STOPS.

| Rank | NAME. | CLUB. | No. Games | Ch's off. | Pr'ct acc. |
|---|---|---|---|---|---|
| 1 | Houck | Athletic | 110 | 589 | .912 |
| 2 | Foster | Allegheny | 29 | 168 | .911 |
| 3 | Nelson | Metropolitan | 110 | 458 | .900 |
| 4 | McLaughlin | Louisville | 96 | 537 | .898 |
| 5 | Macullar | Baltimore | 108 | 491 | .878 |
| 6 | Geer | Brooklyn | 106 | 634 | .871 |
| 7 | { Miller | Toledo | 105 | 509 | .869 |
|   | { Richmond | Columbus | 105 | 455 | .869 |
| 8 | Gleason | St. Louis | 110 | 499 | .868 |
| 9 | { Phillips | Indianapolis | 97 | 523 | .863 |
|   | { Fennelly | Washington, Cincinnati | 87 | 489 | .863 |
| 10 | Cahill | Columbus | 5 | 19 | .862 |
| 11 | Dee | Allegheny | 12 | 49 | .858 |
| 12 | { Reccius | Louisville | 9 | 40 | .850 |
|    | { Corkhill | Cincinnati | 8 | 40 | .850 |
|    | { Peoples | Cincinnati | 48 | 247 | .850 |
| 13 | Schenck | Virginia | 40 | 181 | .835 |
| 14 | White | Allegheny | 61 | 307 | .792 |
| 15 | Donnelly | Indianapolis | 8 | 38 | .790 |
| 16 | Fulmer | Cincinnati | 29 | 118 | .788 |
| 17 | Cline | Louisville | 5 | 22 | .773 |

## LEFT FIELDERS.

| Rank | NAME. | CLUB. | No. Games | Ch's off. | Pr'ct acc. |
|---|---|---|---|---|---|
| 1 | { Mountain | Columbus | 8 | 8 | 1.000 |
|   | { Goldsby | St. L. W. & Va | 5 | 5 | 1.000 |
|   | { Kennedy | Metropolitan | 103 | 165 | .945 |
| 2 | Dundon | Columbus | 13 | 27 | .944 |
| 3 | Morton | Toledo | 102 | 162 | .935 |
| 4 | Mullane | Toledo | 13 | 23 | .914 |
| 5 | Maskrey | Louisville | 97 | 160 | .912 |
| 6 | Mullin | Washington | 5 | 19 | .900 |
| 7 | Farley | Washington | 14 | 28 | .893 |
| 8 | Remson | Brooklyn | 31 | 52 | .585 |
| 9 | O'Day | Toledo | 14 | 17 | .883 |
| 10 | Jones | Cincinnati | 63 | 125 | .875 |
| 11 | Olin | Washington and Toledo | 26 | 30 | .867 |
| 12 | Larkins | Athletic | 30 | 43 | .861 |
| 13 | Miller, L | Toledo | 6 | 7 | .858 |
| 14 | Strief | St. Louis | 42 | 67 | .851 |
| 15 | Reid | Allegheny | 18 | 33 | .849 |
| 16 | O'Neill | St. Louis | 58 | 90 | .834 |
| 17 | Birchal | Athletic | 50 | 99 | .829 |
| 18 | { Glenn | Virginia | 43 | 112 | .822 |
|    | { Walker | Brooklyn | 16 | 28 | .822 |
|    | { York | Baltimore | 68 | 101 | .822 |
| 19 | Peltz | Indianapolis | 106 | 211 | .820 |
| 20 | Cahill | Columbus | 51 | 83 | .820 |
| 21 | Benners | Brooklyn | 49 | 88 | .819 |
| 22 | Morgan | Washington and Va | 16 | 29 | .794 |
| 23 | Carroll | Columbus | 12 | 33 | .788 |
| 24 | Mansell, M. | All., Ath., W. & Va | 41 | 76 | .780 |
| 25 | Cline | Louisville | 7 | 9 | .778 |
| 26 | Clinton | Baltimore | 37 | 48 | .771 |
| 27 | Miller | Allegheny | 48 | 99 | .768 |

## LEFT FIELDERS—Continued.

| Rank. | NAME. | CLUB. | No. Games. | Ch's off. | Pr'ct acc. |
|---|---|---|---|---|---|
| 28 | Berkelback | Cincinnati | 6 | 8 | .750 |
| 29 | Doyle | Allegheny | 23 | 6 | .740 |
| 30 | Coleman | Athletic | 12 | 19 | .737 |
| 31 | Mansell | Cin. and Columbus | 63 | 84 | .703 |
| 32 | Tilly | Toledo | 16 | 22 | .636 |
| 33 | Lane | Toledo | 5 | 14 | .572 |
| 34 | Kiley | Washington | 13 | 27 | .556 |

## CENTER FIELDERS.

| | NAME. | CLUB. | No. Games. | Ch's off. | Pr'ct acc. |
|---|---|---|---|---|---|
| 1 | Browning | Louisville | 24 | 60 | .967 |
| 2 | Romson | Brooklyn | 50 | 113 | .956 |
| 3 | Welsh | Toledo | 104 | 246 | .937 |
| 4 | Holdsworth | Indianapolis | 5 | 25 | .923 |
| 5 | Mountain | Columbus | 6 | 12 | .919 |
| 6 | { Dickerson | Baltimore and Lou | 5 | 11 | .910 |
| 6 | { Mansell | Ath., All'y and Va | 5 | 11 | .910 |
| 7 | Jones | Cincinnati | 50 | 118 | .907 |
| 8 | Walker | Brooklyn | 43 | 86 | .896 |
| 9 | { Larkins | Athletic | 56 | 95 | .895 |
| 9 | { Roseman | Metropolitan | 105 | 189 | .895 |
| 10 | Blakiston | Ath. and Indianapolis | 27 | 55 | .891 |
| 11 | Cline | Louisville | 79 | 171 | .884 |
| 12 | Mann | Columbus | 97 | 166 | .880 |
| 13 | Casey | Baltimore | 38 | 57 | .877 |
| 14 | Trumbull | Washington | 8 | 15 | .867 |
| 15 | Woulfe | Allegheny | 16 | 29 | .863 |
| 16 | Lewis | St. Louis | 72 | 166 | .862 |
| 17 | Johnston | Virginia | 37 | 113 | .859 |
| 18 | Wilson | Brooklyn | 6 | 13 | .847 |
| 19 | Sneed | Indianapolis | 21 | 47 | .830 |
| 20 | Clinton | Baltimore | 67 | 139 | .825 |
| 21 | West | Cincinnati | 33 | 59 | .820 |
| 22 | Mullin | Washington | 27 | 55 | .819 |
| 23 | { Terry | Brooklyn | 7 | 21 | .810 |
| 23 | { McDonald | Allegheny | 11 | 21 | .810 |
| 24 | O'Brien | Athletic | 5 | 15 | .800 |
| 25 | Taylor | Allegheny | 41 | 89 | .787 |
| 26 | Mansell | Toledo, Cin. and Col | 25 | 57 | .772 |
| 27 | Olin | Toledo | 7 | 13 | .770 |
| 28 | Morrison | Indianapolis | 43 | 106 | .765 |
| 29 | Eden | Allegheny | 31 | 52 | .751 |
| 30 | Goldsby | St. L., W. and Va | 13 | 28 | .750 |
| 31 | Lavin | St. Louis | 15 | 23 | .739 |
| 32 | Coleman | Athletic | 14 | 22 | .682 |
| 33 | Krehmeyer | St. Louis | 8 | 10 | .600 |
| 34 | Thompson | Indianapolis | 7 | 12 | .500 |
| 35 | Barr | Washington and Ind | 6 | 5 | .400 |

BASE BALL GUIDE. 53

RIGHT FIELDERS.

| Rank | NAME | CLUB | No. Games | Chances Offered | Percent. Accepted |
|---|---|---|---|---|---|
| 1 | Traffley | Baltimore | 6 | 5 | 1000 |
| 2 | Swartwood | Allegheny | 77 | 308 | .929 |
| 3 | Corkhill | Cincinnati | 94 | 217 | .927 |
| 4 | Knight | Athletic | 109 | 217 | .927 |
| 5 | Brady | Metropolitan | 109 | 204 | .922 |
| 6 | Trumbull | Washington | 5 | 12 | .917 |
| 7 | Morgan | Wash. and Virginia, | 15 | 36 | .917 |
| 8 | Wolf | Louisville | 98 | 202 | .901 |
| 9 | Nicol | St. Louis | 87 | 216 | .894 |
| 10 | Butler | Indianapolis | 7 | 8 | .875 |
| 11 | Cassidy / Poorman | Brooklyn / Toledo | 101 / 92 | 175 / 183 | .869 / .869 |
| 12 | Gardner | Baltimore | 38 | 83 | .868 |
| 13 | York | Baltimore | 16 | 30 | .867 |
| 14 | Weihe | Indianapolis | 58 | 127 | .859 |
| 15 | Dickerson / Goldsby | Balt. and St. Louis / St. L., W. and Va | 15 / 5 | 21 / 7 | .858 / .858 |
| 16 | Caruthers | St. Louis | 10 | 7 | .857 |
| 17 | Lauer | Allegheny | 10 | 20 | .850 |
| 18 | Brown | Columbus | 105 | 204 | .849 |
| 19 | Sommer | Baltimore | 6 | 14 | .843 |
| 20 | Quinton | Virginia | 10 | 19 | .842 |
| 21 | Foutz | St. Louis | 7 | 12 | .834 |
| 22 | T. P. Burnes | Baltimore | 23 | 23 | .827 |
| 23 | Moriarity | Indianapolis | 7 | 9 | .778 |
| 24 | Smith | Washington | 11 | 31 | .774 |
| 25 | Humphries | Washington | 8 | 25 | .760 |
| 26 | Dorgan | Indianapolis and Brook | 30 | 66 | .758 |
| 27 | Mansell | All'y, Ath. and Va | 30 | 37 | .757 |
| 28 | Sneed | Indianapolis | 6 | 12 | .750 |
| 29 | Maskrey | Louisville | 5 | 8 | .750 |
| 30 | Beach | Washington | 7 | 16 | .688 |
| 31 | Woulffe | Cin. and Allegheny | 6 | 14 | .643 |
| 32 | Thompson | Indianapolis | 5 | 9 | .334 |

## THE AMERICAN CLUB RECORDS.

The club records showing the general percentage of base hits to times at the bat, and the percentage of chances accepted to chances offered in the field, show the Athletics in the van in batting averages, though they were only seventh in the pennant race: while in fielding, the Metropolitans take the lead in the averages, as they did in the race.

## CLUB BATTING RECORD.

| Rank | | No. of Games. | Times at Bat. | Runs. | No. of B. H. | Per cent. B. H. to A. B. |
|---|---|---|---|---|---|---|
| 1 | Athletic | 110 | 3986 | 712 | 1120 | .281 |
| 2 | Metropolitan | 112 | 3989 | 734 | 1086 | .272 |
| 3 | Cincinnati | 113 | 4149 | 761 | 1095 | .264 |
| 4 | Louisville | 112 | 4025 | 582 | 1022 | .253 |
| 5 | St. Louis | 110 | 3967 | 660 | 996 | .251 |
| 6 | Columbus | 110 | 3769 | 583 | 899 | .238 |
| 7 | Baltimore | 109 | 3849 | 642 | 910 | .236 |
| 8 | Indianapolis | 110 | 3802 | 462 | 891 | .234 |
| 9 | { Toledo | 109 | 3720 | 463 | 854 | .229 |
|   | { Brooklyn | 109 | 3738 | 476 | 859 | .229 |
| 10 | Virginia | 45 | 1482 | 194 | 327 | .220 |
| 11 | Allegheny | 110 | 3726 | 405 | 798 | .214 |
| 12 | Washington | 63 | 2171 | 248 | 435 | .200 |

## FIELDING RECORD.

| Rank | | No. of Games. | Put out. | Assists. | Errors. | Total Chances Offered | Per cent Chances Accepted. |
|---|---|---|---|---|---|---|---|
| 1 | Metropolitan | 112 | 2949 | 1711 | 383 | 5043 | .925 |
| 2 | { Louisville | 110 | 2892 | 1464 | 412 | 4768 | .914 |
|   | { Athletic | 112 | 3022 | 1547 | 430 | 4999 | .914 |
| 3 | Cincinnati | 113 | 2984 | 1429 | 420 | 4833 | .913 |
| 4 | { Columbus | 110 | 2876 | 1456 | 433 | 4765 | .910 |
|   | { Baltimore | 109 | 2883 | 1655 | 452 | 4990 | .910 |
| 5 | Toledo | 110 | 2830 | 1469 | 454 | 4753 | .905 |
| 6 | St. Louis | 110 | 2963 | 1474 | 480 | 4917 | .903 |
| 7 | Allegheny | 110 | 2817 | 1442 | 518 | 4777 | .892 |
| 8 | Brooklyn | 109 | 2841 | 1437 | 526 | 4804 | .891 |
| 9 | Indianapolis | 110 | 2808 | 1368 | 517 | 4673 | .890 |
| 10 | Virginia | 45 | 1113 | 644 | 238 | 1995 | .881 |
| 11 | Washington | 63 | 1630 | 799 | 393 | 2822 | .861 |

N. B.—All tie games are included.

## THE LEADING BATSMEN AND FIELDERS.

Including those players only who took part in a large majority of the games played by their respective clubs, the nine leading batsmen of the American Association for 1884, are as follows:

BASE BALL GUIDE.  55

| PLAYERS. | CLUBS. | Games Played in. | Average. |
|---|---|---|---|
| Esterbrook | Metropolitan | 112 | 408 |
| Stovey | Athletic | 106 | 404 |
| Orr | Metropolitan | 110 | 352 |
| Browning | Louisville | 105 | 341 |
| Reilly | Cincinnati | 106 | 339 |
| Swartwood | Allegheny | 102 | 330 |
| Fennelly | Wash. and Cincinnati | 90 | 326 |
| Jones | Cincinnati | 113 | 322 |
| Wolf | Louisville | 112 | 303 |

The nine leading fielders in the nine positions according to the same basis of estimate are as follows:

| PLAYERS. | POSITION. | CLUBS. | Games Played in. | Average. |
|---|---|---|---|---|
| Milligan | Catcher | Athletic | 65 | 959 |
| Hecker | Pitcher | Louisville | 76 | 953 |
| Orr | First baseman | Metropolitan | 110 | 977 |
| Creamer | Sec'd " | Allegheny | 98 | 944 |
| Esterbrook | Third " | Metropolitan | 112 | 904 |
| Houck | Short stop | Athletic | 110 | 912 |
| Morton | Left fielder | Toledo | 102 | 935 |
| Welsh | Center fielder | Toledo | 104 | 937 |
| Swartwood | Right fielder | Allegheny | 77 | 929 |

## THE AMERICAN PITCHERS OF 1884.

Some of the most effective work done in the pitcher's "box" in 1884 in the professional arena, was accomplished by a minority of the American Club pitchers, some of whom vied with the best pitchers in the League arena in strategic skill. Noteworthy among these strategists were Keefe and Lynch of the Metropolitan Club, Mathews of the Athletic, White of the Cincinnati, Hecker of the Louisville, Emslie of the Baltimore, and McGinnis of the St. Louis. Those who went in for speed only as their strong point, were Morris of the Columbus, Henderson of the Baltimore, and Taylor of the Athletic. Ninety odd pitchers took part in the American campaign, and fully two-thirds of them went in more for pace as an element of their success rather than strategy. Among the most promising of the candidates for pitching honors for 1884 was young Terry of the Brooklyn Club. Foutz and McKeon, too, of the new class of pitchers did good service in the position. Mountjoy of Cincinnati and Mountain of Columbus also deserve mention for effective work in the box at times. Mullane of Louisville would have been worthy of special mention, but for his discreditable conduct in violating his engagements.

## THE CHAMPIONSHIP RECORDS.

### THE OLD NATIONAL ASSOCIATION RECORD.

Up to 1870 but one National Association existed in the entire country and the last convention held by that organization occurred in that year. In 1871 Mr. Chadwick divided the clubs into two classes, and he organized the first regular professional association in that year, the convention which he called, assembling at Collier's Saloon—the well known actor—on the corner of Broadway and Thirteenth Street, New York, on the night of March 17, 1871. At that convention the first special code of championship rules ever put in operation were adopted, and in that year the first officially recognized championship contests known in the history of the game were played. The season began in May with the Athletic, Boston, Chicago, Cleveland, Forest City Club, Haymakers of Troy, Mutual, Olympic, of Washington, Kekionga and Rockford, Forest City Clubs, in the arena. The Eckfords entered in August, but their games were not counted. The Kekionga games were thrown out owing to illegal games after July. The record which decided the championship of 1871 was as follows:

RECORD FOR 1871.

| CLUB. | Athletic. | Boston. | Chicago. | Mutual. | Olympic. | Haymaker. | Cleveland. | Kekionga. | Rockford. | Games Won. |
|---|---|---|---|---|---|---|---|---|---|---|
| Athletic......................... | .... | 1 | 3 | 3 | 3 | 3 | 3 | 3 | 3 | 22 |
| Boston.......................... | 3 | .... | 1 | 3 | 3 | 3 | 3 | 3 | 3 | 22 |
| Chicago......................... | 2 | 3 | .... | 3 | 3 | 1 | 2 | 3 | 3 | 20 |
| Mutual.......................... | 2 | 2 | 1 | .... | 3 | 1 | 2 | 3 | 3 | 17 |
| Olympic......................... | 0 | 1 | 2 | 1 | .... | 3 | 3 | 3 | 3 | 16 |
| Haymaker....................... | 0 | 2 | 1 | 3 | 2 | .... | 2 | 3 | 2 | 15 |
| Cleveland....................... | 0 | 1 | 1 | 3 | 0 | 2 | .... | 0 | 3 | 10 |
| Kekionga........................ | 0 | 0 | 0 | 1 | 1 | 1 | 3 | .... | 1 | 7 |
| Rockford........................ | 0 | 0 | 0 | 1 | 0 | 1 | 1 | 3 | .... | 6 |
| Games Lost..................... | 7 | 10 | 9 | 18 | 15 | 15 | 19 | 21 | 21 | 135 |

In 1872 the Baltimores entered the list, as also the Atlantics of Brooklyn, and the Troy Club, and Washington sent two clubs, both of which failed, however; the brunt of the battle that year lying between the five clubs of Boston, Baltimore,

New York, Philadelphia and Troy. The result of the pennant race of 1872 was as follows:

RECORD FOR 1872.

| CLUB. | Boston. | Baltimore. | Mutual. | Athletic. | Troy. | Atlantic. | Cleveland. | Mansfield. | Eckford. | Olympic. | National. | Games Won. |
|---|---|---|---|---|---|---|---|---|---|---|---|---|
| Bos on | .... | 7 | 7 | 4 | 2 | 7 | 4 | 3 | 3 | 1 | 1 | 39 |
| Baltimore | 0 | .... | 5 | 4 | 3 | 4 | 4 | 4 | 5 | 2 | 3 | 34 |
| Mutual | 2 | 4 | .... | 6 | 3 | 6 | 2 | 4 | 5 | 1 | 1 | 34 |
| Athletic | 4 | 5 | 3 | .... | 2 | 4 | 3 | 2 | 5 | 1 | 1 | 30 |
| Troy | 1 | 0 | 2 | 0 | .... | 2 | 1 | 4 | 3 | 1 | 1 | 15 |
| Atlantic | 1 | 1 | 2 | 0 | 0 | .... | 0 | 2 | 2 | 0 | 0 | 8 |
| Cleveland | 0 | 1 | 1 | 0 | 0 | 1 | .... | 0 | 1 | 1 | 1 | 6 |
| Mansfield | 0 | 0 | 0 | 0 | 0 | 1 | 1 | .... | 2 | 0 | 1 | 5 |
| Eckford | 0 | 1 | 0 | 0 | 0 | 2 | 0 | 0 | .... | 0 | 0 | 3 |
| Olympic | 0 | 0 | 0 | 0 | 0 | 0 | 0 | 0 | 0 | .... | 2 | 2 |
| National | 0 | 0 | 0 | 0 | 0 | 0 | 0 | 0 | 0 | 0 | .... | 0 |
| Games Lost | 8 | 19 | 20 | 14 | 10 | 27 | 15 | 19 | 26 | 7 | 11 | 176 |

In 1873 the Athletics had a local rival team to meet in the championship arena, in the new Philadelphia Club, which, but for crookedness in its ranks, would have won the championship that year. Baltimore also sent two clubs, and Elizabeth, N. J. entered the lists. The record for 1873 was as follows:

RECORD FOR 1873.

| CLUB. | Boston. | Philadelphia. | Baltimore. | Mutual. | Athletic. | Atlantic. | Washington. | Resolute. | Maryland. | Games Won. |
|---|---|---|---|---|---|---|---|---|---|---|
| Boston | .... | 5 | 7 | 6 | 4 | 8 | 9 | 4 | 0 | 43 |
| Philadelphia | 4 | .... | 6 | 4 | 8 | 7 | 3 | 4 | 0 | 36 |
| Baltimore | 2 | 3 | .... | 6 | 3 | 7 | 6 | 3 | 3 | 33 |
| Mutual | 3 | 4 | 3 | .... | 4 | 7 | 4 | 4 | 0 | 29 |
| Athletic | 5 | 1 | 4 | 5 | .... | 5 | 6 | 2 | 0 | 28 |
| Atlantic | 1 | 2 | 2 | 2 | 4 | .... | 3 | 3 | 0 | 17 |
| Washington | 0 | 2 | 0 | 1 | 0 | 2 | .... | 1 | 2 | 8 |
| Resolute | 1 | 0 | 0 | 0 | 0 | 1 | 0 | .... | 0 | 2 |
| Maryland | 0 | 0 | 0 | 0 | 0 | 0 | 0 | 0 | .... | 0 |
| Games Lost | 16 | 17 | 22 | 24 | 23 | 37 | 31 | 21 | 5 | 196 |

In 1874 Hartford sent a club to compete for the pennant. The Olympic, Kekionga, Rockford, Eckford, Mansfield, Maryland, and Haymakers having retired since 1871 and up to 1873 inclusive. The Chicago Club which had been broken up by the great fire of October, 1871, and had been out of the race in

1872 and 1873, again entered the lists. At the end of the season the record stood as follows:

RECORD FOR 1874.

| CLUB. | Boston. | Mutual. | Athletic. | Philadelphia. | Chicago. | Atlantic. | Hartford. | Baltimore. | Games Won. |
|---|---|---|---|---|---|---|---|---|---|
| Boston........... | | 5 | 8 | 8 | 7 | 6 | 9 | 9 | 52 |
| Mutual........... | 5 | .... | 4 | 1 | 9 | 7 | 8 | 8 | 42 |
| Athletic.......... | 2 | 6 | .... | 9 | 3 | 6 | 5 | 2 | 33 |
| Philadelphia..... | 2 | 5 | 1 | .... | 7 | 6 | 4 | 4 | 29 |
| Chicago.......... | 3 | 1 | 4 | 3 | .. | 4 | 4 | 9 | 27 |
| Atlantic.......... | 4 | 3 | 1 | 3 | 3 | .... | 5 | 3 | 23 |
| Hartford......... | 1 | 2 | 3 | 4 | 1 | 3 | .... | 3 | 17 |
| Baltimore........ | 1 | 1 | 2 | 1 | 1 | 1 | 2 | . | 9 |
| Games Lost...... | 18 | 23 | 23 | 29 | 31 | 33 | 37 | 38 | 232 |

The season of 1875 saw the last of the old National professional Association it being superseded by the League in 1876. In 1875 St. Louis entered the lists and before the season expired there were thirteen competitors in the arena, and things became decidedly mixed, and demoralization set in. The outcome of the contest however, was the success of the Boston Club, which had won the championship each successive season since 1871.

The record of the last season's campaign of the old National Association which closed its season in 1875, was as follows.

RECORD FOR 1875.

| CLUB. | Boston. | Athletic. | Hartford. | St. Louis. | Philadelphia. | Chicago. | Mutual. | New Haven. | Red Stock'gs. | Washington. | Centennial. | Atlantic. | Western. | Games Won. |
|---|---|---|---|---|---|---|---|---|---|---|---|---|---|---|
| Boston........... | ... | 8 | 9 | 7 | 6 | 8 | 10 | 5 | 1 | 5 | 5 | 6 | 1 | 71 |
| Athletic.......... | 2 | ... | 3 | 6 | 8 | 7 | 6 | 7 | 0 | 5 | 2 | 7 | 0 | 53 |
| Hartford......... | 1 | 4 | ... | 5 | 4 | 6 | 8 | 8 | 3 | 4 | 1 | 10 | 0 | 54 |
| St. Louis......... | 2 | 1 | 5 | ... | 5 | 5 | 8 | 2 | 2 | 3 | 0 | 2 | 4 | 39 |
| Philadelphia..... | 0 | 2 | 4 | 5 | ... | 7 | 2 | 4 | 1 | 2 | 3 | 7 | 0 | 37 |
| Chicago.......... | 2 | 1 | 4 | 5 | 3 | ... | 3 | 2 | 4 | 0 | 0 | 2 | 4 | 30 |
| Mutual........... | 0 | 3 | 2 | 0 | 5 | 3 | ... | 4 | 2 | 0 | 2 | 7 | 1 | 29 |
| New Haven...... | 1 | 0 | 1 | 1 | 0 | 1 | 1 | ... | 0 | 1 | 0 | 1 | 0 | 7 |
| Red Stockings... | 0 | 0 | 0 | 0 | 0 | 0 | 0 | ... | | 2 | 0 | 0 | 2 | 4 |
| Washington...... | 0 | 0 | 0 | 0 | 0 | 0 | 4 | 0 | ... | | 0 | 0 | 0 | 4 |
| Centennial....... | 0 | 1 | 0 | 0 | 0 | 0 | 0 | 1 | 0 | 0 | ... | 0 | 0 | 2 |
| Atlantic.......... | 0 | 0 | 0 | 0 | 0 | 0 | 0 | 0 | 0 | 0 | 0 | ... | 0 | 2. |
| Western......... | 0 | 0 | 0 | 0 | 0 | 0 | 0 | 1 | 0 | 0 | 0 | ... | | 1 |
| Games Lost..... | 8 | 20 | 28 | 29 | 31 | 37 | 38 | 39 | 14 | 22 | 13 | 42 | 12 | 333 |

## THE LEAGUE CHAMPIONSHIP RECORD.

### FROM 1876 TO 1884 INCLUSIVE.

The record of the League championship contest each season from 1876—the year the League was organized—to 1884 inclusive, presents a very interesting array of statistics showing the varying features of the several clubs which have entered the League arena within the past nine years. This year completes the first decade in the history of the League organization, and the record of the full period will make up an exceedingly interesting history of professional ball playing in the palmiest days of its history.

In the inaugural year of the League eight clubs entered the lists for championship, the clubs represented being Boston, Hartford, New York, and Philadelphia in the East, and Chicago, Cincinnati, Louisville and St. Louis in the West. The record for that year gave the championship to the Chicago Club, as will be seen by the appended table.

### THE CHAMPIONSHIP RECORD FOR 1876.

| | Chicago | Hartford | St. Louis | Boston | Louisville | Mutual | Athletic | Cincinnati | Games Played | Games Lost | Games Won |
|---|---|---|---|---|---|---|---|---|---|---|---|
| Chicago    | ... | 6 | 4 | 9 | 9 | 7 | 7 | 10 | 66 | 14 | 52 |
| Hartford   | 4 | ... | 4 | 8 | 9 | 4 | 9 | 9  | 68 | 21 | 47 |
| St. Louis  | 6 | 6 | ... | 6 | 6 | 6 | 8 | 7  | 64 | 19 | 45 |
| Boston     | 1 | 2 | 4 | ... | 5 | 8 | 9 | 10 | 70 | 31 | 39 |
| Louisville | 1 | 1 | 4 | 5 | ... | 5 | 6 | 8  | 66 | 36 | 30 |
| Mutual     | 1 | 4 | 1 | 2 | 3 | ... | 3 | 7  | 56 | 35 | 21 |
| Athletic   | 1 | 1 | 0 | 1 | 2 | 4 | ... | 5 | 59 | 45 | 14 |
| Cincinnati | 0 | 1 | 2 | 0 | 2 | 1 | 3 | ... | 65 | 56 | 9 |
| Games Lost | 14 | 21 | 19 | 31 | 36 | 35 | 45 | 56 | 514 | 257 | 257 |

In 1877 the Mutual Club of New York and the Athletic of Philadelphia were not among the contestants, owing to their failure to fulfill their scheduled engagements of the previous season; and consequently only five clubs of the eight which entered the lists in 1876 took part in the championship campaign of 1877. This year Boston went to the front again while Chicago had to be content with the rear rank position, as will be seen from the appended record:

## THE RECORD FOR 1877.

| | Boston. | Louisville. | Hartford. | St. Louis. | Chicago. | Games Played. | Games Lost. | Games Won. |
|---|---|---|---|---|---|---|---|---|
| Boston | .... | 8 | 7 | 6 | 10 | 48 | 17 | 31 |
| Louisville | 4 | .... | 6 | 10 | 8 | 48 | 20 | 28 |
| Hartford | 5 | 6 | .... | 5 | 8 | 48 | 24 | 24 |
| St. Louis | 6 | 2 | 4 | .... | 4 | 48 | 29 | 19 |
| Chicago | 2 | 4 | 7 | 8 | .... | 48 | 30 | 18 |
| Games Lost | 17 | 20 | 24 | 29 | 30 | | 120 | 120 |

In 1878 only six clubs took part in the season's campaign as in 1877; but Providence took the place of Hartford. Indianapolis filled Louisville's place, and Milwaukee that of St. Louis. Once more the championship honors were held by Boston, while Chicago pulled up to a better position than they held in 1877, as the appended record shows:

## THE RECORD FOR 1878.

| | Boston. | Cincinnati. | Providence. | Chicago. | Indianapolis. | Milwaukee. | Games Played. | Games Lost. | Games Won. |
|---|---|---|---|---|---|---|---|---|---|
| Boston | .... | 6 | 6 | 8 | 10 | 11 | 60 | 19 | 41 |
| Cincinnati | 6 | .... | 9 | 10 | 4 | 8 | 60 | 23 | 37 |
| Providence | 6 | 3 | .... | 6 | 10 | 8 | 60 | 27 | 33 |
| Chicago | 4 | 2 | 6 | .... | 8 | 10 | 60 | 30 | 30 |
| Indianapolis | 2 | 8 | 4 | 4 | .... | 8 | 60 | 36 | 24 |
| Milwaukee | 1 | 4 | 4 | 2 | 4 | .... | 60 | 45 | 15 |
| Games Lost | 19 | 23 | 27 | 30 | 36 | 45 | 360 | 180 | 180 |

In 1879 eight clubs once more entered the lists for the League championship, and this number was finally fixed upon as the maximum of membership of the National League. In the place of Indianapolis and Milwaukee Buffalo and Cleveland entered the race, while two new members were taken in from Syracuse and Troy. It was in this year that George Wright left the Boston Club and became the manager of the rival club of that city from Providence, and he signalized the event by winning the pennant from Boston for the Providence Club, the Stars of Syracuse being distanced in the pennant race, while Troy made a very poor show, as the record below proves.

## THE RECORD FOR 1879.

| | Providence. | Boston. | Chicago. | Buffalo. | Cincinnati. | Cleveland. | Troy City. | Syracuse. | Games Played. | Games Lost. | Games Won. |
|---|---|---|---|---|---|---|---|---|---|---|---|
| Providence ............ | .... | 8 | 7 | 6 | 10 | 8 | 10 | 6 | 78 | 23 | 55 |
| Boston ............... | 4 | .... | 4 | 9 | 7 | 10 | 11 | 4 | 78 | 29 | 49 |
| Chicago .............. | 5 | 8 | .. | 6 | 3 | 8 | 8 | 6 | 76 | 32 | 44 |
| Buffalo .............. | 6 | 3 | 6 | .... | 7 | 8 | 11 | 3 | 76 | 32 | 44 |
| Cincinnati............ | 2 | 5 | 8 | 3 | .... | 8 | 9 | 3 | 74 | 36 | 38 |
| Cleveland............. | 4 | 2 | 4 | 4 | 4 | .... | 5 | 1 | 77 | 53 | 24 |
| Troy City............. | 2 | 1 | 3 | 1 | 2 | 6 | .... | 4 | 75 | 56 | 19 |
| Syracuse.............. | 0 | 2 | 0 | 3 | 3 | 5 | 2 | .... | 42 | 27 | 15 |
| Games Lost............ | 23 | 29 | 32 | 32 | 36 | 53 | 56 | 27 | | 288 | 288 |

In 1880 eight clubs again entered the arena, Worcester taking the place of the disbanded Syracuse Stars, which club found their League adversaries altogether too strong for them. This year Chicago went to the front again, Cincinnati falling off so badly in the race that at the finish they were found to be badly distanced, as the record below shows:

## THE RECORD FOR 1880.

| | Chicago. | Providence. | Cleveland. | Troy City. | Worcester. | Boston. | Buffalo. | Cincinnati. | Games Played. | Games Lost. | Games Won. |
|---|---|---|---|---|---|---|---|---|---|---|---|
| Chicago ............... | .... | 9 | 8 | 10 | 10 | 9 | 11 | 10 | 84 | 17 | 67 |
| Providence............. | 3 | .... | 9 | 7 | 6 | 7 | 10 | 10 | 84 | 32 | 52 |
| Cleveland.............. | 4 | 3 | .... | 9 | 6 | 7 | 9 | 9 | 84 | 37 | 47 |
| Troy City.............. | 2 | 5 | 3 | .... | 5 | 5 | 11 | 10 | 83 | 42 | 41 |
| Worcester.............. | 2 | 6 | 6 | 7 | .... | 8 | 3 | 8 | 83 | 43 | 40 |
| Boston................. | 3 | 5 | 5 | 7 | 4 | .... | 9 | 7 | 84 | 44 | 40 |
| Buffalo................ | 1 | 2 | 3 | 1 | 9 | 3 | .... | 5 | 82 | 58 | 24 |
| Cincinnati............. | 2 | 2 | 3 | 1 | 3 | 5 | 5 | .... | 80 | 59 | 21 |
| Games Lost............. | 17 | 32 | 37 | 42 | 43 | 44 | 58 | 59 | | 332 | 332 |

In 1881 no change was made in the League ranks, and the same cities were represented in the pennant race of that year as in 1880. Once more the Chicago Club bore off the season's honors, that club having learned the value of team-work as a potent factor in winning the League championship honors. This year Worcester, which club made so good a fight in 1880, fell off to last place, and Boston also occupied an inferior position in the year's campaign, their falling off during 1880 and 1881 being a feature of the year's events. Then, too, Cincinnati was forced to tender its resignation and Detroit was given that club's place, and the new club made a very good showing in the campaign of '81, as will be seen by the appended record:

RECORD OF 1881.

|  | Chicago. | Providence. | Buffalo. | Detroit. | Troy City. | Boston. | Cleveland. | Worcester. | Games Played. | Games Lost. | Games Won. |
|---|---|---|---|---|---|---|---|---|---|---|---|
| Chicago................. | .... | 9 | 7 | 7 | 8 | 10 | 6 | 9 | 84 | 28 | 56 |
| Providence............ | 3 | .... | 5 | 8 | 6 | 7 | 9 | 9 | 84 | 37 | 47 |
| Buffalo................. | 5 | 7 | .... | 9 | 3 | 8 | 7 | 6 | 83 | 38 | 45 |
| Detroit................. | 5 | 4 | 3 | .... | 7 | 8 | 7 | 7 | 84 | 43 | 41 |
| Troy City............. | 4 | 6 | 9 | 5 | .... | 5 | 6 | 4 | 84 | 45 | 39 |
| Boston................. | 2 | 5 | 4 | 4 | 7 | .... | 8 | 8 | 83 | 45 | 38 |
| Cleveland............. | 6 | 3 | 5 | 5 | 6 | 4 | .... | 7 | 84 | 48 | 36 |
| Worcester............. | 3 | 3 | 5 | 5 | 5 | 8 | 3 | 5 | .... | 82 | 50 | 32 |
| Games Lost........... | 28 | 37 | 38 | 43 | 45 | 45 | 48 | 50 |  | 334 | 334 |

In 1882 the same eight clubs again entered the lists, and for the third time in succession Chicago carried off the championship, with Providence a close second again as they were in '81 and '80. Worcester was again badly distanced, and as a penalty the club was retired at the close of the season. The Troy Club, too, did not show up well this year, and they, too, shared the fate of the Worcesters. The record at the close stood as follows:

RECORD OF 1882.

|  | Chicago. | Providence. | Buffalo. | Boston. | Cleveland. | Detroit. | Troy City. | Worcester. | Games Played. | Games Lost. | Games Won. |
|---|---|---|---|---|---|---|---|---|---|---|---|
| Chicago................. | .... | 8 | 6 | 6 | 9 | 8 | 9 | 9 | 84 | 29 | 55 |
| Providence............ | 4 | .... | 6 | 6 | 8 | 9 | 9 | 10 | 84 | 32 | 52 |
| Buffalo................. | 6 | 6 | .... | 5 | 6 | 5 | 6 | 11 | 84 | 39 | 45 |
| Boston................. | 6 | 6 | 7 | .... | 7 | 4 | 4 | 7 | 84 | 39 | 45 |
| Cleveland............. | 3 | 4 | 6 | 5 | .... | 4 | 9 | 11 | 82 | 40 | 42 |
| Detroit................. | 4 | 3 | 7 | 4 | 7 | .... | 8 | 9 | 83 | 41 | 42 |
| Troy City............. | 3 | 3 | 6 | 8 | 2 | 4 | .... | 9 | 83 | 48 | 35 |
| Worcester............. | 3 | 2 | 1 | 5 | 1 | 3 | 3 | .... | 84 | 66 | 18 |
| Games Lost........... | 29 | 32 | 39 | 39 | 40 | 41 | 48 | 66 |  | 334 | 334 |

In 1883 New York and Philadelphia were elected as League cities in the place of Troy and Worcester, and this time the Boston Club, by a plucky rally toward the close of the season, managed to get in front of Chicago, the latter club being obliged to be content with second place. Neither New York or Philadelphia made much of a show in the campaign, both of them occupying rear positions, as will be seen by the appended record:

RECORD OF 1883.

| | Boston. | Chicago. | Providence. | Cleveland. | Buffalo. | New York. | Detroit. | Philadelphia. | Games Played. | Games Lost. | Games Won. |
|---|---|---|---|---|---|---|---|---|---|---|---|
| Boston............ | .... | 7 | 8 | 10 | 7 | 7 | 10 | 14 | 98 | 35 | 63 |
| Chicago........... | 7 | .... | 7 | 6 | 9 | 9 | 9 | 12 | 98 | 39 | 59 |
| Providence........ | 6 | 7 | .... | 6 | 7 | 9 | 12 | 11 | 98 | 40 | 58 |
| Cleveland......... | 4 | 8 | 8 | .... | 7 | 7 | 9 | 12 | 97 | 42 | 55 |
| Buffalo............ | 7 | 5 | 7 | 7 | .... | 8 | 9 | 9 | 97 | 45 | 52 |
| New York......... | 7 | 5 | 5 | 6 | 5 | .... | 6 | 12 | 96 | 50 | 46 |
| Detroit............ | 4 | 5 | 2 | 5 | 5 | 8 | .... | 11 | 98 | 58 | 40 |
| Philadelphia...... | 0 | 2 | 3 | 2 | 5 | 2 | 3 | .... | 98 | 81 | 17 |
| Games Lost....... | 35 | 39 | 40 | 42 | 45 | 50 | 58 | 81 | | 390 | 390 |

In 1884 the same eight clubs again entered the lists, and this time the Providence Club took the lead of both Boston and Chicago, and came in victors after the most brilliant campaign known in the history of the club, the team toward the close working together as a whole in model style. New York and Philadelphia improved upon their previous season's record, but failed to reach the position in the race they had expected. Cleveland fell off badly in the race, and finally resigned its membership early in the ensuing year. The record for 1884 is as follows:

RECORD OF 1884.

| | Providence. | Boston. | Buffalo. | Chicago. | New York. | Philadelphia. | Cleveland. | Detroit. | Games Played. | Games Lost. | Games Won. |
|---|---|---|---|---|---|---|---|---|---|---|---|
| Providence........ | .... | 9 | 10 | 11 | 13 | 13 | 13 | 15 | 112 | 28 | 84 |
| Boston............ | 7 | .... | 9 | 10 | 8 | 13 | 14 | 12 | 111 | 38 | 73 |
| Buffalo............ | 6 | 6 | .... | 10 | 5 | 11 | 14 | 12 | 111 | 47 | 64 |
| Chicago........... | 5 | 6 | 6 | .... | 12 | 14 | 8 | 11 | 112 | 50 | 62 |
| New York......... | 3 | 8 | 11 | 4 | .... | 11 | 11 | 14 | 112 | 50 | 62 |
| Philadelphia...... | 3 | 3 | 5 | 2 | 5 | .... | 10 | 11 | 112 | 73 | 39 |
| Cleveland......... | 3 | 2 | 2 | 8 | 5 | 6 | .... | 9 | 112 | 77 | 35 |
| Detroit............ | 1 | 4 | 4 | 5 | 2 | 5 | 7 | .... | 112 | 84 | 28 |
| Games Lost....... | 28 | 38 | 47 | 50 | 50 | 73 | 77 | 84 | | 447 | 447 |

In the nine years' history of the League championship struggles a total of 2,682 championship games were won and lost in the League arena, of which but 120 were played in 1876, and but 180 in 1878, while from 1880 to 1883, inclusive, over 300 were played each season, last year's record topping the figure with a total of 447.

## THE AMERICAN ASSOCIATION CHAMPIONSHIP RECORDS.

The American Association was organized at a convention which was held at the Gilsey House, Cincinnati, on Nov. 2, 1881, and it was a successful organization from the very outset. Its first championship campaign was that of the season of 1882, when six clubs of Cincinnati, Louisville, St. Louis, Pittsburg, Baltimore and Philadelphia, entered the lists, the honors of the season being carried off by Cincinnati, as will be seen by the appended record.

### THE RECORD OF 1882.

|  | Cincinnati. | Athletic. | Eclipse. | Allegheny. | St. Louis. | Baltimore. | Won. | Lost. | Played. | Per cent. of Victories. |
|---|---|---|---|---|---|---|---|---|---|---|
| Cincinnati............ | .. | 10 | 11 | 10 | 10 | 14 | 55 | 25 | 80 | .680 |
| Athletic.............. | 6 | .. | 11 | 6 | 11 | 7 | 41 | 34 | 75 | .540 |
| Eclipse............... | 5 | 5 | .. | 10 | 9 | 13 | 42 | 38 | 80 | .520 |
| Allegheny............ | 6 | 10 | 6 | .. | 10 | 7 | 39 | 39 | 79 | .500 |
| St. Louis............. | 6 | 5 | 7 | 6 | .. | 13 | 37 | 43 | 80 | .460 |
| Baltimore............ | 2 | 4 | 3 | 7 | 3 | .. | 19 | 54 | 74 | .260 |
| Games Lost.......... | 25 | 34 | 38 | 39 | 43 | 54 | 233 |  |  |  |

In 1883 eight clubs entered the lists in the American pennant race of that year, the Metropolitans of New York, and the Columbus Club being the new candidates. The season proved to be the most noteworthy for the financial success which marked it, known in the history of the game. The Athletics of Philadelphia bore off the honors, as will be seen by the appended record.

### THE RECORD OF 1883.

|  | Athletic. | St. Louis. | Cincinnati. | Metropolitan. | Louisville. | Columbus. | Allegheny. | Baltimore. | Games Played. | Games Lost. | Games Won. | Per cent. of Victories. |
|---|---|---|---|---|---|---|---|---|---|---|---|---|
| Athletic............ | .. | 9 | 5 | 9 | 7 | 13 | 12 | 11 | 98 | 32 | 66 | .670 |
| St. Louis........... | 5 | .. | 6 | 11 | 8 | 11 | 12 | 12 | 98 | 33 | 65 | .660 |
| Cincinnati......... | 9 | 8 | .. | 4 | 10 | 11 | 9 | 11 | 98 | 36 | 62 | .640 |
| Metropolitan...... | 5 | 3 | 10 | .. | 6 | 11 | 9 | 10 | 96 | 42 | 54 | .560 |
| Louisville.......... | 7 | 6 | 4 | 7 | .. | 9 | 11 | 8 | 97 | 45 | 52 | .530 |
| Columbus.......... | 1 | 3 | 3 | 3 | 5 | .. | 10 | 7 | 97 | 65 | 32 | .330 |
| Allegheny......... | 2 | 2 | 5 | 5 | 3 | 4 | .. | 9 | 98 | 68 | 30 | .300 |
| Baltimore ......... | 3 | 2 | 3 | 3 | 6 | 6 | 5 | .. | 98 | 68 | 28 | .290 |
| Games Lost | 32 | 33 | 36 | 42 | 45 | 65 | 68 | 68 | 389 |  |  |  |

In 1884 twelve clubs entered for the American championship, the new competitors being the Brooklyn, Washington, Toledo and Indianapolis Clubs. The Washingtons disbanded in August, and the Virginia Club of Richmond took its place. The season was not a financial success, only a minority of the clubs making money. The Metropolitan Club bore off the honors in 1884, as will be seen by the appended official record of the Board of Directors.

RECORD OF 1884.

|  | Allegheny. | Athletic. | Baltimore. | Brooklyn. | Cincinnati. | Columbus. | Indianapolis. | Louisville. | Metropolitan. | St Louis. | Toledo. | Washington. | Virginia. | Won. | Played. | Percentage. Won. | Rank. |
|---|---|---|---|---|---|---|---|---|---|---|---|---|---|---|---|---|---|
| Allegheny | | 2 | 0 | 6 | 1 | 1 | 6 | 2 | 1 | 1 | 5 | 4 | 1 | 30 | 108 | .277 | 10 |
| Athletic | 8 | .. | 7 | 6 | 6 | 5 | 6 | 3 | 2 | 3 | 6 | 7 | 2 | 61 | 108 | .564 | 7 |
| Baltimore | 9 | 3 | .. | 5 | 4 | 6 | 9 | 6 | 5 | 5 | 5 | 2 | 4 | 63 | 106 | .594 | 6 |
| Brooklyn | 4 | 3 | 5 | .. | 2 | 3 | 7 | 3 | 1 | 2 | 4 | 3 | 3 | 40 | 104 | .384 | 9 |
| Cincinnati | 8 | 4 | 6 | 8 | .. | 3 | 9 | 5 | 4 | 4 | 7 | 6 | 4 | 68 | 109 | .623 | 5 |
| Columbus | 9 | 5 | 4 | 7 | 7 | .. | 8 | 5 | 4 | 5 | 8 | 5 | 2 | 69 | 108 | .638 | 2 |
| Indianapolis | 4 | 4 | 1 | 3 | 1 | 2 | .. | 1 | 2 | 3 | 3 | 4 | 1 | 29 | 107 | .271 | 11 |
| Louisville | 8 | 6 | 4 | 6 | 5 | 5 | 9 | .. | 3 | 5 | 9 | 4 | 4 | 68 | 108 | .629 | 3 |
| Metropolitan | 9 | 8 | 5 | 9 | 6 | 5 | 8 | 7 | .. | 5 | 5 | 6 | 2 | 75 | 107 | .700 | 1 |
| St. Louis | 9 | 7 | 5 | 7 | 6 | 5 | 6 | 5 | 4 | .. | 5 | 5 | 3 | 67 | 107 | .626 | 4 |
| Toledo | 5 | 3 | 5 | 4 | 3 | 1 | 6 | 1 | 4 | 5 | .. | 5 | 4 | 46 | 104 | .442 | 8 |
| Washington | 1 | 1 | 2 | 1 | 0 | 1 | 2 | 1 | 2 | 1 | 1 | .. | 0 | 12 | 63 | .190 | 12 |
| Virginia | 4 | 0 | 0 | 2 | 0 | 2 | 2 | 1 | 0 | 1 | 0 | 0 | .. | 12 | 42 | .285 | |
| Lost | 78 | 47 | 43 | 64 | 41 | 39 | 78 | 40 | 32 | 40 | 58 | 51 | 30 | | | | |

The following summary shows the order of percentage of victories:

| CLUBS. | Won. | Lost. | Played. | Per Cent. of Victories. |
|---|---|---|---|---|
| Metropolitan | 75 | 32 | 107 | .700 |
| Columbus | 69 | 39 | 108 | .638 |
| Louisville | 68 | 40 | 108 | .629 |
| Cincinnati | 68 | 41 | 109 | .623 |
| St. Louis | 67 | 41 | 107 | .620 |
| Baltimore | 63 | 44 | 107 | .588 |
| Athletic | 61 | 46 | 107 | .570 |
| Toledo | 46 | 58 | 104 | .442 |
| Brooklyn | 41 | 64 | 105 | .390 |
| Allegheny | 31 | 78 | 109 | .284 |
| Indianapolis | 29 | 78 | 107 | .271 |
| Virginia | 24 | 81 | 105 | .228 |
| Totals | 642 | 642 | | |

In '84 the record showed that the twelve clubs of that season had played 641 championship games, including only victories and defeats. The Cincinnati Club won the championship pennant in '82 with a record of 55 victories, Louisville being second with 42, and the Athletics third with 41. The per cent. of victories, however, gave second place to the Athletics. In '83 the Athletics won the pennant with a record of 66 victories, St. Louis being second with 65, and Cincinnati third with 62, the percentage of victories giving them the same relative positions. In '84 the Metropolitans won the pennant with a record of 75 victories, Columbus being second with 69, and Louisville third with 68, the percentage of victories also giving them these relative positions.

For 1885 only eight clubs have entered, and this in future, will be the limit of the Association's membership each season.

### AMERICAN "CHICAGO" GAMES.

No less than seventy-seven of the championship series of contests in the American arena were marked by scores in which one or the other side failed to score a run, the record for 1884 being as follows:

|  | Cincinnati. | Toledo. | Metropolitan. | Baltimore. | Columbus. | St. Louis. | Brooklyn. | Athletic. | Louisville. | Virginia. | Allegheny. | Indianapolis. | Games Won. |
|---|---|---|---|---|---|---|---|---|---|---|---|---|---|
| Cincinnati............... | ... | 1 | 1 | 1 | 0 | 0 | 1 | 0 | 0 | 3 | 2 | 1 | 10 |
| Toledo................... | 1 | ... | 0 | 1 | 0 | 2 | 3 | 0 | 1 | 0 | 1 | 1 | 10 |
| Metropolitan............ | 0 | 0 | ... | 0 | 1 | 2 | 2 | 1 | 0 | 0 | 3 | 1 | 8 |
| Baltimore............... | 2 | 1 | 0 | ... | 0 | 1 | 2 | 0 | 0 | 0 | 1 | 1 | 8 |
| Columbus............... | 0 | 0 | 1 | 0 | ... | 1 | 0 | 0 | 2 | 1 | 2 | 1 | 8 |
| St. Louis................ | 1 | 2 | 1 | 0 | 0 | ... | 1 | 0 | 0 | 1 | 1 | 0 | 7 |
| Brooklyn................ | 0 | 1 | 1 | 0 | 0 | 0 | ... | 1 | 0 | 0 | 1 | 2 | 6 |
| Athletic................. | 0 | 0 | 0 | 0 | 1 | 0 | 0 | ... | 1 | 2 | 0 | 1 | 5 |
| Louisville............... | 0 | 1 | 0 | 0 | 1 | 0 | 1 | 1 | ... | 0 | 1 | 0 | 5 |
| Virginia................. | 0 | 0 | 0 | 0 | 1 | 0 | 1 | 0 | 0 | ... | 0 | 2 | 4 |
| Allegheny.............. | 1 | 0 | 1 | 0 | 0 | 0 | 0 | 0 | 1 | ... | ... | 1 | 4 |
| Indianapolis............ | 0 | 0 | 0 | 0 | 1 | 0 | 0 | 0 | 0 | 0 | ... | ... | 1 |
| Games Lost........ | 5 | 6 | 5 | 2 | 5 | 6 | 11 | 3 | 4 | 8 | 11 | 11 | 77 |

It will be seen that the Western Clubs of Cincinnati and Toledo bore off the palm in this respect, the Pittsburg and Indianapolis Clubs sustaining the most Chicago defeats.

### THE EASTERN LEAGUE SEASON OF 1884.

The Eastern League opened the season of 1884 with eight clubs in the ranks, representing Richmond, Baltimore, Wilmington, Harrisburg, Allentown, Reading, Trenton and

Newark. The championship season had not reached the end of May before the Monumental Club of Baltimore was forced to disband from lack of a paying patronage, the Ironside Club of Lancaster, Pa, filling the vacancy. July saw the retirement of the Harrisburg Club, and also the Actives of Reading. The York Club took the place of the Harrisburgs, and the Atlantics of Long Island City that of the Actives. The Atlantics failed to comply with the rules however, and they were retired after playing two games with the Richmond Club. In August the Richmonds were elected to the American Association to take the place of the disbanded Washington Club, and the same month saw the Wilmington Club go into the Union Association where it died shortly afterward. The five clubs which remained in the Association to the close of the season, were the Trenton, Newark and Allentown of the original eight, and the York and Lancaster Clubs. At the close of the season first place was awarded to the Trenton Club, the Ironsides of Lancaster being second, the Domestics of Newark third, and Allentown and York Clubs fourth and fifth. The official record of the season's play showing all the games played won and lost, is as follows:

| CLUBS. | Active. | Allentown. | Domestic. | Harrisburg. | Ironsides. | Monumental. | Trenton. | Virginia. | Wilmington. | York. | Games Won. |
|---|---|---|---|---|---|---|---|---|---|---|---|
| Active............... | .... | 5 | 3 | 4 | 3 | 0 | 5 | 4 | 2 | 1 | 27 |
| Allentown........... | 4 | .... | 4 | 3 | 7 | 0 | 6 | 5 | 0 | 1 | 30 |
| Domestic............ | 6 | 7 | .... | 2 | 5 | 0 | 4 | 2 | 2 | 4 | 32 |
| Harrisburg.......... | 2 | 2 | 3 | .... | 0 | 2 | 4 | 1 | 1 | 0 | 15 |
| Ironsides........... | 3 | 4 | 6 | 0 | .... | 0 | 5 | 3 | 2 | 7 | 30 |
| Monumental......... | 0 | 0 | 0 | 2 | 0 | .... | 0 | 1 | 0 | 0 | 3 |
| Trenton............. | 4 | 9 | 10 | 2 | 6 | 0 | .... | 6 | 2 | 7 | 46 |
| Virginia............ | 2 | 3 | 6 | 5 | 5 | 2 | 2 | .... | 3 | 0 | 30 |
| Wilmington.......... | 5 | 9 | 6 | 6 | 2 | 6 | 9 | 6 | .... | 0 | 49 |
| York................ | 1 | 2 | 2 | 0 | 3 | 0 | 3 | 0 | 0 | .... | 11 |
| Games Lost. .... | 27 | 41 | 40 | 24 | 31 | 10 | 38 | 28 | 12 | 20 | 273 |

The percentage of the five remaining clubs at the close of the season is as follows: Trenton .547; Ironsides, of Lancaster .488; Domestic, of Newark, .444; Allentown, .422; York, .355.

## THE NORTHWESTERN LEAGUE SEASON OF 1884.

The season of the Northwestern League for 1884 was a decided failure. It began with twelve clubs, but the season was not more than half over before symptoms of financial failure broke it up, and in August it virtually disbanded. An effort was made to carry it through on a smaller basis of representation, but that also proved a failure. The record of the games played up to the virtual breaking up of the League in August is as follows:

| CLUBS. | Evansville. | Fort Wayne. | Grand Rapids. | Milwaukee. | Minneapolis. | Muskegon. | Peoria. | Quincy. | Saginaw. | Stillwater. | St. Paul. | Terre Haute. | Games Won. |
|---|---|---|---|---|---|---|---|---|---|---|---|---|---|
| Evansville............ | .. | 3 | 1 | 2 | 2 | 4 | 1 | 2 | 2 | 3 | 3 | 4 | 27 |
| Fort Wayne........... | 0 | .. | 1 | 2 | 4 | 4 | 2 | 2 | 2 | 1 | 2 | 3 | 23 |
| Grand Rapids......... | 2 | 5 | .. | 4 | 5 | 6 | 4 | 3 | 2 | 4 | 4 | 7 | 46 |
| Milwaukee............ | 1 | 4 | 2 | .. | 8 | 2 | 1 | 2 | 5 | 5 | 8 | 3 | 41 |
| Minneapolis.......... | 1 | 2 | 1 | 1 | .. | 5 | 4 | 3 | 2 | 2 | 3 | 3 | 27 |
| Muskegon............. | 1 | 2 | 0 | 4 | 2 | .. | 1 | 2 | 1 | 5 | 3 | 2 | 23 |
| Peoria................ | 2 | 4 | 2 | 5 | 3 | 5 | .. | 0 | 2 | 5 | 6 | 4 | 38 |
| Quincy............... | 1 | 4 | 2 | 3 | 5 | 4 | 4 | .. | 2 | 7 | 8 | 5 | 45 |
| Saginaw.............. | 1 | 5 | 2 | 3 | 6 | 5 | 4 | 4 | .. | 6 | 6 | 4 | 46 |
| Stillwater............ | 0 | 4 | 2 | 1 | 3 | 1 | 1 | 1 | 0 | .. | 2 | 6 | 21 |
| St Paul............... | 0 | 4 | 2 | 2 | 2 | 3 | 2 | 2 | 0 | 3 | .. | 4 | 24 |
| Terre Haute.......... | 0 | 3 | 0 | 3 | 2 | 1 | 1 | 1 | 1 | 0 | 2 | .. | 14 |
| Games Lost.......... | 9 | 40 | 15 | 30 | 42 | 40 | 25 | 22 | 19 | 41 | 47 | 45 | 375 |

## THE UNION ASSOCIATION.

The record of the financially disastrous inaugural campaign of the Union Association for 1884 is appended by way of record. This Association was organized ostensibly in opposition to the working of the reserve rule in the League and the American Association. But its season had not proceeded far before it opened its doors to contract breakers from the clubs of the other Associations which had entered the national agreement. This was the commencement of its downfall. In May the Altoona Club of the Association disbanded, and in August the Keystone Club followed suit, as did the disastrous failure of the Chicago Unions, which club was transferred to Pittsburg. The latter part of the season saw clubs from Wilmington, Milwaukee and St. Paul enter the Union ranks; only one club paid its expenses even during the season, and that was the National of Washington.

The following is a complete record of all the championship games played during the season, commencing on April 17 and ending on Oct. 19:

BASE BALL GUIDE.                        69

| CLUBS. | Altoona. | Baltimore. | Boston. | Pittsburg. | Cincinnati. | Keystone. | National. | St. Louis. | Kansas City. | Wilmington. | Milwaukee. | St. Paul. | Total Won. |
|---|---|---|---|---|---|---|---|---|---|---|---|---|---|
| Altoona............... | ... | 1 | 1 | 0 | 0 | 1 | 3 | 0 | 0 | 0 | 0 | 0 | 6 |
| Baltimore............. | 3 | ... | 10 | 6 | 3 | 10 | 12 | .1 | 10 | 1 | 0 | 0 | 56 |
| Boston................ | 1 | 6 | ... | 4 | 5 | 8 | 12 | 8 | 8 | 4 | 2 | 0 | 58 |
| Pittsburg............. | 0 | 6 | 8 | ... | 6 | 3 | 4 | 1 | 12 | 0 | 0 | 0 | 40 |
| Cincinnati............ | 3 | 11 | 11 | 8 | ... | 8 | 10 | 2 | 10 | 2 | 0 | 3 | 68 |
| Keystone.............. | 3 | 2 | 3 | 5 | 0 | ... | 4 | 0 | 4 | 0 | 0 | 0 | 21 |
| National.............. | 1 | 4 | 4 | 8 | 6 | 8 | ... | 3 | 8 | 4 | 1 | 0 | 47 |
| St. Louis............. | 8 | 13 | 8 | 11 | 14 | 8 | 13 | ... | 10 | 4 | 0 | 2 | 91 |
| Kansas City........... | 0 | 2 | 4 | 3 | 0 | 0 | 4 | 0 | ... | 0 | 0 | 1 | 14 |
| Wilmington............ | 0 | 0 | 0 | 0 | 1 | 0 | 1 | 0 | 0 | ... | 0 | 0 | 2 |
| Milwaukee............. | 0 | 3 | 2 | 0 | 0 | 0 | 3 | 0 | 0 | 0 | ... | 0 | 8 |
| St. Paul.............. | 0 | 0 | 0 | 0 | 0 | 0 | 0 | 1 | 1 | 0 | 0 | ... | 2 |
| Total Lost............ | 19 | 48 | 51 | 45 | 35 | 46 | 66 | 16 | 63 | 15 | 3 | 6 | 413 |

Percentage:—St. Louis .85, Milwaukee .72, Cincinnati ·.66, Baltimore .53, Boston .53, Chicago .47, National .41, Keystone .31, St. Paul .25, Altoona .24, Kansas City .17, Wilmington .11. No official records were kept, and no club legally won the pennant.

## THE PROFESSIONAL CHAMPIONSHIP NINES FROM 1871 TO 1884 INCLUSIVE.

### LEAGUE CHAMPIONS.

Before the organization of the first Professional National Association, there was no recognized code of rules governing any championship contest in the base ball arena, only a nominal title existing prior to 1871, and even that was frequently disputed. The original champions of the old amateur class of clubs, which existed at the home of base ball, in New York and its suburbs, was the Atlantic Club, of Brooklyn, the champion team of that club, when it was in its palmiest amateur days, being M. O'Brien, pitcher; Boerum, catcher; Price, John Oliver and Charlie Smith on the bases; Dick Pearce, shortstop, and P. O'Brien, Archy McMahon and Tice Hamilton in the out-field. This was in 1860, when they won the championship from the Excelsiors. When they defeated the Mutuals and Eckfords, in 1864, their champion team was Pratt, pitcher; Ferguson, catcher; Start, Crane and Smith on the bases; Pearce, at short-field, and Chapman, Joe Oliver and Sid Smith in the out-field. The Eckfords held the nominal title in 1862 and '63, and in 1869 the Cincinnati Red Stockings were indisputably the champions of the United States. Their team, in that year, included Asa Brainard, as pitcher; **D.** Allison, as catcher; Gould, Sweazy and Waterman, on the bases; George Wright, as short-stop, and Leonard, Harry Wright and McVey in the outfield. In 1870 the title was claimed by the Mutuals and Chicagos, and the disputed claim was never settled.

In 1871 the Professional National Association was organized, and then was begun the first series of championship matches under an official code of rules known in the history of professional ball-playing. From this year to 1876, when the National League was organized, the winning teams were as follows:

1871, Athletic—McBride, pitcher; Malone, catcher; Fisler, Reach and Meyerle on the bases; Radcliff, short-stop; Cuthbert, Sensenderfer and Heubel in the outfield.

1872, Boston—A. G. Spalding, pitcher; C. A. McVey, catcher; Chas. Gould, Ross Barnes and Harry Schafer on the bases; Geo. Wright, short-stop; Andy Leonard, Harry Wright and Fraley Rogers in the outfield.

1873, Boston—A. G. Spalding, pitcher; Jas. White, catcher; James O'Rourke, Barnes and Schafer on the bases; George Wright, short-stop; Leonard, Harry Wright and Manning in the outfield.

1874, Boston—A. G. Spalding, pitcher; McVey, catcher; Jas. White, Barnes and Schafer on the bases; Geo. Wright, short-stop; Leonard, Hall and Jas. O'Rourke in the outfield.

1875, Boston—A. G. Spalding, pitcher; James White, catcher; Latham, Barnes and Schafer on the bases; George Wright, short-stop; Leonard, Jas. O'Rourke and Manning in the outfield.

From 1876 to 1883, inclusive, the winning teams in the League arena were as follows:

1876, Chicago—A. G. Spalding, pitcher; Jas. White, catcher; McVey, Barnes and Anson on the bases; Peters, short-stop; Glenn, Hines and Addy in the outfield.

1877, Boston—Bond, pitcher; Brown, catcher; Jas. White, Geo. Wright and Morrill on the bases; Sutton, short-stop; Leonard, Jas. O'Rourke and Schafer in the outfield.

1878, Boston,—Bond, pitcher; Snyder, catcher; Morrill, Burdock and Sutton on the bases; Geo. Wright, short-stop; Leonard, Jas. O'Rourke and Manning in the outfield.

1879, Providence—Ward, pitcher; Brown, catcher; Start, McGeary and Hague on the bases; Geo. Wright, short-stop; York, Hines and Jas. O'Rourke in the outfield.

1880, 1881 and 1882, Chicago—Corcoran and Goldsmith, pitchers; Flint, catcher; Anson, Quest and Williamson on the bases; Burns, short-stop; Dalrymple, Gore and Kelly in the outfield.

1883, **Boston**—Whitney and Buffinton, pitchers; Hines

and Hackett, catchers; Morrill, Burdock and Sutton on the bases; Wise, short-stop; and Hornung, Smith and Radford in the outfield.

1884, Providence—Radbourne, pitcher; Gilligan and Nava, catchers; Start, Farrell and Denny on the bases; Irwin, short-stop, and Carroll, Hines and Radford on the outfield.

### AMERICAN CHAMPIONS.

The American champion team of 1882 was that of the Cincinnati Club, and it included the following players: Snyder c.; White, p.; Stearns, 1st b.; McPhee, 2d b.; Carpenter, 3d b.; Fulmer, s.s.; Sommer, l. f.; Jones, c. f., and Corkhill, r. f., with Powers, McCormick and Wheeler as extra men. The champion team of 1883 was that of the Athletic Club of Philadelphia, and it included the following players: Rowen, c.; Matthews, p.; Stovey, 1st b.; Stricker, 2d b.; Bradley, 3d b.; Moynahan, s. s.; Birchall, l. f.; Blackiston, c. f.; Knight, r. f., with O'Brien, Corey and Jones as extra men.

The champion team of 1884 was that of the Metropolitan Club, which team included Halbert, c.; Keefe, p.; Orris, Troy, 2d b.; Esterbrook, 3d b.; Nelson, s.-s.; Kennedy, l. f.; Roseman, c. f.; Brady, r. f., with Keep and Lynch as extra players.

## THE INTER-COLLEGIATE ASSOCIATION.

### CHAMPIONSHIP RECORD FOR 1884.

The Inter-collegiate Association began its history at the meeting of college delegates on Dec. 6, 1879, when six of the Eastern State Colleges were represented at the convention, viz: Harvard, Yale, Princeton, Amherst, Dartmouth and Brown. As a majority at the convention voted to exclude college players from their nines who took part as players in professional club teams, Yale ultimately withdrew from the Association, and only five clubs entered for the Inter-collegiate Association pennant. Yale afterward arranged a series of eight matches with three of the five clubs, and only lost one game out of the eight. They virtually won the championship honors of the season, though Princeton won the Association pennant of 1880. The official record of the games played under the auspices of the Association, up to 1883 inclusive, is a follows:

| 1880. | Won. | Lost. | 1881. | Won. | Lost. |
| --- | --- | --- | --- | --- | --- |
| Princeton | 6 | 2 | Yale | 7 | 3 |
| Brown | 5 | 3 | Harvard | 6 | 4 |
| Dartmouth | 4 | 4 | Princeton | 6 | 4 |
| Harvard | 3 | 5 | Brown | 4 | 6 |
| Amherst | 2 | 6 | Dartmouth | 4 | 6 |
|  |  |  | Amherst | 3 | 7 |
|  | 20 | 20 |  | 30 | 30 |

| 1882. | Won. | Lost. | 1883. | Won. | Lost. |
|---|---|---|---|---|---|
| Yale | 8 | 3 | Yale | 7 | 1 |
| Princeton | 7 | 4 | Princeton | 6 | 2 |
| Harvard | 5 | 5 | Amherst | 4 | 4 |
| Amherst | 4 | 6 | Harvard | 2 | 6 |
| Brown | 4 | 6 | Brown | 1 | 7 |
| Dartmouth | 3 | 7 | | | |
| | 31 | 31 | | 20 | 20 |

It will be seen that each of the above seasons saw the Princeton team well up in the front, while only in two seasons was Harvard among the leaders.

In 1880 Yale's record in their contests with the Inter-collegiate clubs was as follows:

```
May  12  Yale vs. Princeton, at Princeton...................... 9—0
June  9  Yale vs. Princeton, at New Haven...................... 8—1
May  15  Yale vs. Harvard, at New Haven.......................21—4
 "   29  Yale vs. Harvard, at Cambridge........................ 2—1
June 28  Harvard vs. Yale, at New Haven........................ 3—1
 "   30  Yale vs. Harvard, at Cambridge........................ 3—0
May  22  Yale vs. Amherst, at Amherst.......................... 8—0
June  5  Yale vs. Amherst, at New Haven........................14—3
```

The above were, of course, outside games, Yale not being a member of the Inter-collegiate Association that year. But the series were practically championship contests. The full record of the season, including Yale games, was as follows:

### RECORD FOR 1880.

| | Yale. | Princeton. | Brown. | Dartmouth. | Harvard. | Amherst. | Games Won. | Games Lost. | Games Played. |
|---|---|---|---|---|---|---|---|---|---|
| Yale | .... | 2 | 0 | 0 | 2 | 2 | 6 | 1 | 7 |
| Princeton | 0 | .... | 1 | 2 | 2 | 1 | 6 | 4 | 10 |
| Brown | 0 | 1 | .... | 1 | 1 | 2 | 5 | 3 | 8 |
| Dartmouth | 0 | 0 | 1 | .... | 2 | 1 | 4 | 4 | 8 |
| Harvard | 1 | 0 | 1 | 0 | .... | 2 | 4 | 7 | 11 |
| Amherst | 0 | 1 | 0 | 1 | 0 | .... | 2 | 8 | 10 |
| Games Lost | 1 | 4 | 3 | 4 | 7 | 8 | 27 | | |

In 1881 Yale re-entered the Inter-collegiate Association and has remained in it ever since. Yale won the honors after a close fight with Harvard and Princeton, as the appended record shows:

RECORD FOR 1881.

|  | Yale. | Harvard. | Princeton. | Brown. | Dartmouth. | Amherst. | Games Won. | Games Lost. | Games Played. |
|---|---|---|---|---|---|---|---|---|---|
| Yale | .... | 1 | 1 | 2 | 1 | 2 | 7 | 3 | 10 |
| Harvard | 1 | .... | 1 | 1 | 2 | 1 | 6 | 4 | 10 |
| Princeton | 1 | 1 | .... | 1 | 2 | 1 | 6 | 4 | 10 |
| Brown | 0 | 1 | 1 | .... | 1 | 1 | 4 | 6 | 10 |
| Dartmouth | 1 | 0 | 0 | 1 | .... | 2 | 4 | 6 | 10 |
| Amherst | 0 | 1 | 1 | 1 | 0 | .... | 3 | 7 | 10 |
| Games Lost | 3 | 4 | 4 | 6 | 6 | 7 | 30 | | |

In 1882 the contest between Yale and Princeton was very close, Harvard falling back in the race. Yale finally won, as the appended record shows:

RECORD FOR 1882.

|  | Yale. | Princeton. | Harvard. | Amherst. | Brown. | Dartmouth. | Games Won. | Games Lost. | Games Played. |
|---|---|---|---|---|---|---|---|---|---|
| Yale | .... | 2 | 1 | 2 | 1 | 2 | 8 | 3 | 11 |
| Princeton | 1 | .... | 2 | 1 | 1 | 2 | 7 | 4 | 11 |
| Harvard | 1 | 0 | .... | 2 | 2 | 0 | 5 | 5 | 10 |
| Amherst | 0 | 1 | 0 | .... | 2 | 1 | 4 | 6 | 10 |
| Brown | 1 | 1 | 0 | 0 | .... | 2 | 4 | 6 | 10 |
| Dartmouth | 0 | 0 | 2 | 1 | 0 | .... | 3 | 7 | 10 |
| Games Lost | 3 | 4 | 5 | 6 | 6 | 7 | 31 | | |

In 1883 the majority of the clubs acted very unjustly to Dartmouth, and the result was that that club was forced to withdraw from the pennant race of that year; and the Dartmouth Club were not at all disappointed to find Harvard—which Club had been mainly instrumental in driving Dartmouth out of the field—near last in the pennant race of that year. Yale again won the honors, with Princeton once more a good second, as the appended record shows:

RECORD FOR 1883.

|  | Yale. | Princeton. | Amherst. | Harvard. | Brown. | Games Won. | Games Lost. | Games Played. |
|---|---|---|---|---|---|---|---|---|
| Yale | .... | 1 | 2 | 2 | 2 | 7 | 1 | 8 |
| Princeton | 1 | .... | 1 | 2 | 2 | 6 | 2 | 8 |
| Amherst | 0 | 1 | .... | 1 | 2 | 4 | 4 | 8 |
| Harvard | 0 | 0 | 1 | .... | 1 | 2 | 6 | 8 |
| Brown | 0 | 0 | 0 | 1 | .... | 1 | 7 | 8 |
| Games Lost | 1 | 2 | 4 | 6 | 7 | 20 | | |

In 1884 justice was shown Dartmouth and that Club resumed its proper place in the Association. But in consequence of being out of the arena in 1883 they had lost material strength and consequently had to occupy last place in the race. Last season Princeton fell off badly in the pennant race, while Harvard made quite a good fight of it, they coming in second for the first time since 1881, as will be seen by the appended record:

### RECORD FOR 1884.

|  | Yale. | Harvard. | Amherst. | Brown. | Princeton. | Dartmouth. | Games Won | Games Lost. | Games Played. |
|---|---|---|---|---|---|---|---|---|---|
| Yale............ | .... | 1 | 2 | 2 | 2 | 2 | 9 | 2 | 11 |
| Harvard........ | 2 | .... | 1 | 1 | 2 | 2 | 8 | 3 | 11 |
| Amherst........ | 0 | 1 | .... | 2 | 1 | 2 | 6 | 4 | 10 |
| Brown.......... | 0 | 1 | 0 | .... | 2 | 2 | 5 | 5 | 10 |
| Princeton....... | 0 | 0 | 1 | 0 | .... | 1 | 2 | 8 | 10 |
| Dartmouth...... | 0 | 0 | 0 | 0 | 1 | .... | 1 | 9 | 10 |
| Games Lost..... | 2 | 3 | 4 | 5 | 8 | 9 | 31 | | |

A summary of the above records gives the appended figures of total games won and lost, with the victories won each year:

| CLUBS. | 1880 | 1881 | 1882 | 1883 | 1884 | Won | Lost. |
|---|---|---|---|---|---|---|---|
| Yale............ | 6 | 7 | 8 | 7 | 9 | 37 | 10 |
| Princeton....... | 6 | 6 | 7 | 6 | 2 | 27 | 22 |
| Harvard........ | 4 | 6 | 5 | 2 | 8 | 25 | 25 |
| Brown.......... | 5 | 4 | 4 | 1 | 5 | 19 | 27 |
| Amherst........ | 2 | 3 | 4 | 4 | 6 | 19 | 29 |
| Dartmouth...... | 4 | 4 | 3 | 0 | 1 | 12 | 26 |
|  | 27 | 30 | 31 | 20 | 31 | 139 | 139 |

## OFFICIAL SCHEDULE OF THE AMERICAN COLLEGE BASE BALL ASSOCIATION.

### CHAMPIONSHIP SERIES, 1884.

| May | 1 | Brown vs. Harvard, at Cambridge; Umpire, Gaffney......... | 1- 8 |
| " | 3 | Yale vs. Brown, at Providence; Umpire, Gaffney............ | 8- 3 |
| " | 7 | Amherst vs. Harvard, at Cambridge; Umpire, Tilden........ | 9- 8 |
| " | 9 | Brown vs. Dartmouth, at Hanover; Umpire, Tilden......... | 5- 3 |
| " | 10 | Princeton vs. Amherst, at Amherst; Umpire, Gaffney........ | 4- 5 |
| " | 12 | Princeton vs. Harvard, at Cambridge; Umpire, Donovan..... | 4- 5 |
| " | 13 | Princeton vs. Brown, at Providence; Umpire, Gaffney....... | 5-10 |
| " | 14 | Yale vs. Dartmouth, at New Haven; Umpire, Gaffney....... | 6- 2 |
| " | 16 | Princeton vs. Dartmouth, at Princeton; Umpire, Donovan... | 11- 2 |
| " | 17 | Harvard vs. Yale, at New Haven; Umpire, Gaffney......... | 8- 7 |
| " | 17 | Dartmouth vs. Princeton, at Princeton; Umpire, Donovan... | 6- 3 |
| " | 19 | Harvard vs. Amherst, at Amherst; Umpire, Tilden.......... | 13- 1 |
| " | 21 | Amherst vs. Brown, at Providence; Umpire, Tilden......... | 5- 4 |
| " | 23 | Harvard vs. Brown, at Providence; Umpire, Gaffney......... | 6-10 |
| " | 24 | Yale vs. Amherst, at Amherst; Umpire, Donovan............ | 17- 4 |
| " | 24 | Harvard vs. Princeton, at Princeton; Umpire, Tilden........ | 15- 3 |
| " | 30 | Yale vs. Princeton, at New York; Umpire, Cronin.......... | 16- 3 |
| " | 31 | Dartmouth vs. Amherst, at Amherst; Umpire, Gaffney...... | 3-12 |

BASE BALL GUIDE. 75

June  2  Dartmouth vs. Yale, at New Haven; Umpire, Tilden........11-12
 "    4  Brown vs. Princeton, at Princeton; Umpire, Tilden.......... 5- 3
 "    5  Amherst vs. Yale, at New Haven; Umpire, Cronin. ........ 3- 4
 "    6  Amherst vs. Princeton, at Princeton; Umpire, Gaffney...... 3- 6
 "   11  Dartmouth vs. Harvard, at Cambridge; Umpire, Donovan... 1- 6
 "   12  Dartmouth vs. Brown, at Providence; Umpire, Donovan..... 8-14
 "   14  Harvard vs. Dartmouth, at Cambridge; Umpire, Tilden......14- 2
 "   16  Brown vs. Amherst, at Amherst; Umpire, Donovan......... 1- 6
 "   17  Brown vs. Yale, at New Haven; Umpire, Cronin............ 6- 9
 "   19  Princeton vs. Yale, at New York; Umpire, Cronin........... 0- 9
 "   21  Yale vs. Harvard, at Cambridge; Umpire, Donovan.......... 4-17
 "   24  Amherst vs. Dartmouth, at Hanover; Umpire, Gaffney......10- 8
 "   27  Yale vs. Harvard, at Brooklyn; Umpire, Gaffney........ ... 4- 2

UMPIRES.—Jno. H. Gaffney, No. 377 Main St., Worcester, Mass.  Otis Tilden, Brockton, Mass.  T. H. Donovan, Letter Carrier 74, Boston P. O. D. Cronin, No. 765 Washington St., Boston, Mass.

The above is a correct schedule of the championship series of 1884, together with the umpires appointed by the Judiciary Committee.  G. W. WADSWORTH,  Sec'y A. C. B. B. A.

The Exhibition games were as follows:

May 10  Yale vs. Harvard, at Cambridge........ ..................... 8-1
June 18  Harvard vs. Brown, at Providence...........................14-2
 "   24  Yale vs. Harvard, at New Haven............................ 6-2

The full detailed record of the championship season of 1884— similar in form to that given exclusively in the Guide of 1884 —is appended.  It shows not only the games won and lost by each club, but the date of each game and the scores.

|            | Yale. | Harvard. | Amherst. | Brown. | Princeton. | Dartmouth. | Games Won. |
|---|---|---|---|---|---|---|---|
| Yale........... |  | June 27, 4-2. | May 24, 17-4. June 5, 4-3. | May 3, 8-3. June 17, 9-6. | May 30, 16-3. June 19, 9-0. | May 14, 6-2. June 2, 12-11. | 9 |
| Harvard......... | May 17, 8-7. June 21, 17-4. |  | May 19, 13-10 | May 1, 8-1. | May 12, 5-4. May 24, 15-3. | June 11, 6-1. June 14, 14-2. | 8 |
| Amherst ......... |  | May 7, 9-8. |  | May 21, 5-4. June 16, 6-1. | May 10, 5-4. | May 31, 12-3. June 25, 10-8. | 6 |
| Brown........... |  | May 23, 10-6. |  |  | May 13, 10-5. June 4, 5 3. | May 9, 5-3. June 12, 14-8. | 5 |
| Princeton........ |  |  | June 6, 6-3. |  |  | May 16, 11-2. | 2 |
| Dartmouth....... |  |  |  |  | May 17, 6-3. |  | 1 |
| Games Lost...... | 2 | 3 | 4 | 5 | 8 | 9 | 31 |

## THE COLLEGE AVERAGES.

The official data for making up the averages of the College Clubs of 1884 were not of a very reliable character, the official scoring, except in a minority of instances, not having been up to the required mark. In fact, the existing system of College Club averages ought to be improved upon by the College Clubs themselves, and they should not follow the professional methods so much as they do when there is such a field for improvement. In making up the fielding percentage, wild pitches and passed balls have been counted errors, while bases on called balls have not been classed with errors.

### YALE.

| PLAYERS. | POSITION. | Games Played in. | Batting Average. | Fielding Average. |
|---|---|---|---|---|
| Terry | Second base | 11 | 404 | 814 |
| Souther | Catcher | 9 | 310 | 941 |
| Brigham | Left field | 11 | 326 | 758 |
| Bremner | Center field | 10 | 312 | 714 |
| McKee | Right field | 11 | 255 | 867 |
| Oliver | Short stop | 10 | 256 | 733 |
| Hopkins | Third base | 11 | 255 | 795 |
| Booth | Pitcher | 11 | 224 | 943 |
| Stewart | First base | 11 | 239 | 978 |

### HARVARD.

| PLAYERS. | POSITION. | Games Played in. | Batting Average. | Fielding Average. |
|---|---|---|---|---|
| Coolidge | Second base | 10 | 340 | 887 |
| Phillips | Third base | 11 | 294 | 737 |
| Winslow | Center field | 11 | 292 | 938 |
| Nichols | Pitcher | 9 | 275 | 929 |
| Tilden | Left field | 11 | 269 | 529 |
| Allen | Catcher | 10 | 271 | 979 |
| Smith | First base | 9 | 259 | 971 |
| Le Moyne | Right field | 11 | 244 | 969 |
| Baker | Short stop | 11 | 240 | 873 |

### AMHERST.

| PLAYERS. | POSITION. | Games Played in. | Batting Average. | Fielding Average. |
|---|---|---|---|---|
| Stuart | Center field | 10 | 378 | 935 |
| Taylor | Short stop | 10 | 292 | 843 |
| Marble | Third base | 10 | 279 | 909 |
| Kimball | Left field | 10 | 261 | 846 |
| Sullivan | Catcher | 10 | 214 | 937 |
| Buffum | Second base | 10 | 209 | 850 |
| Harris | Pitcher | 10 | 231 | 899 |
| Wheeler | Right field | 10 | 171 | 824 |
| Gardner | First base | 8 | 152 | 938 |

## BASE BALL GUIDE. 77

### BROWN.

| | | | | |
|---|---|---|---|---|
| Bassett | Third base | 10 | 317 | 847 |
| Shedd | Left field | 10 | 262 | 829 |
| Chase | First base | 10 | 256 | 933 |
| Durfee | Right field | 10 | 292 | 727 |
| Seagraves | Center field | 10 | 255 | 857 |
| Clark | Catcher | 8 | 219 | 969 |
| Wadsworth | Short stop | 10 | 211 | 825 |
| Gunderson | Pitcher | 10 | 209 | 967 |
| Doron | Second base | 10 | 231 | 847 |

### PRINCETON.

| | | | | |
|---|---|---|---|---|
| Shaw | Right field | 6 | 345 | 925 |
| A. Moffatt | Pitcher | 9 | 302 | 941 |
| Toller | Center field | 7 | 219 | 875 |
| W. Moffatt | First base | 7 | 240 | 921 |
| Van Arsdale | Third base | 7 | 207 | 500 |
| Cooper | Short stop | 10 | 195 | 783 |
| Van Etten | Catcher | 10 | 171 | 889 |
| Reynolds | Left field | 10 | 133 | 833 |
| Harlan | Second base | 10 | 125 | 841 |

### DARTMOUTH.

| | | | | |
|---|---|---|---|---|
| G. O. Nettleton | Third base | 10 | 326 | 746 |
| Springfield | Left field | 10 | 293 | 882 |
| Hale | First base | 10 | 279 | 972 |
| Chellis | Second base | 10 | 268 | 824 |
| Nutt | Right field | 6 | 217 | 818 |
| McCarty | Short stop | 10 | 214 | 754 |
| Fellows | Center field | 9 | 206 | 857 |
| F. Nettleton | Pitcher | 10 | 158 | 981 |
| Thomas | Catcher | 10 | 111 | 918 |

### BEST FIELDING RECORDS.

| | | |
|---|---|---|
| Pitcher | F. H. Nettleton, of Dartmouth | .981 |
| Catcher | Allen, of Harvard | .979 |
| 1st Base | Stewart, of Yale | .978 |
| 2d Base | Coolidge, of Harvard | .887 |
| 3d Base | Marble, of Amherst | .909 |
| Short Stop | Baker, of Harvard | .873 |
| Left Field | Springfield, of Dartmouth | .882 |
| Center Field | Stuart, of Amherst | .935 |
| Right Field | LeMoyne, of Harvard | .969 |

The following are the victories of each in 1884:

### YALE.

| | | | | |
|---|---|---|---|---|
| 1 | May 3 | Yale vs. Brown | | 8- 3 |
| 2 | " 14 | " " Dartmouth | | 6- 2 |
| 3 | " 24 | " " Amherst | | 17- 4 |
| 4 | " 30 | " " Princeton | | 16- 3 |
| 5 | June 2 | " " Dartmouth | | 12-11 |
| 6 | " 5 | " " Amherst | | 4- 3 |
| 7 | " 17 | " " Brown | | 9- 6 |
| 8 | " 19 | " " Princeton | | 9- 0 |
| 9 | " 27 | " " Harvard | | 4- 2 |

## HARVARD.

| | | | | | |
|---|---|---|---|---|---|
| 1 | May 1 | Harvard vs. Brown | | | 8- 1 |
| 2 | " 12 | " " Princeton | | | 5- 4 |
| 3 | " 17 | " " Yale | | | 8- 7 |
| 4 | " 19 | " " Amherst | | | 13-10 |
| 5 | " 24 | " " Princeton | | | 15- 3 |
| 6 | June 11 | " " Dartmouth | | | 6- 1 |
| 7 | " 11 | " " Dartmouth | | | 14- 2 |
| 8 | " 21 | " " Yale | | | 17- 4 |

## AMHERST.

| | | | | | |
|---|---|---|---|---|---|
| 1 | May 7 | Amherst vs. Harvard | | | 9- 8 |
| 2 | " 10 | " " Princeton | | | 5- 4 |
| 3 | " 21 | " " Brown | | | 5- 4 |
| 4 | " 31 | " " Dartmouth | | | 12- 3 |
| 5 | June 16 | " " Brown | | | 6- 1 |
| 6 | " 24 | " " Dartmouth | | | 10- 8 |

## BROWN.

| | | | | | |
|---|---|---|---|---|---|
| 1 | May 9 | Brown vs. Dartmouth | | | 5- 3 |
| 2 | " 13 | " " Princeton | | | 10- 5 |
| 3 | " 23 | " " Harvard | | | 10- 6 |
| 4 | June 4 | " " Princeton | | | 5- 3 |
| 5 | " 12 | " " Dartmouth | | | 14- 8 |

## PRINCETON.

| | | | | |
|---|---|---|---|---|
| 1 | May 16 | Princeton vs. Dartmouth | | 11- 2 |
| 2 | June 5 | " " Amherst | | 6- 3 |

## DARTMOUTH.

| | | | |
|---|---|---|---|
| 1 | May 17 | Dartmouth vs. Princeton | 6-3 |

## CLUB AVERAGES.

| COLLEGES. | Batting Average. | Batting Rank. | Fielding Average. | Fielding Rank. | General Average. | Rank. |
|---|---|---|---|---|---|---|
| Amherst | 246 | 4 | 887 | 1 | 567 | 1 |
| Yale | 287 | 1 | 838 | 5 | 563 | 2 |
| Harvard | 257 | 2 | 861 | 3 | 559 | 3 |
| Brown | 250 | 3 | 867 | 2 | 559 | 4 |
| Dartmouth | 245 | 5 | 859 | 4 | 552 | 5 |
| Princeton | 205 | 6 | 827 | 6 | 516 | 6 |

The above are the official averages of the American College Base Ball Association, for the season of 1884.

(Signed)      G. W. WADSWORTH,

Secretary.

## THE ANNUAL MEETING.

The annual meeting of the American College Base Ball Association, took place at the Massasoit House, Springfield, on March 14, 1884.

The convention was called to order by Mr. Crocker, of Harvard, at 10 A. M., the colleges in the Association being represented as follows: Amherst, G. W. Wadsworth, W. F. Wilcox and E. P. Harris; Brown, A. T. Wall, G. M. Wadsworth and Norman S. Dike; Harvard, S. V. LeMoyne and Adams Crocker; Princeton, C. S. Clark and A. Moffat; Yale, Henry C. Hopkins, Walter C. Camp and N. G. Williams, Jr.

The following officers were then elected: For President of the Asssociation, Adams Crocker, of Harvard; 1st Vice-President, N. G. Williams, Jr., of Yale; 2d Vice-President, N. S. Dike, of Brown; Secretary and Treasurer, G. W. Wadsworth, of Amherst.

The report of the former Secretary and Treasurer, Mr. Harlan of Princeton, was then read by Mr. Clark, of Princeton, and was accepted. The pennant for the season of 1883 was then unanimously voted to Yale.

Representatives of St. John's College, Fordham, N. Y., applied for admission to the Association, and Dartmouth applied for readmission. The application of St. John's College was rejected by a vote of 4 to 1.

It was moved that a delegation be appointed to inform Dartmouth that their admission was conditional on their playing their games on the home grounds of their opponents.

A recess was then taken to give the committee on Dartmouth, time to consult.

In fifteen minutes the meeting was called to order, and the committee on Dartmouth, reported that Dartmouth had accepted the offer and agreed to play both the Harvard games at Cambridge, both the Yale games at New Haven, and both the Princeton games at Princeton.

The Dartmouth delegates, Messrs. N. A. McClary, A. E. Nutt and G. O. Nettleton, were then admitted.

The Constitution was then discussed and amended, as published in the College records for 1884. It was moved that all championship games at Providence, be played on the Providence National League Club grounds, when the Providence Club is not there.

The playing rules of the National League were adopted with these exceptions: The seven ball rule was retained, the foul balk rule was retained, and a foul bound catch is to be out.

A recess was then taken to give the Committee on Umpires time to consult. At 4:15 the meeting was again called to order, and the committee reported that three umpires and one reserve umpire would be elected, and suitable salaries agreed upon by the judiciary committee, through the mail.

The official schedule, as announced in the College records, was then read by the Secretary and adopted.

The convention adjourned at 5:30 P. M.

G. W. WADSWORTH Secretary.

## 1884.

### OFFICERS OF THE ASSOCIATION.

AMHERST—G. W. WADSWORTH, President; R. T. FRENCH, JR., Scorer.

BROWN—CHAS. G. KING, President; CRAWFORD HILL, Scorer.

DARTMOUTH—B. P. GEORGE, President; H. C. BULLARD, Scorer.

HARVARD—T. J. COOLRIDGE, President; LEIGH BONSAL, Scorer.

PRINCETON—PAUL KIMBALL, President; WM. HALL, JR., Scorer.

YALE—N. G. WILLIAMS, JR., President; H. R. WAGNER, Scorer.

The following are the players of the ex-clubs and the positions they occupied in 1884.

| YALE. | HARVARD. | AMHERST. |
|---|---|---|
| Hopkins, 3 b., capt. | Coolidge, 2 b. | Taylor, s. s. |
| Terry, 2 b. | Baker, s. s. | Stuart, c. f. |
| Bremner, c. f. | Phillips, 3 b. | Sullivan, c. |
| Souther, c. | Le Moyne, r. f., capt. | Kimball, l. f. |
| Booth, p. | Tilden, l. f. | Marble, 3 b. |
| Stewart, 1 b. | Allen, c. | Buffum, 2 b. |
| Brigham, l. f. | Smith, 1 b. | Wheeler, r. f. |
| McKee, r. f. | Winslow, p. & c. f. | Gardiner, 1 b. |
| Oliver, s. s. | Nichols, c. f. & p. | Harris, p., capt. |

| BROWN. | PRINCETON. | DARTMOUVH. |
|---|---|---|
| Durfee, r. f., capt. | A. Moffat, p. | G. O. Nettleton, 3 b. |
| Seagrave, c. f. | Edwards, 2 b. | Springfield, l. f. capt. |
| Bassett, 3 b. | W. Moffatt, 1 b. | Hale, 1 b. |
| Chase, 1 b. | Harlan, c., capt. | Chellis, 2 b. |
| Shead, l. f. | Toler, c., capt. | Fellows, c. f. |
| Gunderson, p. | Cooper, s. s. | McCarthy, s. s. |
| Doran, 2 b. | Shaw, s. s. | Nutt, r. f. |
| Clark, c. | Reynolds, l. f. | F. H. Nettleton, p. |
| Wadsworth, s. s. | Van Etten, 3 b. | Thomas, c. |

## THE NORTHWESTERN COLLEGE ASSOCIATION.

This Association was formed three years ago with a view of bringing about a closer acquaintance and more frequent intercourse between the various Western Colleges than had before existed. As a rule athletics in Western Colleges are in a very backward condition, this condition being principally due to the fact that the Colleges are comparatively isolated, and, moreover, feel the want of that rivalry and competition so essential to excellence in any department. It was thought that this step would in a large measure overcome the difficulty. The result has been most encouraging, especially as regards the base ball interests.

The first year saw only half-organized, half-disciplined nines in the field; even Ann Arbor nine, which did not lose a game, had only a fairly good amateur team in the field that season. Since then there has been a steady improvement, and the nines of last season would bear a comparison with the best amateur nines of the country. The prospects for the season of 1885 are very good, and a corresponding improvement may be looked for.

There seems to be a growing sentiment in favor of the readmission of Ann Arbor into the Association. Most of the other colleges feeling as though they would like, once more, to "lock horns" with an antagonist, who downed them so easily the first year of the Association.

### THE CHAMPIONSHIP RECORD FOR 1884.

The contest for the championship of the Northwestern College Base Ball Association for 1884, was competed for by four clubs only, viz.: The University of Wisconsin, the Racine College the Northwestern University and the Beloit College, the result being the success of the Wisconsin University team, as will be seen by the appended record:

|  | Wisconsin. | Racine. | Northwestern | Beloit. | Games Won. | Games Lost. | Games Played. |
|---|---|---|---|---|---|---|---|
| Wisconsin........................ |  | 1 | 2 | 2 | 5 | 1 | 6 |
| Racine........................... | 1 |  | 1 | 2 | 4 | 2 | 6 |
| Northwestern................... | 0 | 1 |  | 1 | 2 | 4 | 6 |
| Beloit............................. | 0 | 0 | 1 |  | 1 | 5 | 6 |
| Games Lost.................... | 1 | 2 | 4 | 5 | 12 |  |  |

The championship contests began on May 3, at Beloit, and ended on June 7, at Evanston, during which period twelve games were played. Only three of these were marked by single-figure victories, the best-played game of the series being that of May 3 at Beloit, between the Wisconsin University nine and the Beloit College nine, the former winning by three to two only. The next best game was that of May 12 at Madison, when the Wisconsin University nine found it difficult to defeat the Racine College nine by 4 to 3. The other single-figure game was that of June 7, at Evanston, when the Beloit College nine defeated the Northwestern University nine. The full record of the score is appended:

| | | | |
|---|---|---|---|
| May | 3 | W. of W. vs. B. C., at Beloit | 3—2 |
| " | 3 | N. W. vs. R. C., at Racine | 19—1 |
| " | 10 | R. C. vs. B. C., at Beloit | 14—63 |
| " | 12 | W. of W. vs. R. C., at Madison | 4—3 |
| " | 17 | N. W. vs. B. C., at Beloit | 24—8 |
| " | 19 | W. of W. vs. N. W., at Madison | 14—6 |
| " | 23 | W. of W., vs. N. W., at Evanston | 12—10 |
| " | 28 | R. C. vs. W. of W., at Racine | 19—8 |
| " | 31 | R. C. vs. N. W., at Evanston | 13—5 |
| " | 31 | W. of W. vs. B. C., at Madison | 10—5 |
| June | 6 | R. C. vs. B. C., at Racine | 10—1 |
| " | 7 | B. C. vs. N. W., at Evanston | 9-7 |

The nine players who excel in the fielding averages are as follows:

| PLAYERS. | CLUBS. | POSITION. | Games Played. | Fielding Average. |
|---|---|---|---|---|
| Crooks | Racine | Catcher | 6 | .910 |
| Cowdrick | Northwestern | Pitcher | 2 | .937 |
| Kramer | Wisconsin | First baseman | 6 | .965 |
| Steele | Racine | Second " | 6 | .944 |
| Lunt | " | Third " | 6 | .936 |
| Reed | Beloit | Short-stop | 6 | .900 |
| Huxford | Northwestern | Left field | 6 | .909 |
| Harvey | Racine | Center field | 6 | .950 |
| Smith | Beloit | Right " | 6 | .923 |

The official record sent us by Secretary Waldo is as follows:

| PLAYERS AND POSITION. | CLUB. | Games Played. | Batting Average. | Fielding Average. | Rank in Fielding. |
|---|---|---|---|---|---|
| Huxford, l. f. | N. W. U | 6 | .500 | .909 | 9 |
| Arnd, p | N. W. U | 5 | .500 | .866 | 12 |
| Chase, s. s. | N. W. U | 3 | .444 | .818 | 19 |
| Wright, r. f. | R. C | 6 | .423 | .916 | 6 |
| Crooks, c | R. C | 6 | .393 | .910 | 8 |
| Parkinson, 3 b | U. of W | 5 | .391 | .833 | 16 |
| Steele, 2 b | R. C | 6 | .320 | .944 | 2 |
| Welsh, 3 b | B. C | 6 | .320 | .652 | 29 |
| Harvey, c. f. | R. C | 6 | .308 | .950 | 3 |
| Lewis, c. f. | N. W. U | 4 | .294 | .714 | 25 |
| Swasey, 3 b | N. W. U | 4 | .294 | .571 | 32 |
| Lunt, 3 b | R. C | 6 | .290 | .936 | 4 |
| Waldo, c | U. of W | 6 | .269 | .856 | 13 |
| Lansing, 2 b | B. C | 6 | .250 | .900 | 10 |
| Plummer, 2 b | N. W. U | 6 | .240 | .833 | 17 |
| Rice, s. s. | B. C | 6 | .240 | .678 | 26 |
| Farr, p | B. C | 6 | .230 | .550 | 34 |
| Ide, c | N. W. U | 6 | .222 | .847 | 14 |
| Brown, c. f. | U. of W | 6 | .222 | .666 | 27 |

BASE BALL GUIDE.   83

| PLAYERS AND POSITION. | CLUB. | Games Played. | Batting Average. | Fielding Average. | Rank in Fielding. |
|---|---|---|---|---|---|
| Smith, 1 b & r. f............... | B. C........... | 6 | .208 | .923 | 5 |
| Alderman, 2 b................... | U. of W....... | 6 | .208 | .655 | 28 |
| Connolly, p..................... | U. of W....... | 6 | .182 | .818 | 20 |
| Tomlinson, 1 b.................. | N. W. U....... | 6 | .179 | .843 | 15 |
| Parker, r. f..................... | U. of W....... | 6 | .176 | .722 | 23 |
| Van Tassel, c. f................. | B. C........... | 6 | .174 | .454 | 36 |
| Thompson, s. s.................. | U. of W....... | 6 | .173 | .652 | 30 |
| Reed, s. s...................... | B. C .......... | 6 | .160 | .900 | 11 |
| Chandler, l. f................... | U. of W....... | 6 | .143 | .833 | 18 |
| Whitehead, c.................... | B. C........... | 6 | .134 | .766 | 22 |
| Holborn, 3b..................... | R. C........... | 6 | .115 | .578 | 31 |
| Russell, 1 b..................... | B. C.......... | 6 | .107 | .914 | 7 |
| Kershaw, l. f.................... | R. C........... | 6 | .107 | .715 | 24 |
| Kramer, 1 b..................... | U. of W....... | 6 | .087 | .965 | 1 |
| Johnson, sub.................... | R. C........... | 3 | .083 | .500 | 35 |
| Holden, r. f..................... | N. W. U....... | 4 | .000 | .571 | 33 |
| Pellett, l. f..................... | B. C........... | 6 | .000 | .777 | 21 |

PLAYED IN LESS THAN THREE GAMES.

| | | | | | |
|---|---|---|---|---|---|
| Cook, s. s...................... | N. W. U....... | 1 | .333 | .400 | 65 |
| Goode, c........................ | N. W. U... | 1 | .250 | .833 | 4 |
| Rankins, s. s.................... | N. W. U.  ... | 1 | .250 | .500 | 2 |
| Sibley, 1 b...................... | R. C........... | 3 | .222 | .917 | |
| Cowdrick, p.................... | N. W. U....... | 2 | .125 | .937 | 1 |
| Helmuth, 1 b.................... | N. W. U....... | 1 | .000 | .900 | 8 |
| Castel, 3 b...................... | N. W. U....... | 1 | .000 | .250 | 3 |
| Bright, sub..................... | R. C........... | 2 | .000 | .000 | 7 |
| Canner, r. f..................... | U. of W ...... | 1 | .000 | .000 | 9 |

## THE UMPIRING OF 1884.

### NEW POINTS OF PLAY DEVELOPED.

The umpiring in the League arena in 1884 was not marked by as great a degree of improvement in the work as was expected under the amended rules; only a minority of the occupants of the position of Umpire on the League staff showing themselves competent to discharge the onerous duties required of them. The fact is, until the position is properly protected, and Umpires are made perfectly independent of all club influences, it will be difficult, if not impossible to secure men to act as Umpires who are fully competent in every respect to act in the position. It is one of the necessities of our national game, that the duties of the Umpire should exceed in their multiplicity and importance those of the Referee or Umpire in any other sport in vogue. For this reason the position nas become one requiring almost as much special training and instruction to excel in it as that of the most important field position in the game. Indeed, it is far easier to find a fitting occupant for the leading position in a first class professional nine than it is to find a suitable candidate for the onerous position of Umpire. In the early days of the game the Umpire had far less important points to decide upon than he now has, and more power for arbitrary decisions. Year by year, however, the revised rules of the game have lessened the opportunities for discretionary action, and transferred to the rules themselves what was formerly entirely in the hands of the Umpire to decide upon. Nevertheless, while much of the responsibility formerly attached to the position has been removed, there still remains enough to make it very important that the occupant of the place should be a man well posted in the matter of cor.ectly defining the existing laws of the game. Moreover, it is equally as essential that the Umpire should be a man who has the courage of his convictions and the determination to do his duty in the position at all costs. One of the erroneous opinions in vogue in regard to filling the position is that the best men for umpire are experienced players. No matter how skillful a player may be, however, it does not follow that he is therefore competent to act as Umpire. Some of the poorest Umpires we have ever seen have been professional players, men who have acquired a knowledge of the rules by hearsay only, and who seldom or never look at a base ball book. Whereas, on the other hand, we have seen some of the best of umpiring done by men who had but little practical knowledge of the game, but who, by studying the works on the game and thereby attaining a familiarity with the true intent and meaning of each rule, had made themselves thoroughly acquainted with the duties of the position.

As usual several new points in umpiring were developed during the season of 1884; rules of doubtful interpretation having been discovered, as well as points of play not covered by express rules. For instance, in the Providence-Chicago game of June 28, Umpire McLean found out a special point not covered by the rules. The case was this. The Providence nine were at the bat, with Denny on first base and Carroll about to strike. Five balls and two strikes had been called, when in the next ball delivered the Umpire called a balk on the pitcher. The latter delivered the ball, on which the balk was called, over the home base and at the height called for, but it being a balked ball the Umpire decided it as not a fair ball, and therefore the sixth called ball, and he not only gave Denny his base—the second—on the balk, but also sent Carroll to first on the sixth called ball. At the first look the decision appeared to be a sound one: but in reality it was not, for the important reason that the ball on which the balk was made was delivered to the bat before the penalty of the balk had been duly enforced by the runner on first base taking his second base, the ball delivered before this had been done, being a dead ball under the rules, and therefore not one to be called.

Another new point was developed in the Chicago-Boston game of June 21, in which a dispute occurred on a claim of the Boston captain to put in a substitute in the place of Manning who was disabled by a lame ankle. When Manning sprained his ankle in the field instead of retiring at once he kept on playing, and it was this fact which led the Chicago captain to object to the substitution of Buffinton for Manning, when the latter's ankle began to swell and pain him from use after the sprain, and he had to retire. As no substitute was allowed Captain Morrell played with one man short in the out-field, Manning really being disabled. The point in this case was that under rule 22 of the code it is requisite that each side must have *nine* men in the field during a game, and if they play with less they simply violate an express rule of the game, and thereby render themselves amenable to a forfeited game.

A new point was developed in the Chicago-Detroit game of July 29, in the case of the batsman—Ziller—while striking at the ball, missing it with the bat, but striking it with his body. As the ball by this means was sent out of the reach of the catcher, and in consequence a base was run, the question arose as to whether the decision should be the call of "dead ball" or one strike. Rule 30 defines a ball "striking the batsman's person, while standing in his position, *and without its being struck at*," as a dead ball. It was so decided in this case by Umpire Decker, and the runner who had taken his base on the play, was sent back to the base he left. Under a strict construction of the rule the act of striking at the ball prevented it from being called a "dead ball" from its having hit the body of the batsman, and consequently only the strike should have been called, and the runner have been allowed the base he ran on the play. The rule requires amending so as to prevent the batsman from wilfully allowing the ball to strike him in order to afford the runner a chance to make a base. Section 5 of rule 51 looks as if it covered the point; the rule in question covering the act of the batsman's hindering the catcher—but that only applies when the hindrance is made without any "effort to make a fair hit," whereas this ball was struck at and missed.

Another new point developed was that which occurred in the Chicago-Buffalo game of Aug. 11, in which a fielder was wilfully obstructed in putting a runner out. The Chicago nine were at the bat, and after the retirement of Dalrymple the first striker, Gore, made a base-hit, and Kelly followed with a short hit ball to Richardson near second base. The latter fielded the ball sharply and had ample time afforded him to have made a double play on a "force off" First touching Gore as he was running to second, he was about to throw out Kelly at first base when Gore running back toward first base suddenly turned and ran into Richardson, thereby preventing his throwing the ball until it was too late to throw Kelly out at first base. The Umpire decided both men out under the spirit of rule 68, which virtually makes him sole judge of the law and master of the field. This empowers him to decide under the law of equity on all cases not expressly covered by the wording of the rules. In this case there was no doubt as to the fact that but for Gore's willful obstruction, Richardson could easily have put out Kelly; and it was within the spirit of the law governing the power of the Umpire to judge all violations of fair play, to inflict the penalty he did in this case.

## THE PROFESSIONAL UMPIRE SYSTEM.

The problem of securing the best Umpire service in the professional arena, is each season approaching nearer a satisfactory solution. The system of having salaried Umpires first went into practical operation in 1882, and though the rules governing the League staff of Umpires of that year were rather crude, they have been improved upon each year since. The American Association adopted the League plan of salaried Umpires in 1883, and now the rules which govern the system in both organizations are virtually the same. This year the President of the League has the business of appointing Umpires solely in his hands, as also the American Association President, who in addition can remove an Umpire at his option, provided the Umpire violates a rule of the Association. It is a difficult task to secure men for the position who are fully competent for the service, and therefore the duties of the two Presidents in this respect are rather onerous.

## INSTRUCTIONS TO UMPIRES.

### ON CALLING STRIKES.

In rendering judgment on called strikes the Umpire must be fully satisfied that the ball not struck at was not delivered to the bat so as to plainly pass directly over the home base; and if so delivered was not, at the same time, sent in at the height called for by the batsman. There must be no doubt in the mind of the umpire as to the ball's passing over the base; if there is then such doubt must be given in favor of the batsman. The same rule of judgment, too, must govern the decision in reference to the height of the ball; that is, it must plainly be sent in within the boundary lines of a "high" or a "low" ball, as called for, or, in case of any doubt, the decision must be in favor of the batsman. The relative advantage of the positions of attack and defense as possessed by the pitcher and batsman under the rules, lies with the attack; and therefore all doubtful points in giving judgment in decisions must be given in favor of the defense, especially in calling "strikes" on balls not struck at.

### ON CALLING BALLS.

The same rule must govern the Umpire's decisions in judging "called balls" as in the case of called strikes; that is, the Umpire must call balls on every ball that is not plainly "*over the home base*," as well as within the boundary of the height called for by the batsman. In judging of called balls, too, he should fix upon some particular point of the batsman's person as a guide to him in judging the height of the ball.

There are three specially defined boundaries descriptive of "high," "low," and "high or low balls," the latter being a ball sent in at any height between the highest and lowest boundary lines, which are shoulder-high and knee-high. A "*high*" ball must be sent in above the line of the waist or "belt" of the batsman—the latter being the legal boundary—and not above the line of his shoulder. A "*low*" ball must be sent in not lower than the line of his knee, nor higher than the line of his belt. These are all the expressly defined balls under the rules which the Umpire has to judge of in calling balls; and according to these definitions a ball sent in above the line of the batsman's shoulder, or below the line of his knee, must be judged as a called ball, regardless of the fact of the ball's being, at the same time, plainly sent in over the home base. Then, too, in the case of a "high" ball being called for and the ball be sent in even with the line of the belt, a "ball" must be called, as the rule defining a "high" ball requires it to be sent in "higher than the belt of the batsman;" while, in the case of a call for a "low" ball, a ball sent in at the height of the belt—or what is called a "waist" ball—would be a fair ball, provided, of course, that it was, at the same time, sent in "over the home base," the latter being an imperative requirement in all cases in judging of "high" or "low" balls.

In fixing upon the points of "knee," the "belt" or the "shoulder" of the batsman, the Umpire should closely watch the movements of the batsman as to his bending his knee or body in striking at the ball, in order to vary the height of the defined lines. It is quite a difficult matter to define the exact height of a ball in the case of judging balls which cross the line of the batsman's belt, and the Umpire must bear in mind the fact of its being necessary for him to be pretty sure that the ball was plainly sent in "high" or "low" as called for, or otherwise, in the case of any doubt on the question, the decision must be rendered in favor of the defense. If, after being asked to name the ball he wants, the batsman declines to indicate any particular ball, the Umpire must call strikes on the batsman whenever he fails to hit at any ball sent in over the home base, which is not lower than one foot distant from the ground and not higher than the batsman's shoulder; and he cannot call "balls" on any balls thus delivered to the bat.

### THE METHOD OF DELIVERY.

The Umpire has nothing to decide upon in regard to the manner of delivering the ball to the bat as regards either the form of a "pitch," a "jerk," an *"underhand"* or *"overhand" throw* of the ball, or of the round-arm delivery as in bowling in cricket, as all of these forms of delivery are legal under the code. He has, therefore, only to watch the movement of the feet of the pitcher, in the act of delivery, to see that he fully conforms to the rule which requires him to have *both feet on the ground* within the lines of his position from the time that he takes his stand within the said lines to make the first motion of his form of delivery, until the ball leaves his hand. In watching the pitcher's feet during this period the Umpire needs only to watch the forward foot, as the backward foot cannot be lifted until the ball has left the pitcher's hand, inasmuch as it is from the pressure of this foot on the ground that he derives the power to give the last impetus to the ball. The Umpire, therefore, has only to watch the forward foot to see that that is not slipped forward, for the slipping or sliding of the foot forward is prohibited. In fact, the Umpire must see that this foot is not moved in any way; if it is he must promptly declare the penalty inflicted for a violation of the rule. This is the only point in the delivery of the ball by the pitcher which the Umpire has to regard before the ball leaves the pitcher's hands on its way to the bat, as far as a legal delivery is concerned outside of the question of a "balk."

### THE QUESTION OF A BALK.

The newly worded rule defining a "balk" relieves the Umpire from all doubt as to a correct definition of the rule, as will be seen by the appended rule itself:

"*A balk is made whenever the pitcher, when about to deliver the ball to the bat, while standing within the lines of his position, makes any one of the series of motions he habitually makes in so delivering the ball, and then fails to deliver the ball to the bat.*"

Every pitcher has a series of movements which he invariably makes preliminary to the ball's leaving his hand on its way to the bat; and under the above rule if he makes any one of these preliminary motions and then fails to pitch the ball directly to the bat, he commits a balk. All throwing to bases by the pitcher should be done by signal, and it is necessary that all such throwing should be done before he gets into his regular form to deliver to the bat.

The pitcher, under the new rule of keeping his feet on the ground while in the act of pitching, when getting into position to deliver the ball, first takes his stand with his feet apart and ready braced for his throw of the ball to the bat. While in this position, and before making any motion to throw to the bat, he can, of course, throw to a base, just as he can while simply standing still in his position before taking his stride to get ready for a regular delivery. But after taking this preparatory stride and getting himself ready to pitch, he must not make a single motion to throw to the bat and then throw to a base, or he must have a balk called on him. In throwing to base, therefore, under the new rule, the pitcher should do the most of his throwing while standing with his feet close together, and while in this position he cannot well commit a balk. But the moment he takes his stride ready to pitch the ball the Umpire must closely watch his every motion when runners are on bases, as then it is that his liability to "balk" begins.

### ON PUTTING OUT BASE RUNNERS.

It is imperative on the part of the Umpire that in rendering decisions on the putting out of base runners at *first base*, and also when "forced off," that the rule requiring the ball to be held by the base player while touching the base "*before*" the runner touches the base should be strictly enforced according to the precise letter of the rule. If the ball be thus held simultaneously with the runner's touching the base, the Umpire must decide the runner as "*not out.*" It must be plain to the Umpire that the ball was held by the base player *before* the runner touched the base, or his decision must be rendered in favor of the runner. This applies to every other base as well as the first in case of a "force off" or in returning to bases on foul balls.

### MAKING BASES ON THE RUN.

Rules 54 and 55 state that the base runner is entitled to take bases, and to return to them without being put out for being off a base, under certain conditions, one of which is that "*he do so on the run.*" The object of this rule is simply to avoid delays in the game either intentionally or otherwise. In the case of this running to a base when returning on a foul ball, it does not follow that if the base runner fails to run back he must therefore be decided out; his failure to run in such case simply takes away from him the exemption from being put out in so returning, leaving him in the position of taking the ordinary risks of regular base running. The exemption from being put out in returning to bases applies only in the case of a declared "*dead ball,*" a "*foul ball*" not caught on the fly, and the calling of a "*foul strike.*" The exemption applies in taking bases, in all cases where the batsman is given his base on called balls, or if any runner is thereby "forced off;" or if the Umpire calls a "balk:" or if the pitched ball passes the catcher and touches any fence or building which stands less than ninety feet distant from the home base, or if the runner be prevented from making a base by any plainly wilful obstruction by a fielder, or if a fielder stop or catch a batted ball with his hat or cap, or his jacket, or any loose part of his dress.

### OVER RUNNING FIRST BASE.

The Umpire should watch the base runner closely when the latter overruns first base, so as to be sure that he makes no effort to run to second before returning to retouch first base, for in such case the base runner ceases to be exempt from being put out while off the base. The Umpire, too, should see that the base runner, in over-running the base, touches it, for should he not do so he is not exempted from the penalty. Of course, to be put out when forfeiting the exemption referred to in the rule, the base runner must be put out by being touched by the fielder with his hand holding the ball. The base runner, after overrunning first base, cannot wait and return and retouch the base at his leisure; he must do it at once.

### ON CATCHES MADE.

It is a difficult point to decide the question of the making of a legal catch of the ball under the existing wording of the rule in which a catch is defined as a "momentarily held" ball. In rendering decisions on this point the Umpire must be governed, to a considerable extent, by the peculiar circumstances attendant upon the making of the catch. There is comparatively but little doubt as to the character of a catch, or of the nature of a failure to hold the ball sufficiently as to constitute a legal catch under the rule, under the varying circumstances of a game, except in the case of a "force off," that is, when it becomes a point of skillful play to purposely drop a fly ball or miss a catch in order to force a base runner to leave a base. In all such latter cases the Umpire must regard the purposely dropped half-caught ball as a ball "momentarily held" as defined in the rule. Even under this construction he will have to watch the action of the fielder pretty closely to see that a really accidentally dropped fly ball is not made to serve the purpose of a willfully missed catch, in order to effect the failure to make the catch by the throwing out of the runner on the subsequent "force off." The Umpire must make it a rule to require all fielders, striving to change an out on a fair catch into a "force off," by refusing to make the catch, to let the fly-ball touch the ground before he grasps it to throw to a base for a "force off."

## THE NEW RULE ON BALK.

The rules applicable to "balking" differ in the American code from those of the League. The former include the following sections:

RULE 25. *A Balk* is

(1) A motion made by the pitcher to deliver the ball to the bat without delivering it, and shall be held to include any and every accustomed motion with the hands, arms or feet, or position of the body assumed by the pitcher in his delivery of the ball, except the ball be accidentally dropped.

(3) Any motion to deliver the ball, or the delivering of the ball to the bat by the pitcher when any part of his person is upon ground outside the lines of his position. This shall include all preliminary motions with the hands, arms or feet.

The new rule governing the act of a base runner's hitting a fair hit ball is as follows:

RULE 42, Sec. 13. If a fair hit ball strike him before it has touched the hands or person of a fielder he shall be declared out, and in such case no base shall be run unless forced, and no run be scored.

The changes in the scoring rules only apply to sundry definitions, such as the following:

All "battery errors" are to go in the summary and to be excluded from the error column.

A wild pitch is a battery error, even if it lets in a run.

A passed ball is a battery error, even if it lets in a run.

A missed third strike which allows the batsman to make first base is a passed ball, and therefore a battery error.

A base given on balls, or by hitting the batsman with the ball is a battery error.

When the batsman misses the third strike and reaches first base through no fault of the pitcher, the pitcher is to be credited n the summary with a "struck out."

## THE BATSMAN' POSITION.

### UNDER THE LEAGUE RULE.

At the December convention of the National League in 1884, an important amendment was made to the rule defining the batsman's position; first in widening the position from three to four feet, and secondly in placing the line of the position nearest the home base at six inches from the corner of the base instead of one foot as before. This was done to afford the batsman greater freedom of movement in facing for a hit to right field, and also to enable him to stand nearer the base in reaching for out curve balls. The new lines are shown in the appended diagram.

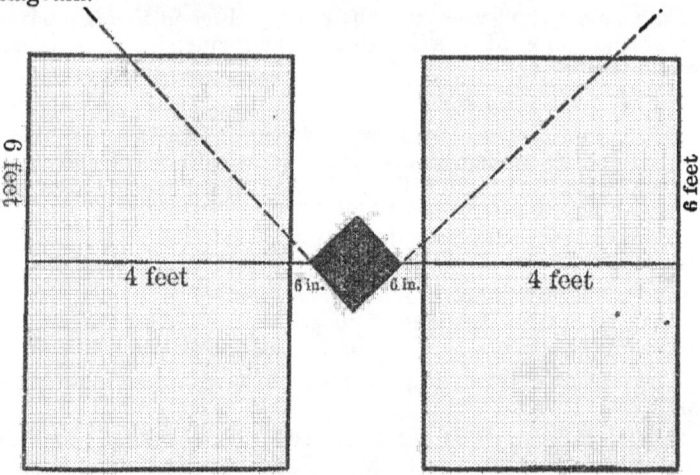

It will be seen that the home base line is now exactly nine feet in length from the outside lines of the two positions; the batsman can step three feet forward of the base line or three feet back of it; and he can stand four feet distant from the home base or within six inches of it.

## UNDER THE AMERICAN RULE.

The lines of the batsman's position under the American code of rules, were not changed at the December convention of 1884, and they remain as shown in the appended diagram.

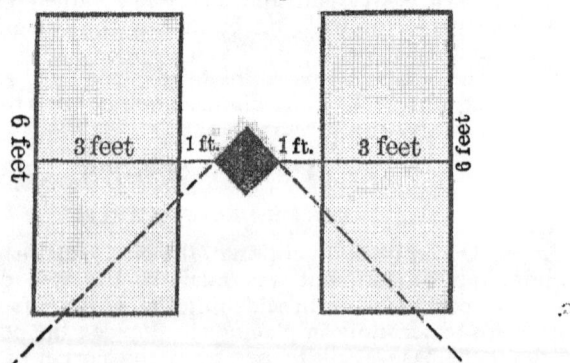

## THE PRESIDENT'S DUTIES.

A new departure was made by both the National League and the American Association at their respective conventions of 1884, and that was in the important amendments made to their constitutions in regard to the duties assigned to their Presidents. Especially was this the case in reference to the special powers given the President of the American Association. The experience of 1884 had plainly shown the value of having an executive head to the American Association, who should be entirely free from club influences; and it was also desirable that an official should be at command to adjudicate upon a certain class of disputes and of violations of Association rules, who should have direct power to carry out the laws of the institution so as to obviate the delays incident to a regular process of appeal. Then, too, the marked executive ability exhibited by President Mills of the League, in settling disputed points, and also explaining the correct definition of doubtful rules, presented an example of effective work in the Presidential position which the American Clubs were desirous of benefiting by in their Association. To cover all these points effectually an amendment was made to the American constitution which provided for the election of a President of the Association who should be a salaried official, and as such entirely free from the entangling influences which are attached to the position of a presiding officer selected from the members of one or other of the American clubs. Singularly enough the League convention was forced into following this plan of individualizing the office of President, as it were, by the fact of the retirement of Mr. A. G. Mills from the League Presidency. Fortunately they found in the person of their tried and most efficient Secretary the very individual for the emergency; and the prompt and unanimous election of N. E. Young as President of the National League, was but a well merited compliment to a most deserving official. To him, too, was assigned the complex duties of President, Secretary and Treasurer of the League, together with special supervisory control over the League staff of Umpires. The "new departure" as far as the League was concerned, therefore, was but the natural following of a path which circumstances obliged the convention to take. With the American Association "change of base," however, came the trial of a very important experiment, inasmuch as with the newly created office—a salaried official instead of the ordinarily elected President—a new system of government of the American Club ranks was inaugurated, which if successfully carried out could not but prove greatly advantageous to the future welfare of the Association. In 1884 the President of the American Association was simply the nominal head of the organization, whose sphere of control was far more limited than that of the Association's Secretary. This year the President of that association will have duties of a very onerous nature to discharge, as will be seen from the appended extract from the revised constitution, giving the amended section of article five.

"SECTION 1. To the President shall be delegated special powers, which shall be absolute and unquestioned, unless revoked by a two-thirds vote of the Board of Directors, as provided for in Section 4 of this article.

"SEC. 2. He shall appoint a staff of Umpires, to the number required by the playing rules, and shall report the same to the Association at the annual December meeting, subject to the approval of a majority of the clubs. *He shall also have the sole* power to remove any of the acting Umpires at any time, and fill the vacancy immediately. He shall assign all Umpires by telegraph, in the discharge of their duties, and neither he nor the Umpires so assigned shall disclose the nature or location of said assignment until said Umpires shall have reported for duty at the city stipulated: Provided, that no Umpire shall be assigned to Umpire more than four consecutive championship games at the same city. *It shall be his duty to compel each Umpire to enforce the letter and meaning of each playing rule strictly, upon penalty of the removal of said Umpire for refusing so to do.* To this end he shall be allowed a sum not to exceed $500 for traveling expenses each season, to be paid out of the treasury, and shall be required to file with the Secretary monthly an itemized statement of all such expenditures.

"SEC. 3. It shall be his duty at various times, as may seem best to him, to visit the various ball fields of the clubs of this Association, during the progress of championship games, and personally inform himself whether the playing and field rules are enforced by the clubs and Umpires.

"SEC. 4. Whenever he shall have *positive* evidence that any player, manager or Umpire of the Association has been guilty of public drunkenness, or has publicly engaged in a broil or fight, or has in any manner brought disgrace upon the profession of base ball playing by his open conduct, the President shall immediately suspend said player, Umpire or manager for a stipulated period of time, who, during the term of said suspension, shall be ineligible to play in or umpire any game of ball or manage the affairs of any club as party to the National Agreement. Provided, that if said player, Umpire or manager, or the President of the club to which the said player or manager is under consract desires to appeal to the Board of Directors for a removal of said suspension, it may be done in this manner: Said appellant shall, within five days from the date of the suspension, notify the Secretary in writing that he desires a trial before the Board of Directors. Said notification shall in each instance be accompanied by a cash deposit from said appellant of two hundred dollars, which, in the event of the Board sustaining the suspension, shall be used toward paying the traveling and incidental expenses of the Board of Directors incurred in such appeal; the residue, if any there be, to go into the general treasury. But if upon inquiry and an examination of the proof, the appellant be sustained by a two-thirds vote of the Board, and the ineligible party ordered reinstated, then said sum of $200 shall be returned to said appellant by the Secretary and the expenses of the Board in said trial shall be borne by the Association. And in no instance shall the Secretary notify the members of the Board of Directors of such appeal, or call them together to hear such appeal, unless the said sum of deposit above named be actually placed in his possession.

"SEC. 5. The President shall be permitted to draw a salary from the Association of $1,800, to be paid to him by the Secretary in twelve equal installments upon the 1st day of each month, commencing with Feb. 1 of each official year; and to meet the payment of said salary and of said traveling expenses of said President, each club of this Association shall pay to the Secretary upon or before the 20th day of each month, beginning with the 20th day of January, after each annual meeting, the sum of twenty-five dollars."

The most important feature of this schedule of Presidential duties is that which entrenches upon the constitutional rule— Article 6, Sec. 1—which gives to each club " *the right to regulate its own affairs, to make its own contracts, to establish its own rules, and to discipline, punish, suspend or expel its own Manager, players or other employes.*" The giving the President the right to appoint and remove Umpires at his option is one thing; but in adding the power to suspend a club manager or player under the conditions of the fourth section of the above rules, is a question open to serious objection. Still it may work satisfactorily. It certainly will if it does away with that crying evil, "kicking" against the decisions of Umpires, which was so objectionable a feature of the season of 1884.

## DRUNKENNESS IN THE RANKS.

Prior to the organization of the National League professional ball playing suffered greatly from several then existing evils prominent among which was "crookedness" among the club players, this evil being almost entirely due to the malign influence of pool gambling, the primary cause of all dishonesty in sports. But this evil was got rid of by the League after a hard fight; and now pool gambling is prohibited on every respectable professional ball ground in the country; and, moreover, every player found guilty of crooked work is forever debarred from employment in any professional club in the United States, every professional association having adopted the League rules punishing dishonest players.

Next to "crooked" play was the evil of drunkenness in the ranks, and this, we regret to state is still in existence, it being the most conspicuous evil that was connected with professional ball playing during 1884. This trouble has proved to be not only destructive to the morale of every club team in which it exists, but it is a powerful barrier to the financial success of the club whose team is injured by drunken players among them. Season after season for the past three years, have clubs besome bankrupt solely through the failure of their teams to accomplish successful field work owing to the presence of two or three drunkards in their team. Even one such member demoralizes a nine to such a degree as to offset all the advantages the team possesses in other respects. Club after club has adopted stringent rules against drunkenness in their teams, which have been enforced for a time, but owing to the frequent condoning of offenses the rules have become almost dead letters. Experience plainly points out the fact that there is but one remedy for this evil and that is total abstinence from the first day of the season to the last, and this rule should be enforced by costly pecuniary penalties, ending with suspension from service for an entire season when the violation is repeated. As for the class of habitual drinkers they should be driven from the ranks of the fraternity forever, just as Jim Devlin, Al Nichols, Craver, and others were for their proved dishonesty. Until this is done our professional clubs will never be free from the trouble drunken players cause them. Honesty in professional ball playing has been given a premium, and no man of questionable integrity of character can find employment in any professional club that is controlled by honorable men. Let temperance also be placed on the premium list by refusing to employ any player in the habit of drinking liquor. It is useless to point out to players of drinking habits the folly of the evil course they are pursuing. Treat them with all the kindly consideration possible by condoning their faults, they will only return it with more indulgence. The example of the folly of their course has no effect in preventing indulgence. Look at the case of young Eagan, the former pitcher of the League Club of Troy, who was taken in hand by the Brooklyn Club and given the means of reformation which would have made a man of him. What was his return for the help given him to rise out of the gutter of dissipation? Let his disgraceful death within prison walls point the moral of his wretched folly, as Devlin's death in low poverty did that of the results of dishonesty on the ball field. Self-preservation by the professional clubs requires that the strong hand of convention law be brought to bear on this existing evil. The hundreds of thousands of dollars invested as capital in base ball stock companies can no longer be placed in jeopardy by the continued trifling with this growing evil. Every base ball city in the land suffered from it in 1884 to a more or less extent, and it undoubtedly bankrupted a third of the clubs which encountered financial failure last season. Whatever may be said about prohibition in political circles, most assuredly it is the only law which should prevail on the subject in the ranks of the professional fraternity, from April to November each base ball year.

## CLIQUES IN CLUBS.

We regret to state that cliqueism prevailed among the professional clubs of 1884 to an extent which proved damaging to thorough team work in their nines. When this obstacle to successful management exists, the organization of a well trained and disciplined team is out of the question. The trouble in this respect is, that in nearly every professional team there will be found one or more players who are not contented with doing faithful service in the one position in the team which they are competent to fill, but are continually striving either to become captains, or, aiming higher, to ultimately work themselves into the manager's place. To do this they plan and contrive in every way to make the captain or the manager they are ambitious to replace fail in his efforts to discharge his duties satisfactorily. Of course, all this weakens the team as an effective corps in their working together as a team, and the failure is charged not to the real cause but to the unoffending captain or manager's incompetency. When this clique "racket" is not worked in the interests of some selfish aspirant for managerial control, it appears in the form of "clans" in the team who specially favor this or that one of the two "batteries" of the club. Here is a pitcher, for instance, who is really a very effective man in the position, as far as his special skill in the delivery of the ball is concerned; who, not satisfied with legitimately earning the handsome salary paid him, wants to control the entire team; leaving the manager to be a mere figurehead in his position, or limiting him to attend only to the outside business of the club. Such a pitcher goes to work to get a clique of "heelers" among the players, who will help him in his "little game," and the result is that each "battery" in the club have their special supporters in the team, and each clique works for the advantage of their pet "battery," at the cost of the general interests of the team as a whole. This cliqueism finds apt illustration in the instances of the McCormick clique in the League Club of Cleveland, and in the rivalry between Radbourne and Sweeny in the Providence team. It is one of the greatest obstacles to the efforts of a really competent manager to get his team into thorough practical working order; and until some means are contrived to check its growth in p o-fessional club nines successful team work is out of the question.

One cause of cliquiesm and its dissensions in clubs is the interference of some one or other club director with the work of running the team by the regularly appointed manager. Mr. A, for instance, thinks that the pitcher of the club, whom he regards as the most effective man in the possition, is not put in the "box" often enough; while Mr. B. thinks that non success of the team is largely due to the fact that his pet pitcher is left out of the nine far too often for its good. The respective pitchers in question are not slow to perceive this difference of opinion which prevails among the governing officials of the club; and utterly disregarding the behests of the manager they go to work to scheme for the advancement of their own special interests, and with this comes the growth of cliques in the team, and a division in the ranks which is fatal to thorough team work. In the face of such barriers to successful field work as these cliques present, how is it possible for a manager to run the team to the best of his ability, or even for a captain to general the nine in the field successfully. The trouble with this business is that the mischief works quietly and beneath the surface, the general patrons of the club only being aware that something or other is going wrong without knowing what the cause is. As the business of running a professional club advances with experience, these obstacles to financial success will ultimately disappear. In the interim, however, they tend to ruin the prospects of many a club which starts out at the commencement of a season with every prospect of financial prosperity.

## THE QUESTION OF ADVANCE MONEY.

The improvidence of a majority of professional players has come to be as familiar a factor in the business of engaging their services at the end of a season for an ensuing campaign as is the question of their individual ability to excel in their home positions; the result of their imprudence and want of economy bringing about the annual demands for advance money when they are engaged for an ensuing season's service. It is astonishing how many professionals there are who neglect, in the heyday of their harvest season, to provide for the exigencies of their idle winter term. Men receiving salaries which ought to enable them to live in comfort through the winter by what they earn in the summer, somehow or other find themselves almost penniless at the end of each November; and hence has come the yearly demand for advances on the salaries to be paid them the ensuing season. This question of advance money has grown to be a very important one, and also a very serious one, and the various baseball stock companies are this year considering whether it is not advisable to put a stop to it entirely. As it stands at present the player evidently has the best of the situation. If the company fails to pay its players their just financial dues, the players have the laws of the association, to which their club belongs, to protect them, together with the additional safeguard of the protective influence of the Arbitration Committee under the terms of the national agreement. But what protection has the stock company if the player chooses to "go back on them" after receiving advance money, as a number of players did in 1884 when they left the League and American Clubs to take service in Union Association Clubs. It is timely to bring this subject up for discussion, for it has come to have a very important bearing on the business of reorganizing club teams for an ensuing season's work in the field.

## THE MULLANE CASE.

The "Mullane Case" which occupied considerable attention at the American Association convention in December, 1884, merits passing notice in the GUIDE from the fact of the lesson it teaches of the folly of a dishonorable course of conduct by a professional player. A. J. Mullane, a noted pitcher of the American Association clubs, made himself notorious early in the season of 1884 by "jumping" his contract with the St. Louis Union Club, and leaving its service to play in the Louisville team of 1884. In the fall of the year he left the Louisville Club under a promise to sign with the American Club of St. Louis, and then broke his written pledge to that club to sign with the Cincinnati Club under the influence of a higher salary, together with an advance of $2,000 down. This case came up before the convention through charges made by the St. Louis Club, and after a full hearing the convention adopted the following resolution.

*Whereas*, A. J. Mullane having been found guilty of conduct calculated to bring discredit on the professional fraternity, and of setting an example of sharp practice almost equivalent to actual dishonesty, therefore it is

*Resolved*, That the Board of Directors feel that such conduct cannot be passed by without punishment, and they therefore decree the suspension of said A. J. Mullane for and during the season of 1885; and they also require that he shall refund to the Cincinnati Club, before Jan. 1, 1885, $1,000 of the money advanced to him by that club; and, furthermore, that said Mullane shall not be eligible to play base ball in any professional club during the season of 1885, the violation of this decree to be punished by final expulsion.

## THE IMPORTANCE OF SKILLFUL FIELDING.

A correct analysis of the play of the championship teams in the professional arena each season, shows very plainly that fielding is the most important element of success in winning matches. For instance, taking the appended table as a basis—which shows the total runs, earned runs and first base hits scored by each of the League clubs in their championship matches, as also fielding average of each club; it will be seen at a glance how important an element of success the splendid team work of the Providence Club was in winning the championship of 1884.

|  | Total Runs. | Total Earned Runs. | Total First Base Hits. | Fielding Average. |
|---|---|---|---|---|
| Providence | 665 | 262 | 987 | 876 |
| Boston | 684 | 267 | 1067 | 885 |
| Buffalo | 710 | 297 | 1093 | 861 |
| Chicago | 834 | 398 | 1164 | 828 |
| New York | 693 | 262 | 1055 | 826 |
| Philadelphia | 549 | 172 | 934 | 848 |
| Cleveland | 458 | 196 | 930 | 828 |
| Detroit | 443 | 163 | 822 | 835 |

This table shows that four clubs excelled the Providence team in total runs; three in earned runs, and four in base hits. The three leading teams, it will be seen, excelled all the others in their fielding averages, while in batting averages all three were beaten by others of the eight clubs.

## THE DEATHS OF 1884.

We add this year to the GUIDE, a brief notice of the deaths of well known ball players—amateur and professional—which took place during the season of 1884.

On Feb. 7th, Ed. Sullivan, a professional pitcher of Pittsburg, Pa., was accidentlaly killed from being run over by a locomotive.

On Feb. 16th, Theodore F. Kelly, the old second baseman of the amateur Active Club of New York twenty years ago, died at Jacksonville, Fla.

On March 3d, Jas. Sullivan, a professional pitcher of Allegheny, Pa., was accidentally killed from falling from a window of his residence.

On March 16th, A. F. Craft, a well known professional player of St. Louis, died.

On May 3d, that fine young College player, R. W. Lovering of the Harvard Club nine, died at Boston.

On June 2d, Anson B. Taylor, the old out-fielder of the Mutual Club nine of New York of twenty odd years ago, died in New York.

On June 12th, the veteran pitcher of the old Eckford Club of 1858, Frank Pidgeon, was run over and killed on the Hudson River Railroad near High Bridge, New York.

On June 14th, Edward R. Pennington, the veteran second baseman of the Eureka Club of New York in 1862, and the son of Ex-Governor Pennington of New Jersey, died at Newark, N. J.

On July 11th, W. B. Smiley, the professional second baseman of the Virginia Club team of 1884, died of disease of the heart at Baltimore, Md.

On July 22nd, Mr. John McDonough, a professional catcher, died at Mt. Clemens.

On July 30th, David Baurgim, an amateur pitcher, committed suicide at Camden, N. J.

On Sept. 7th, Arthur Daniels, a prominent amateur player of San Francisco, died in that city.

On Sept. 19th, Frank A. Leonard, a disabled amateur pitcher died in Boston, from disease of the shoulder, caused by excessive muscular exertion of his arm in pitching.

On Sept. 27th, Isaac P. Wilkins, the old short stop of the Athletic Club of 1866, died of typhoid fever at his residence in Montgomery Co., Pa.

On Oct. 10th, Chas. Householder, of the Union Club of Pittsburg, fell off the roof of a house while at work, and sustained injuries which resulted in his death shortly afterward.

On Nov. 3d, Jas. E. Powers, an old amateur player of the Eagle Club of New York of fifteen years ago, and an Ex-Alderman of Brooklyn, died in that city.

On Nov. 13th, William Sullivan, a professional player of the Holyoke Club, died of apoplexy in that city.

On Dec. 6th, Robt. Crandal, a veteran empoye of the Cincinnati Club, died in Cincinnati.

On Dec.    J. Ford Evans, a highly esteemed Director of the Cleveland Club, and formerly its President, died of the heart disease in that city.

On Dec. 12th, Geo. M. Reeder, the President of the Eastern Base Ball Club of Easton, Pa., died in that city.

## THE CLUB MANAGERS OF 1884.

The League Club managers of 1884 were Messrs. Bancroft of the Providence Club; Morrill of the Boston; O'Rourke of the Buffalo; Price of the New York; Anson of the Chicago; Harry Wright of the Philadelphia; Hackett of the Cleveland, and Chapman of the Detroit.

The American Association managers of 1884 were Messrs. Mutrie of the Metropolitan; Schmelz of the Columbus; Walsh of the Louisville; Williams of the St. Louis; Snyder of the Cincinnati; Barnie of the Baltimore; Simmons of the Athletic; Morton of the Toledo; Doyle, of the Brooklyn; McKnight of the Allegheny; D. O. Leaxy, of the Indianapolis, and Hollingshead of the Washington.

## CONFIDENCE THE ELEMENT OF SUCCESS.

Confidence is the one great element of success in a base ball team. It causes batsmen to "bunch their hits," and to punish even first-class pitchers. It inspires a supporting team to help a favorite pitcher to be effective, and it brings about a successful rally in a hard uphill fight. In fact, it is the basis of success in a team's work. Without it good batsmen strike out to poor pitchers; first-class fielders become "rattled" in critical periods of a contest, and a lack of confidence in their team's pitcher causes his supports to fall off in their effectiveness. With confidence to aid them a second-class nine can whip a first-class team which lacks confidence in their work. It was the secret of the old Atlantic's success twenty odd years ago. It was the very basis of the brilliant career of the Cincinnatis of 1869, and it gave the Bostons the championship in 1883, and it gave the pennant of 1884 to the club which possessed it most, and that was the Providence Club.

## BASE BALL TRAVELING.

The estimated distances traveled by the League Clubs in completing their championship schedule games in 1884 was as follows:

|   | No. of Miles Traveled. | Longest Jump. |
|---|---|---|
| Chicagos | 7,482 | 1,038 |
| Bostons | 7,148 | 1,038 |
| Providences | 6,648 | 735 |
| Philadelphias | 6,617 | 822 |
| New Yorks | 6,465 | 912 |
| Detroits | 6,383 | 735 |
| Clevelands | 5,876 | 682 |
| Buffalos | 5,516 | 912 |

The estimated distances traveled by the clubs of the American Association in their championship schedule were as follows:

|  | No. of Miles Traveled. | Longest Jump. |
|---|---|---|
| Brooklyns | 8,564 | 1,055 |
| Metropolitans | 8,497 | 883 |
| St. Louis | 8,438 | 944 |
| Toledos | 8,030 | 719 |
| Athletics | 7,685 | 1,065 |
| Cincinnatis | 7,389 | 757 |
| Baltimores | 7,123 | 689 |
| Columbus | 6,862 | 638 |
| Louisvilles | 6,795 | 883 |
| Alleghenys | 6,703 | 444 |
| Indianapolis | 6,523 | 825 |
| Washingtons | 6,265 | 904 |

## BASE RUNNING.

The season of 1884 in the earlier part of it, was marked by some every excellent base running; but toward the close of the season the strange action taken by the majority of Umpires in interpreting the rule defining a balk in such manner as virtually to nullify the intended effect of the rule, proved so much of an obstacle to successful base running that even a steal to second base with a poor thrower behind the bat became difficult. This season the new rule has removed this obstacle to base running and therefore better work may be confidently looked for in this important department of the game.

Each season's experience only shows more and more the fact that good base running is one of the most important essentials of success in winning games. It is a difficult task to get to first base safely in the face of the effectual fire from a first-class club battery, backed up by good support in the field; but it is still more difficult when the base is safely reached, to secure the other three bases without the aid of the succeeding batsmen. The fact is, a greater degree of intelligence is required in the player who would excel in base running than is needed either in fielding or in batting. Any soft-brained heavy weight can occasionally hit a ball for a home run, but it requires a shrewd, intelligent player, with his wits about him, to make a successful base runner. Indeed, base running is the most difficult work a player has to do in the game. To cover in-field positions properly, a degree of intelligence in the players is required which is not characteristic of the majority of players as a general rule; but to excel in base running such mental qualifications are required as only a small minority are found to possess. Presence of mind; prompt action on the spur of the moment; quickness of perception, and coolness and nerve, are among the requisites of a successful base runner.

Players habitually accustomed to hesitate to do this, that or the other, in attending to the varied points of a game, can never become good base runners. There is so little time allowed to judge of the situation that prompt action becomes a necessity with the base runner. He must "hurry up" all the time. Then, too, he must be daring in taking risks, while at the same time avoiding recklessness in his running. Though fast running is an important aid in base running, a fast runner who lacks judgment, coolness, and, in fact, "headwork" in his running, will not equal a poor runner who possesses the nerve and intelligence required for the work. The great point in the art of base running is to know when to start, and to start promptly when the favorable opportunity is offered. One difficulty a base runner, trying to steal to second, invariably encounters, is his having to watch either the pitcher or catcher closely. He cannot watch both carefully, and therefore he must make his selection as to which player he will look after. If the catcher is an accurate and swift thrower to the bases, he is the man to be attended to. But if the pitcher is one who has a method of delivery which includes a number of special movements which occupy more than the ordinary time in delivering the ball, then he is the man to watch, for he will surely afford the runner the required opportunity to steal a base or to secure a balk, if the runner only plays his part properly. A sharp base runner can bother a pitcher exceedingly by skillful dodging. It requires no small amount of nerve and coolness for a pitcher to watch a runner closely, and at the same time play the strategical points of his pitching with full effect.

# INDEX

—TO—

## RULES AND REGULATIONS.

|  | RULE. |
|---|---|
| The Ground | 1 |
| The Infield | 2 |
| The Bases | 3 |
| The Foul Lines | 4 |
| The Pitcher's Lines | 5 |
| The Catcher's Lines | 6 |
| The Captain's Lines | 7 |
| The Players' Lines | 8 |
| The Players' Bench | 9 |
| The Batsman's Lines | 10 |
| The Three Feet Lines | 11 |
| The Lines Must be Marked | 12 |
| The Ball | 13 |
|     of what composed (1) | 13 |
|     furnished by Home Club (2) | 13 |
|     replaced if injured (3) | 13 |
|     " " lost (4) | 13 |
| The Bat | 14 |

### FIELD RULES.

| | |
|---|---|
| Open Betting and Pool Selling Prohibited | 15 |
| Sale of Liquor Prohibited | 16 |
| No Person Allowed on Field During Game | 17 |
| Players not to Sit with Spectators | 18 |
| Penalty for Insulting Umpire | 19 |
| Penalty for not Keeping Field Clear | 20 |
| Restriction as to Addressing Audience | 21 |

## INDEX TO PLAYING RULES.

### THE PLAYERS AND THEIR POSITIONS.

|  | RULE. |
|---|---|
| Nine Players on each Side.......................... | 22 |
| Players' Positions................................. | 23 |
|     in the Field............................(1) | 23 |
|     at the Bat .............................(2) | 23 |
| Order of Batting....................................(3) | 23 |
| Restriction as to Occupying Catcher's Lines..........(4) | 23 |

### DEFINITIONS.

| | |
|---|---|
| A High Ball........................................ | 24 |
| A Low Ball........................................ | 25 |
| A High or Low Ball................................ | 26 |
| A Fair Ball........................................ | 27 |
| An Unfair Ball..................................... | 28 |
| A Balk............................................ | 29 |
| A Dead Ball....................................... | 30 |
| A Block........................................... | 31 |
| A Fair Hit........................................ | 32-34 |
| A Foul Hit........................................ | 33-34 |
| A Strike.......................................... | 35 |
| A Foul Strike..................................... | 36 |
| "Play"........................................... | 37 |
| "Time".......................................... | 38 |
| "Game"......................................... | 39 |
| An Inning........................................ | 40 |
| A Time at Bat.................................... | 41 |
| Legal or Legally................................. | 42 |

### THE GAME.

| | |
|---|---|
| Number of Innings................................ | 43 |
| Drawn Game...................................... | 44 |
| Forfeited Game................................... | 45 |
| "No Game"...................................... | 46 |
| Substitute, when Allowed......................... | 47 |
| Choice of First Innings........................... | 48 |
| When Umpire Must Call "Play".................. | 49 |
| Game Must Begin when "Play" is Called........ | 49 |
| When Umpire May Suspend Play................. | 49 |
| "    "    "    Terminate Game............... | 49 |
| Rain, effect of, in Terminating Game.............(4) | 43 |
| "    "    "    "    "    "........................ | 44 |
| "    "    "    "    "    "............................ | 46 |
| "    Definition of........................... | 49 |
| "    Umpire's Duty in Case of................ | 49 |
| Batsman Must Call for Ball He Wants.............. | 50 |

|  | RULE. |
|---|---|
| What Umpire Must Count and Call | 50 |
| When Batsman is Out | 51 |
| "        "        becomes Base-Runner | 52 |
| Base-Runner must touch Bases in Order | 53 |
| "        "        when entitled to hold Base | 53 |
| "        '        "        "        take one Base | 54 |
| "        "        "        required to return to Base | 55 |
| No Substitute Allowed for Base-Runner | 56 |
| When Base-Runner is Out | 57 |
| When Umpire shall, without appeal, declare player "Out" | 58 |
| When Ball is not in Play until Returned to Pitcher | 59 |
| Block, effect of | 60 |
| Run, when to be Scored | 61 |
| Fines on Pitcher | 62 |
| "     "  any Player ............63 (4,) 68, | 69 |
| Player not to Address Umpire | 63 |
| "     "     "     Audience | 21 |
| "     "  use Improper Language......(4) | 68 |
| "  to Obey Umpire's Orders......(4) | 68 |

## THE UMPIRE.

|  |  |
|---|---|
| Selection of Umpire | 64 |
| Disqualification of Umpire......(3) | 64 |
| Removal of Umpire......(4) | 64 |
| Duties as to Materials of Game......(1) | 65 |
| "     "  Ground Rules......(1) | 65 |
| "     "  Reversal of Decision......(2) | 65 |
| Changing Umpire during Game | 66 |
| Expulsion of Umpire | 67 |
| Umpire's Jurisdiction and Powers | 68 |
| Umpire to give Notice of Fine......(5,) (6) | 68 |
| "     "     "     "  Forfeited Game......(6) | 68 |
| Special Penalties | 69 |
| SCORING REGULATIONS | 70 |

## CONSTRUCTION AND AMENDMENTS.

|  |  |
|---|---|
| Construction of Rules | 71 |
| Amendment of Rules | 72 |

# PLAYING RULES

—OF THE—

# NATIONAL LEAGUE

—OF—

## Professional Base Ball Clubs;

### 1885.

ADOPTED IN PURSUANCE OF SECTION 51 OF THE LEAGUE CONSTITUTION.

## CLASS I.

### THE MATERIALS OF THE GAME.

RULE 1. *The Ground* must be an inclosed field, sufficient in size to enable each player to play in his position as required by these Rules.

RULE 2. *The Infield* must be a space of ground thirty yards square.

RULE 3. *The Bases* must be

(1) Four in number, and designated as First Base, Second Base, Third Base and Home Base.

(2) The Home Base must be of white rubber or white stone, twelve inches square, so fixed in the ground as to be even with the surface, and so placed in the corner of the infield that two of its sides will form part of the boundaries of said infield.

(3) The First, Second and Third Bases must be canvas bags, fifteen inches square, painted white, and filled with some soft material, and so placed that the center of each shall be upon a separate corner of the infield, the First Base at the right, the Second Base opposite, and the Third Base at the left of the Home Base.

(4) All the Bases must be securely fastened in their positions, and so placed as to be distinctly seen by the Umpire.

RULE 4. *The Foul Lines* must be drawn in straight lines from the outer corner of the Home Base, through the center of the positions of First and Third Bases, to the boundaries of the Ground.

RULE 5. *The Pitcher's Lines* must be straight lines forming the boundaries of a space of ground, in the infield, six feet long by four feet wide, distant fifty feet from the center of the Home Base, and so placed that the six feet lines would each be two feet distant from and parallel with a straight line passing through the center of the Home and Second Bases. Each corner of this space must be marked by a flat iron plate or stone, six inches square, fixed in the ground, even with the surface.

RULE 6. *The Catcher's Lines* must be drawn from the outer corner of the Home Base, in continuation of the Foul Lines, straight to the limits of the Ground back of the Home Base.

RULE 7. *The Captain's Lines* must be drawn from the Catcher's Lines to the Limits of the Ground, fifteen feet from and parallel with the Foul lines.

RULE 8. *The Players' Lines* must be drawn from the Catcher's Lines to the limits of the Ground, fifty feet from and parallel with the Foul Lines.

RULE 9. *The Players' Benches* must be furnished by the home club, and placed upon a portion of the ground outside the Players' Lines. They must be twelve feet in length, and immovably fastened to the ground. At the end of each bench must be immovably fixed a bat-rack, with fixtures for holding twenty bats; one such rack must be designated for the exclusive use of the Visiting Club, and the other for the exclusive use of the Home Club.

RULE 10. *The Batsman' Lines* must be straight lines forming the boundaries of a space on the right, and of a similar space on the left of the Home Base, six feet long by four feet wide extending three feet in front of and three feet behind the center of the Home Base, and with its nearest line distant six inches from the Home Base.

RULE 11. *The Three Feet Lines* must be drawn as follows: From a point on the Foul Line from Home Base to First Base, and equally distant from such bases, shall be drawn a line on Foul Ground, at a right angle to said Foul Line, and to a point three feet distant from it; thence running parallel with said Foul Line, to a point three feet distant from the center of the First Base; thence in a straight line to the center of the First Base, and thence upon the Foul Line to the point of beginning.

RULE 12. *The lines designated* in Rules 4, 5, 6, 7, 8, 10 and 11 must be marked with chalk or other suitable material, so as to be distinctly seen by the Umpire. They must all be so marked their entire length, *except* the Captain's and Players' Lines, which must be so marked for a distance of at least thirty-five yards from the Catcher's Lines, or to the limits of the grounds.

RULE 13. *The Ball.*

(1) Must not weigh less than five nor more than five and one-quarter ounces avoirdupois, and measure not less than nine nor more than nine and one-quarter inches in circumference. It must be composed of woolen yarn, and contain not more than one ounce of vulcanized rubber in mould form, and be covered with leather. It must be furnished by the Secretary of the League, whose seal shall be final evidence of the legality of the ball.*

(2) In all games the ball or balls played with shall be furnished by the Home Club, and become the property of the winning club.

(3) Should the ball become out of shape, or cut or ripped so as to expose the yarn, or in any way so injured as to be unfit for fair use in the opinion of the Umpire, on being appealed to by either Captain, a new ball shall at once be called for by the Umpire.

(4) Should the ball be lost during the game, the Umpire shall, at the expiration of five minutes, call for a new ball.

RULE 14. *The Bat.*

(1) Must be made wholly of wood, except that the handle may be wound with twine, not to exceed eighteen inches from the end.

(2) It must be round, except that a portion of the surface may be flat on one side, must not exceed two and one-half inches in diameter in the thickest part, and must not exceed forty-two inches in length.

## CLASS II.

### FIELD RULES.

RULE 15. *No Club* shall allow open betting or pool selling upon its grounds, nor in any building owned or occupied by it

*I hereby certify that the Spalding League Ball, manufactured by A. G. Spalding & Bros., of Chicago and New York, has been adopted as the official ball of the National League for 1885, and must be used in all championship games.

N. E. YOUNG,
Sec'y National League.

## PLAYING RULES.     111

RULE 16. *No Club* shall sell or allow to be sold upon its grounds, nor in any building owned or occupied by it, any spirituous, vinous or malt liquors.

RULE 17. *No person* shall be allowed upon any part of the field during the progress of the game, in addition to *the nine players on each side and the umpire, except such officers of the law as may be present in uniform to preserve the peace.*

RULE 18. *Players in uniform* shall not be permitted to seat themselves among the spectators.

RULE 19. *The umpire* is the sole judge of play, and is entitled to the respect of the spectators, and any person offering any insult or indignity to him, must be promptly ejected from the grounds.

RULE 20. *Every Club* shall furnish sufficient police force upon its own grounds to preserve order, and in the event of a crowd entering the field during the progress of a game, and interfering with the play in any manner, the Visiting Club may refuse to play further until the field be cleared. If the ground be not cleared within fifteen minutes thereafter, the Visiting Club may claim, and shall be entitled to, the game by a score of nine runs to none (no matter what number of innings have been played).

RULE 21. No Umpire, Manager, Captain or Player shall address the audience during the progress of a game, except in case of necessary explanation.

## CLASS III.

### THE PLAYERS AND THEIR POSITIONS.

RULE 22. *The Players* of each club, in a match game, shall be nine in number, one of whom shall be the Captain

RULE 23. *The Players' Positions* shall be

(1) When in the field (designated "Fielders" in these Rules) such as may be assigned them by their Captain, *except* that the Pitcher must take his position within the Pitcher s Lines, as defined in Rule 5.

(2) When their side goes to the bat they must immediately seat themselves upon the Players' Bench, and remain there until the side is put out, *except* when batsman or base-runner. All bats not in use must be kept in the bat racks, and the two players next succeeding the Batsman, in the order in which they are named on the Score, must be ready with bat in hand to promptly take position as batsman: *Provided*, That the Captain, and one assistant only, may occupy the space between the Players' Lines and the Captain's Lines, to coach Base-Runners.

(3) The Batsmen must take their positions within the Batsman's Lines, as defined in Rule 10, in the order in which they are named on the Score, which must contain the batting order of both nines and must be followed, except in case of disability of a player, in which case the substitute must take the place of the disabled player in the batting order.

(4) No player of the side at bat, *except* when Batsman, shall occupy any portion of the space within the Catcher's Lines as defined in Rule 6.

## CLASS IV.
### DEFINITIONS.

RULE 24. *A High Ball* is a ball legally delivered by the Pitcher, over the Home Base, higher than the belt of the Batsman, but not higher than his shoulder.

RULE 25. *A Low Ball* is a ball legally delivered by the Pitcher, over the Home Base, not higher than the Batsman's belt, nor lower than his knee.

RULE 26. *A High or Low Ball* is a ball legally delivered by the Pitcher, over the Home Base, not higher than the Batsman's shoulder, nor lower than his knee.

RULE 27. *A Fair Ball* is a ball delivered by the Pitcher while standing wholly within the lines of his position, and facing the batsman, with both feet touching the ground while making any one of the series of motions he is accustomed to make in delivering the ball to the bat, the ball, so delivered, to pass over the home base and at the height called for by the batsman. A violation of this rule shall be declared a "Foul Balk" by the umpire, and two Foul Balks shall entitle the batsman to take first base.

RULE 28. *An Unfair Ball* is a ball delivered by the Pitcher as in Rule 27, except that the ball does not pass over the Home Base, or does not pass over the Home Base at the height called for by the Batsman.

RULE 29. *A Balk* is

(1) If the Pitcher, when about to deliver the ball to the bat, while standing within the lines of his position, make any one of the series of motions he habitually makes in so delivering the ball to the bat, without delivering it.

(2) If the ball be held by the Pitcher so long as to delay the game unnecessarily; or,

(3) If delivered to the bat by the Pitcher when any part of his person is upon ground outside the lines of his position.

RULE 30. *A Dead Ball* is a ball delivered to the bat by the Pitcher, that touches the Batsman's bat, without being struck at, or any part of the Batsman's person while standing in his position, without being struck at, or any part of the Umpire's person, without first passing the Catcher.

Rule 31. *A Block* is a batted or thrown ball that is stopped or handled by any person not engaged in the game.

Rule 32. *A Fair Hit* is a ball batted by the Batsman, standing in his position, that first touches the ground, the First Base, the Third Base, the part of the person of a player, or any other object that is in front of or on either of the Foul Lines, or (*exception*) batted directly to the ground by the Batsman, standing in his position, that (whether it first touches Foul or Fair Ground) bounds or rolls within the Foul Lines, between Home and First, or Home and Third Bases, without first touching the person of a player.

Rule 33. *A Foul Hit* is a ball batted by the Batsman, standing in his position, that first touches the ground, the part of the person of a player, or any other object that is behind either of the Foul Lines, or that strikes the person of such Batsman, while standing in his position, or (*exception*) batted directly to the ground by the Batsman, standing in his position, that (whether it first touches Foul or Fair Ground) bounds or rolls outside the Foul Lines, between Home and First, or Home and Third Bases, without first touching the person of a player.

Rule 34. When a batted ball passes outside the grounds, the Umpire shall decide it fair should it disappear within, or foul should it disappear outside of the range of the foul lines, and Rules 32 and 33 are to be construed accordingly.

Rule 35. *A Strike* is

(1) A ball struck at by the Batsman without its touching his bat; or,

(2) A ball legally delivered by the Pitcher at the height called for by the Batsman, and over the Home Base, but not struck at by the Batsman.

Rule 36. *A Foul Strike* is a ball batted by the Batsman when any part of his person is upon ground outside the lines of the Batsman's position.

Rule 37. *Play* is the order of the Umpire to begin the game, or to resume play after its suspension.

Rule 38. *Time* is the order of the Umpire to suspend play. Such suspension must not extend beyond the day of the game.

Rule 39. *Game* is the announcement by the Umpire that the game is terminated.

Rule 40. *An Inning* is the turn at bat of the nine players representing a Club in a game, and is completed when three of such players have been put out as provided in these Rules.

Rule 41. *A time at bat* is the term at bat of a batsman. It begins when he takes his position, and continues until he is put out, or becomes a base runner.

Rule 42. *Legal, or Legally*, signifies as required by these rules.

## CLASS V.

#### THE GAME.

Rule 43. *A Game* shall consist of nine innings to each contesting nine, except that:

(1) If the side first at bat scores less runs in nine innings than the other side has scored in eight innings, the game shall then terminate.

(2) If the side last at bat in the ninth innings scores the winning run before the third man is out, the game shall then terminate.

(3) If the score be a tie at the end of nine innings to each side, play shall only be continued until the side first at bat shall have scored one or more runs than the other side, in an equal number of innings; or until the other side shall score one more run than the side first at bat.

(4) If the Umpire calls "Game" on account of darkness or rain at any time after five innings have been completed by both sides, the score shall be that of the last equal innings played, *unless* the side second at bat shall have scored one or more runs than the side first at bat, in which case the score of the game shall be the total number of runs made.

Rule 44. *A Drawn Game* shall be declared by the Umpire when he terminates a game, on account of darkness or rain, after five equal innings have been played, if the score at the time is equal on the last even innings played; but (*exception*) if the side that went second to bat is then at the bat, and has scored the same number of runs as the other side, the Umpire shall declare the game drawn, without regard to the score of the last equal innings.

Rule 45. *A Forfeited Game* shall be declared by the Umpire, in favor of the Club not in fault, in the following cases:

(1) If the nine of a club fail to appear upon the field, or, being upon the Field, fail to begin the game within five minutes after the Umpire has called "Play" at the hour appointed for the beginning of the game.

(2) If, after the game has begun, one side refuses or fails to continue playing, *unless* such game has been suspended or terminated by the Umpire.

(3) If, after play has been suspended by the Umpire, one side fails to resume playing within five minutes after the Umpire has called "Play."

(4) If, in the opinion of the Umpire, any one of these Rules is willfully violated.

Rule 46. "*No Game*" shall be declared by the Umpire if he shall terminate play, on account of rain or darkness, before five innings on each side are completed.

Rule 47. *A Substitute* shall not be allowed to take the place of any player in a game, *unless* such player be disabled in the game then being played, by reason of illness or injury.

Rule 48. *The Choice of First Innings* shall be determined by the two Captains.

Rule 49. *The Umpire* must call "Play" at the hour appointed for beginning a game. The game must begin when the Umpire calls "Play." When he calls "Time," play shall be suspended until he calls "Play" again, and during the interim no player shall be put out, base be run, or run be scored. The Umpire shall suspend play only for an accident to himself, or a player; (but in case of accident to a Fielder, Time shall not be called until the ball be returned to, and held by the Pitcher, standing in his position); or in case rain falls so heavily that the spectators are compelled, by the severity of the storm, to seek shelter, in which case he shall note the time of suspension, and, should such rain continue to fall thirty minutes thereafter, he shall terminate the game. The Umpire shall also declare every "Dead Ball," "Block," "Foul Hit," "Foul Strike," and "Balk."

Rule 50. *The Batsman, on taking his position*, must call for a "High Ball," a "Low Ball," or a "High or Low Ball," and the Umpire shall notify the Pitcher to deliver the ball as required; such call shall not be changed after the first ball delivered. The Umpire shall count and call every "Unfair Ball" delivered by the Pitcher, and every "Dead Ball," if also an "Unfair Ball," as a "Ball;" and he shall also count and call every "Strike." Neither a "Ball" nor a "Strike" shall be called or counted until the ball has passed the Home Base.

Rule 51. *The Batsman is out:*

(1) If he fails to take his position at the bat in his order of batting, unless the error be discovered, and the proper Batsman takes his position before a fair hit has been made, and in such case the balls and strikes called will be counted in the time at bat of the proper Batsman.

(2) If he fails to take his position within one minute after the Umpire has called for the Batsman.

(3) If he makes a Foul Hit, and the ball be momentarily held by a fielder before touching the ground, provided it be not caught in a fielder's hat or cap, or touch some object other than the fielder before being caught.

(4) If he makes a Foul Strike.

(5) If he plainly attempts to hinder the Catcher from fielding the ball, evidently without effort to make a fair hit.

RULE 52. *The Batsman becomes a Base Runner*

(1) Instantly after he makes a Fair Hit.

(2) Instantly after six Balls have been called by the Umpire

(3) Instantly after three Strikes have been declared by the Umpire.

(4) Instantly after two "Foul Balks" have been declared by the umpire.

RULE 53. *The Base-Runner must touch each Base in regular order*, viz: First, Second, Third and Home Bases, and when obliged to return, must do so on the run, and must retouch the base or bases in reverse order. He shall only be considered as holding a base after touching it, and shall then be entitled to hold such base until he has legally touched the next base in order, or has been legally forced to vacate it for a succeeding Base Runner.

RULE 54. *The Base Runner shall be entitled, without being put out, to take one Base, provided he do so on the run*, in the following cases:

(1) If, while he was Batsman, the Umpire called six Balls.

(2) If the Umpire awards a succeeding Batsman a base on six balls, and the Base Runner is thereby forced to vacate the base held by him.

(3) If the Umpire calls a Balk.

(4) If the umpire calls two "Foul Balks."

(5) If a ball delivered by the Pitcher pass the Catcher and touch any fence or building within ninety feet of the Home Base.

(6) If he be prevented from making a base by the obstruction of an adversary.

(7) If a Fielder stop or catch a batted ball with his hat or any part of his dress.

RULE 55. *The Base Runner shall return to his Base*, and shall be entitled to so return without being put out, provided he do so on the run.

(1) If the Umpire declares a Foul Hit, and the ball be not legally caught by a Fielder.

(2) If the Umpire declares a Foul Strike.

(3) If the Umpire declares a Dead Ball, unless it be also the sixth Unfair Ball, and he be thereby forced to take the next base, as provided in Rule 54 (2).

RULE 56. *The Base Runner shall not have a substitute run for him.*

RULE 57. *The Base Runner is out:*

(1) If, after three strikes have been declared against him

PLAYING RULES. 117

while Batsman, and the Catcher fails to catch the third-strike ball, he plainly attempts to hinder the Catcher from fielding the ball.

(2) If, having made a Fair Hit while Batsman, such fair-hit ball be momentarily held by a Fielder, before touching the ground or any object other than a Fielder: *Provided*, It be not caught in the Fielder's hat or cap.

(3) If, when the Umpire has declared three Strikes on him while Batsman, the third-strike ball be momentarily held by a Fielder before touching the ground: *Provided*, It be not caught in a Fielder's hat or cap, or touch some object other than a Fielder before being caught.

(4) If, after three Strikes or a Fair Hit, he be touched with the ball in the hand of a Fielder before such Base Runner touches First Base.

(5) If, after three Strikes or a Fair Hit, the ball be securely held by a Fielder, while touching First Base with any part of his person, before such Base Runner touches First Base.

(6) If, in running the last half of the distance from Home Base to First Base, he runs outside the Three Feet Lines, as defined in Rule 11, *except* that he must do so if necessary to avoid a Fielder attempting to field a batted ball, and in such case shall not be declared out.

(7) If, in running from First to Second Base, from Second to Third Base, or from Third to Home Base, he runs more than three feet from a direct line between such bases to avoid being touched by the ball in the hands of a Fielder; but in case a Fielder be occupying the Base Runner's proper path, attempting to field a batted ball, then the Base Runner shall run out of the path and behind said Fielder, and shall not be declared out for so doing.

(8) If he fails to avoid a Fielder attempting to field a batted ball, in the manner prescribed in (6) and (7) of this Rule, or if he, in any way, obstructs a Fielder attempting to field a batted ball: *Provided*, That if two or more Fielders attempt to field a batted ball, and the Base Runner comes in contact with one or more of them, the Umpire shall determine which Fielder is entitled to the benefit of this Rule, and shall not decide the Base Runner out for coming in contact with any other Fielder.

(9) If, at any time while the ball is in play, he be touched by the ball in the hand of a Fielder, unless some part of his person is touching a base he is entitled to occupy, provided the ball be held by the Fielder after touching him; *but (exception as to First Base)*, in running to First Base, he may overrun said base without being put out for being off said base, after

first touching it, provided he returns at once and retouches the base, after which he may be put out as at any other base. If, in overrunning First Base, he also attempts to run to Second Base, he shall forfeit such exemption from being put out.

(10) If, when a Fair or Foul Hit ball is legally caught by a Fielder, such ball is legally held by a Fielder on the base occupied by the Base Runner when such ball was struck (or the Base Runner be touched with the ball in the hands of a Fielder), before he retouches said base after such Fair or Foul Hit ball was so caught. *Provided*, That the Base Runner shall not be out in such case, if, after the ball was legally caught as above, it be delivered to the bat by the Pitcher before the Fielder holds it on said base, or touches the Base Runner with it

(11) If, when a Batsman becomes a Base Runner (*except as provided in Rule 54*), the First Base, or the First and Second Bases, or the First, Second and Third Bases, be occupied, any Base Runner so occupying a base shall cease to be entitled to hold it, until any following Base Runner is put out, and may be put out at the next base or by being touched by the ball in the hands of a Fielder in the same manner as in running to First Base, at any time before any following Base Runner is put out.

(12) If a Fair Hit ball strike him, he shall be declared out and in such case no base shall be run unless forced, and no run be scored.

(13) If, when running to a base or forced to return to a base, he fail to touch the intervening base or bases, if any, in the order prescribed in Rule 53, he may be put out at the base he fails to touch, or by being touched by the ball in the hand of a Fielder, in the same manner as in running to First Base. *Provided*, That he shall not be declared out unless the Captain of the fielding side claim such decision before the ball is delivered to the bat by the Pitcher.

(14) If, when the Umpire calls "Play," after any suspension of a game, he fails to return to and touch the base he occupied when "Time" was called before touching the next base.

RULE 58. *The Umpire shall declare the Batsman or Base Runner out, without waiting for an appeal for such decision*, in all cases where such player is put out in accordance with these rules, *except* as provided in Rule 57, (10), (13) and (14).

RULE 59. *In case of a Foul Strike, Foul Hit not legally caught flying, Dead Ball, or Base Runner put out for being struck by a fair-hit ball*, the ball shall not be considered in play until it is held by the Pitcher standing in his position.

PLAYING RULES. 119

RULE 60. *Whenever a Block occurs*, the Umpire shall declare it, and Base Runners may run the bases without being put out, until after the ball has been returned to and held by the Pitcher standing in his position.

RULE 61. *One Run shall be scored* every time a Base Runner, after having legally touched the first three bases, shall touch the Home Base before three men are put out. If the third man is forced out, or is put out before reaching First Base, a run shall not be scored.

RULE 62. *If the Pitcher causes the ball to strike the Batsman*, and the Umpire be satisfied that he does it intentionally, he snall fine the Pitcher therefor in a sum not less than Ten Dollars, nor more than Fifty Dollars. (See League Contract paragraph 11).

RULE 63. *No Player except the Captain or his assistant shall address the Umpire* concerning any point of play, and any violation of this Rule shall subject the offender to a fine of five dollars by the Umpire.

## CLASS VI.

### THE UMPIRE.

RULE 64. A staff of four League umpires shall be selected by the Secretary before the 1st day of May.

(1) Applications for such positions will be received by the Secretary until the 1st day of March.

(2) A written contract shall be made with each of the four umpires selected, stipulating for his service from May 1 to Oct. 15, at a salary of one thousand dollars for such period, payable in equal monthly payments, at the expiration of each month of service. He shall also be allowed and paid his actual expenses while absent from his home in the service of the League.

(3) He shall be under the sole control and direction of the Secretary, from whom he will receive all assignments to duty and all instructions regarding the interpretation of the playing rules, and the Secretary shall see that he is proficient in the discharge of his duties, and that he shall appear in proper dress when acting as umpire.

(4) In the event of the failure of such umptre to umpire a game assigned to him, it shall be the duty of the Secretary to provide a substitute to umpire such game, and, in such case, there shall be deducted from the next monthly payment to the League Umpire the sum of twelve dollars for each game as-

signed to him, which, for any reason, he shall have failed to umpire.

(5) It shall be the duty of each League Club to accept as Umpire for any championship game such League Umpire or substitute as the Secretary shall assign to such game, and only in the event of the failure of the League Umpire or substitute so assigned to appear at the hour appointed for the beginning of such game, shall the duty devolve upon the visiting club to designate an Umpire for such game.

(6) Any League Umpire shall be subject to removal by the Secretary at any time, and in the event of the resignation, removal or expulsion of any League Umpire the Secretary shall have power to appoint a suitable person to fill the vacancy thus created.

RULE 65. *The Umpire's Duties*, in addition to those specified in the preceding Rules, are:

(1) Before the commencement of a Match Game, the Umpire shall see that the rules governing all the materials of the game are strictly observed. He shall ask the Captain of the Home Club whether there are any special ground rules to be enforced, and if there are, he shall see that they are duly enforced, provided they do not conflict with any of these Rules. He shall also ascertain whether the fence directly in the rear of the Catcher's position is distant ninety feet from the Home Base. A fair batted ball that goes over the fence at a less distance than two hundred and ten feet from home base shall entitle the batsman to two bases, and a distinctive line shall be marked on the fence at this point.

The Umpire shall not reverse his decision on any point of play upon the testimony of any player engaged in the game, or upon the testimony of any bystander.

(2) It shall be the duty of the Umpire to decide whether the grounds are in proper condition, and the weather suitable for play.

RULE 66. *The Umpire shall not be changed* during the progress of a Match Game, except for reason of illness or injury.

Rule 67. *Any League Umpire who shall in the judgment of the President of the League be guilty* of ungentlemanly conduct or of selling, or offering to sell, a game of which he is umpire, shall thereupon be removed from his official capacity and placed under the same disabilities inflicted upon expelled players by the Constitution of the League. (See also Constitution, Sec. 42).

RULE 68. *The Umpire's Jurisdictions and Powers*, in addition to those specified in the preceding Rules, are:

(1) The gentleman selected to fill the position of Umpire must keep constantly in mind the fact that upon his sound discretion and promptness in conducting the game, compelling players to observe the spirit as well as the letter of the Rules,

## PLAYING RULES.   121

and enforcing each and every one of the Rules, largely depends the merit of the game as an exhibition, and the satisfaction of spectators therewith. He must make his decisions distinct and clear, remembering that every spectator is anxious to hear such decision. He must keep the contesting nines playing constantly from the commencement of the game to its termination, allowing such delays only as are rendered unavoidable by accident, injury or rain. He must, until the completion of the game, require the players of each side to promptly take their positions in the field as soon as the third hand is put out, and must require the first striker of the opposite side to be in his position at the bat as soon as the fielders are in their places.

(2) The players of the side "at bat" must occupy the portion of the field allotted them, subject to the condition that they must speedily vacate any portion thereof that may be in the way of the ball, or any fielder attempting to catch or field it. The triangular space behind the Home Base is reserved for the exclusive use of the Umpire, Catcher and Batsman, and the Umpire must prohibit any player of the side "at bat" from crossing the same at any time while the ball is in the hands of the Pitcher or Catcher, or is passing between them, while standing in their positions.

(3) Section 9 of the League Constitution makes the League Umpire a member of the League. During the progress of a game he is the sole representative of the League, to see that the game is played and determined solely on its merits, and these Rules invest him with ample powers to accomplish this purpose. In the performance of his duties he must remember that his sole allegiance is due to the League.

(4) The Umpire is master of the Field from the commencement to the termination of the game, and must compel the players to observe the provisions of all the Playing Rules, and he is hereby invested with authority to order any Player to do or omit to do any act, as he may deem it necessary to give force and effect to any and all of such provisions, and power to inflict upon any player disobeying any such order a fine of not less than five nor more than fifty dollars for each offense, and to impose a similar fine upon any player who shall use abusive, threatening or improper language to the Umpire, audience, or other player, and when the Umpire shall have so punished the player, he shall not have the power to revoke or remit the penalty so inflicted. (See League Contract, paragraph 11).

(5) The Umpire shall at once notify the Captain of the offending player's side of the infliction of any fine herein provided for, and the club to which such player belongs shall, upon receipt of a notice of said fine from the Secretary of

the League, within ten days transmit the amount of such fine to the Secretary of the League.

(6) In case the Umpire imposes a fine on a player, or declares a game forfeited, he shall transmit a written notice thereof to the Secretary of the League within twenty-four hours thereafter; and if he shall fail to do so, he shall forfeit his position as League Umpire, and shall forever thereafter be ineligible to umpire any League game.

RULE 69. For the special benefit of the patrons of the game, and because the offenses specified are under his immediate jurisdiction, and not subject to appeal by players, the attention of the Umpire is particularly directed to possible violations of the purpose and spirit of the Rules, of the following character:

1. Laziness or loafing of players in taking their places in the field, or those allotted them by the Rules when their side is at the bat, and especially any failure to keep the bats in the racks provided for them; to be ready (two men) to take position as Batsmen, and to remain upon the Players' Bench, except when otherwise required by the Rules.

2. Any attempt by players of the side at bat, by calling to a fielder, other than the one designated by his Captain, to field a ball, or by any other equally disreputable means seeking to disconcert a fielder.

3. Indecent or improper language addressed by a player to the audience, the Umpire, or any player.

In any of these cases the Umpire should promptly fine the offending player.

4. The Rules make a marked distinction between hindrance of an adversary in fielding a batted or a thrown ball. This has been done to rid the game of the childish excuses and claims formerly made by a Fielder failing to hold a ball to put out a Base Runner, but there may be cases of a Base Runner so flagrantly violating the spirit of the Rules and of the Game in obstructing a Fielder from fielding a thrown ball, that it would become the duty of the Umpire, not only to declare the Base Runner "out" (and to compel any succeeding Base Runners to hold their bases), but also to impose a heavy fine upon him. For example: If the Base Runner plainly strike the ball while passing him, to prevent its being caught by a Fielder: if he hold a Fielder's arms so as to disable him from catching the ball, or if he knock the Fielder down for the same purpose.

5. In the case of a "Block," if the person not engaged in the game should retain possession of the ball, or throw, or kick it beyond the reach of the Fielders the Umpire should call

# PLAYING RULES. 123

"Time," and require each Base Runner to stop at the last base touched by him, until the ball be returned to the Pitcher, standing in his position.

6. The Umpire must call "Play" at the exact time advertised for beginning a game, and any player not then ready to take the position allotted him, must be promptly fined by the Umpire.

7. The Umpire is only allowed, by the Rules, to call "Time" in case of an accident to himself or a player, or in case of rain, as defined by the Rules. The practice of players suspending the game to discuss or contest a decision with the Umpire, is a gross violation of the Rules, and the Umpire should promptly fine any player who interrupts the game in this manner.

## CLASS VII.

### Scoring.

RULE 70. *In Order to Promote Uniformity in Scoring* Championship Games, the following instructions, suggestions and definitions are made for the benefit of scorers of League clubs, and they are required to make the scores mentioned in Section 67 of the League Constitution in accordance therewith

*Batting.*

(1) The first item in the tabulated score, after the player's name and position, shall be the number of times he has been at bat during the game. Any time or times where the player has been sent to base on called balls shall not be included in this column.

(2) In the second column should be set down the runs made by each player.

(3) In the third column should be placed the first base hits made by each player. A base hit should be scored in the following cases.

When the ball from the bat strikes the ground between the foul lines, and out of reach of the fielders.

When a hit is partially or wholly stopped by a fielder in motion, but such player cannot recover himself in time to handle the ball before the striker reaches First Base.

When the ball is hit so sharply to an infielder that he cannot handle it in time to put out a man. In case of doubt over this class of hits, score a base hit and exempt fielder from the charge of an error.

When a ball is hit so slowly toward a fielder that he cannot handle it in time to put out a man.

(4) In the fourth column should be placed to the credit of each player the total bases made by him off his hits.

*Fielding.*

(5) The number of opponents put out by each player shall be set down in the fifth column. Where a striker is given out by the Umpire for a foul strike, or because he struck out of his turn the put-out shall be scored to the Catcher.

(6) The number of times the player assists shall be set down in the sixth column. An assist should be given to each player who handles the ball in a run-out or other play of the kind.

An assist should be given to a player who makes a play in time to put a runner out, even if the player who should complete the play fails, through no fault of the player assisting.

And generally an assist should be given to each player who handles the ball from the time it leaves the bat until it reaches the player who makes the put-out, or in case of a thrown ball, to each player who throws or handles it cleanly, and in such a way that a put-out results or would result if no error were made by the receiver.

An assist shall be given the pitcher when the batsman fails to hit the ball on the third strike, and the same shall also be entered in the summary under the head of "struck out."

(7) An error should be given for each misplay which allows the striker or base-runner to make one or more bases, when perfect play would have insured his being put out.

An error should be given to the pitcher when the batsman is given first base on "called balls."

In scoring errors off batted balls, see (3) of this rule.

Wild pitches and passed balls shall be charged to the pitcher and catcher respectively, in the error column, and shall also appear in the summary."

## CLASS VIII.

### CONSTRUCTION AND AMENDMENTS.

RULE 71. No section of these Rules shall be construed as conflicting with or affecting any article of the Constitution of the League.

RULE 72. *No Amendment* or change of any of these Rules shall be made, except in the manner provided in the Constitution of the League.

BASE BALL GUIDE. 125

## OFFICERS AND PLAYERS.

The following is an official list of the Officers of the National League of Professional Base Ball Clubs, and Officers and Players of Clubs, members thereof, for the season of 1885, so far as completed, to March 10, 1885.

N. E. YOUNG, PRES. and SEC., Box 536, Washington, D. C.

### DIRECTORS.

A. J. REACH, JNO. B. DAY, SPENCER CLINTON, and JNO. B. MALONEY.

### BOSTON BASE BALL ASSOCIATION, OF BOSTON, MASS.

A. H. SODEN, *President*,     J. B. BILLINGS, *Treasurer*,
*No. 116 Water St.*     *Box 1756.*

| | | |
|---|---|---|
| Manning, James H. | Burdock, J. J. | C. G. Buffinton, |
| Whitney, J. E. | Gunning, Thos. F. | Sutton, E. B. |
| Davis, John A. | Hornung, Jos. | Hines, M. P. |
| Wise, S. W. | Morrill, J. F. | |

### BUFFALO BASE BALL CLUB, OF BUFFALO, N. Y.

JOSIAH JEWETT, *President.*     GEO. H. HUGHSON, *Secretary,*
*No. 11 White Building.*

| | | |
|---|---|---|
| Crowley, Wm. | Myers, Geo. D. | McCauley, J. A. |
| Richardson, H. | Hengle, E. J. | Force, D. W. |
| Brouthers, D. | Serad, Wm. T. | Galvin, J. F. |
| Blakiston, R. | Rowe, John C. | Connor, John |
| Lillie, J. J. | | |

### CHICAGO BALL CLUB, OF CHICAGO, ILL.

A. G. SPALDING, *President*,     JNO. A. BROWN, *Secretary.*
*No. 108 Madison St.*

| | | |
|---|---|---|
| Clarkson, J. G. | Sutcliffe, E. E. | Williamson, E. N. |
| Pfeffer, Fred. | Anson, A. C. | Marr, Chas. |
| Corcoran, L. J. | Beard, O. P. | Kelly, M. J. |
| Gore, Geo. F. | Sunday, W. A. | Flint, F. S. |
| Burns, Thos. E. | Dalrymple, A. | Brown, Jos. |

## DETROIT BASE BALL ASSOCIATION, OF DETROIT, MICH.

Joseph A. Marsh, *President.*  Robt. H. Leadley, *Secretary,*
  *P. O. Box 122.*

| | | |
|---|---|---|
| Weidman, Geo. E. | Hanlon, Edward | Bennett, C. W. |
| Morton, C. H. | Meinke, F. W. | Wood, Geo. A. |
| Getzein, Chas. | Dorgan, J. F. | Farrell, J. F. |
| Phillips, Marr | Scott, M. P. | |

## PROVIDENCE BASE BALL ASSOCIATION, OF PROVIDENCE, R. I.

Henry T. Root, *President.*  J. E. Allen, *Box 73.*

| | | |
|---|---|---|
| Lovett, T. J. | Irwin, A. A. | Murray, U. J. |
| Farrell, John | Bancroft, F. C. | Carroll, C. |
| Start, Jos. | Gilligan, B. | Denny, Jeremiah |
| Crane, E. N. | Radbourn, Chas. | Bassett, C. E. |
| Daily, C. F. | Radford, P. R. | |

## NEW YORK BALL CLUB, OF NEW YORK CITY.

Jno. B. Day, *President, No. 121 Maiden Lane.*

| | | |
|---|---|---|
| Gerhardt, J. J. | McKinnon, A. | O'Rourke, J. H. |
| Ewing, Wm. | Welch, M. | Conner, R. |
| Richardson, D. | Gillespie, P. | |

## PHILADELPHIA BALL CLUB, OF PHILADELPHIA, PENN.

A. J. Reach, *President,*  Jno. I. Rogers, *Secretary,*
  *No. 23 So. 8th St.*  *No. 138 So. 6th St.*
  Harry Wright, *Manager, No. 710 Oxford St.*

| | | |
|---|---|---|
| Foster, E. E. | Cusick, Andrew | Daily, E. M. |
| Fogarty, J. G. | Myers, Albert | Andrews, Geo. E. |
| Purcell, W. A. | Ganzell, C. W. | Nolan, E. S. |
| Vinton, W. M. | Malvey, Jos. | Clements, Jno. |
| Ferguson, C. J. | Lynch, Thos. J. | Bastian, C. J. |

## ST. LOUIS ATHLETIC ASSOCIATION, OF ST. LOUIS, MO.

H. V. Lucas, *President, 2527 Cass Ave.*

| | | |
|---|---|---|
| Sullivan, F. P. | Baker, Geo. F. | Quinn, Joseph |
| Bandle, F. W. | Colgan, W. H. | Lewis, Fred'k. |
| O'Donnell, Wm. | Staples, Jos. F. | Henry J. Boyle. |

# BASE BALL GUIDE. 127

## THE AMERICAN ASSOCIATION.

The teams of this organization will be made up as follows:

### ATHLETIC.

| | | |
|---|---|---|
| Taylor, W. H. | Matthews, R. | Co ey, F. |
| Milligan, J. | Cushman, E. L. | Houck, S. P. |
| Fusselbach, E. | Stovey, H. D. | Larkin, H. |
| O'Brien, J. | Stricker, J. A. | Knight, A. |
| Coleman, J. | Strief, G. A. | |

### BALTIMORE BALL CLUB, OF BALTIMORE, MD.

| | | |
|---|---|---|
| Trott, S. W. | Nava, V. | Traffley, W. |
| Henderson, H. | Emslie, R. D. | Stearns, D. E. |
| Creamer, G. | Manning, T. E. | Muldoon, M. |
| Sommer, J. J. | Casey, D. P. | Burns, T. P. |
| Macullar, C. F. | | |

### BROOKLYN BALL CLUB, OF BROOKLYN, N. Y.

| | | |
|---|---|---|
| Kreig, W. F. | Hayes, J. J. | Porter, H. |
| Harkins, J. J. | Terry, W. H. | Phillips, W. B. |
| Smith, G. J. | Pinkney, G. B. | McClellan, W. H. |
| Swartwood, C. E. | Hotaling, P. J. | Cassidy, J. P. |

### CINCINNATI BALL CLUB, OF CINCINNATI.

| | | |
|---|---|---|
| Peoples, J. E. | Powers, Phil. | Snyder, C. M. |
| White, W. H. | Mullane, A. J. | Shallix, Gus. |
| Mountjoy, W. | Reilly, J. G. | McPhee, J. A. |
| Carpenter, W. W. | Fennelly, T. J. | Clinton, J. L. |
| Jones, C. W. | | Corkhill, J. S. |

### LOUISVILLE BALL CLUB, OF LOUISVILLE, KY.

| | | |
|---|---|---|
| Sullivan, D. C. | Whiting, E. | Blake, N. L. |
| Crotty, J. | Cross, A. C. | Noe, C. W. |
| Reccius, P. | Hecker, G. J. | Neagle, J. |
| Kerins, J. A. | Geer, R. | McLaughlin, T. |
| Browning, T. | Miller, J. A. | Maskrey, L. |
| Wolf, W. | | Hart, J. A. |

### METROPOLITAN BALL CLUB, NEW YORK CITY.

| | | | |
|---|---|---|---|
| Holbert, W. H. | Reipschlager, C. | Lynch, J. H. | |
| Becannon, J. M. | Orr, D. | Troy, J. | |
| Nelson, J. | Kennedy, E. | Roseman, J. | Brady, S. |

### PITTSBURG BALL CLUB, OF PITTSBURG, PA.

| | | |
|---|---|---|
| Carroll, C. H. | Kemmler, R. | Miller, J. F, |
| Mountain, F. H. | Morris, F. | O'Day, H. M. |
| Field, J. | Smith, C. M. | Kuehne, W. J. |
| Whitney, A. W. | Mann, T. J. | Brown, T. G.   Eden, C. M. |

### ST. LOUIS BALL CLUB, OF ST. LOUIS, MO.

| | | |
|---|---|---|
| Broughton, C. C. | Krehmeyer, C. L, | Robinson, W. H. |
| Bushong, A. J. | Foutz, Dave | McGinnis, Geo. |
| O'Neill, J. E. | Caruthers, R. L. | Comiskey, C. A. |
| Barkley, W. S. | Latham, W. A. | Gleason, W. |
| Welch, C. | Nichol, H. | |

## Record of Championship Games Played during the Season of 1884.

| Date 1884 | | Names of Contestants. | Winning Club | Winning Club | Losing Club |
|---|---|---|---|---|---|
| May | 1 | Boston vs. Buffalo | Boston | 5 | 3 |
| " | 1 | New York vs. Chicago | New York | 15 | 3 |
| " | 1 | Providence vs. Cleveland | Cleveland | 2 | 1 |
| " | 1 | Philadelphia vs. Detroit | Philadelphia | 13 | 2 |
| " | 2 | Philadelphia vs. Detroit | Philadelphia | 3 | 0 |
| " | 2 | Boston vs. Buffalo | Boston | 11 | 10 |
| " | 2 | New York vs. Chicago | New York | 13 | 6 |
| " | 2 | Providence vs. Cleveland | Providence | 5 | 2 |
| " | 3 | " Buffalo | Providence | 3 | 0 |
| " | 3 | Philadelphia vs. Chicago | Philadelphia | 9 | 8 |
| " | 3 | Boston vs. Cleveland | Boston | 11 | 2 |
| " | 3 | New York vs. Detroit | New York | 11 | 3 |
| " | 5 | " " | " | 3 | 1 |
| " | 5 | Boston vs. Cleveland | Boston | 9 | 3 |
| " | 5 | Philadelphia vs. Chicago | Chicago | 12 | 7 |
| " | 5 | Providence vs. Buffalo | Providence | 5 | 2 |
| " | 6 | Boston vs. Buffalo | Buffalo | 3 | 2 |
| " | 7 | " " | Boston | 7 | 0 |
| " | 8 | Philadelphia vs. Chicago | Chicago | 13 | 0 |
| " | 8 | New York vs. Detroit | New York | 8 | 4 |
| " | 9 | " " | | 5 | 0 |
| " | 9 | Philadelphia vs. Chicago | Chicago | 7 | 4 |
| " | 9 | Providence vs. Buffalo | Providence | 3 | 1 |
| " | 9 | Boston vs. Cleveland | Boston | 6 | 2 |
| " | 10 | New York vs. Cleveland | New York | 8 | 2 |
| " | 10 | Philadelphia vs. Buffalo | Buffalo | 9 | 7 |
| " | 10 | Providence vs. Chicago | Providence | 9 | 1 |
| " | 10 | Boston vs. Detroit | Boston | 3 | 2 |
| " | 12 | " " | " | 7 | 0 |
| " | 12 | Providence vs. Chicago | Chicago | 5 | 0 |
| " | 12 | Philadelphia vs. Buffalo | Philadelphia | 12 | 1 |
| " | 12 | New York vs. Cleveland | New York | 4 | 0 |
| " | 13 | Philadelphia vs. Cleveland | Philadelphia | 6 | 1 |
| " | 13 | New York vs. Buffalo | New York | 20 | 5 |
| " | 13 | Boston vs. Chicago | Boston | 5 | 3 |
| " | 13 | Providence vs. Detroit | Providence | 4 | 1 |
| " | 14 | " " | " | 25 | 3 |
| " | 14 | Boston vs. Chicago | Boston | 4 | 2 |
| " | 14 | New York vs. Buffalo | New York | 4 | 0 |
| " | 14 | Philadelphia vs. Cleveland | Cleveland | 7 | 5 |
| " | 15 | New York vs. Cleveland | New York | 7 | 1 |
| " | 15 | Philadelphia vs. Buffalo | Philadelphia | 25 | 5 |
| " | 15 | Providence vs. Chicago | Providence | 7 | 5 |
| " | 15 | Boston vs. Detroit | Boston | 11 | 9 |
| " | 16 | " " | Detroit | 4 | 2 |
| " | 16 | Providence vs. Chicago | Providence | 4 | 1 |
| " | 16 | hiladelphia vs. Buffalo | Buffalo | 9 | 0 |
| " | 16 | New York vs. Cleveland | New York | 6 | 3 |

## LEAGUE CHAMPIONSHIP GAMES.

### Record of Championship Games.—*Continued.*

| Date 1884 | | Names of Contestants. | Winning Club | Runs Scored. Winning Club. | Losing Club. |
|---|---|---|---|---|---|
| May | 17 | Philadelphia vs. Cleveland | Philadelphia .. | 16 | 2 |
| " | 17 | New York vs. Buffalo | Buffalo | 4 | 1 |
| " | 17 | Boston vs. Chicago | Boston | 9 | 7 |
| " | 17 | Providence vs. Detroit | Providence | 5 | 2 |
| " | 19 | " " | " | 4 | 2 |
| " | 19 | Boston vs. Chicago | Boston | 4 | 2 |
| " | 19 | New York vs. Buffalo | New York | 17 | 8 |
| " | 19 | Philadelphia vs. Cleveland | Cleveland | 5 | 0 |
| " | 20 | " Boston | Boston | 3 | 0 |
| " | 20 | New York vs. Providence | Providence | 2 | 1 |
| " | 21 | " " | " | 3 | 0 |
| " | 21 | Philadelphia vs Boston | Boston | 3 | 1 |
| " | 21 | Cleveland vs. Chicago | Cleveland | 2 | 1 |
| " | 21 | Buffalo vs. Detroit | Buffalo | 12 | 3 |
| " | 22 | " " | " | 8 | 7 |
| " | 22 | Cleveland vs. Chicago | Cleveland | 3 | 0 |
| " | 22 | Philadelphia vs. Providence | Providence | 12 | 4 |
| " | 22 | New York vs. Boston | New York | 7 | 1 |
| " | 23 | " " | " | 8 | 7 |
| " | 23 | Philadelphia vs. Providence | Providence | 8 | 1 |
| " | 23 | Cleveland vs. Chicago | Chicago | 5 | 0 |
| " | 23 | Buffalo vs. Detroit | Buffalo | 2 | 1 |
| " | 24 | Cleveland vs. Detroit | Detroit | 14 | 2 |
| " | 24 | Buffalo vs. Chicago | Buffalo | 8 | 4 |
| " | 24 | Philadelphia vs. Boston | Boston | 13 | 0 |
| " | 24 | New York vs. Providence | Providence | 19 | 5 |
| " | 26 | " " | " | 10 | 4 |
| " | 26 | Philadelphia vs. Boston | Boston | 10 | 4 |
| " | 26 | Buffalo vs. Chicago | Buffalo | 4 | 0 |
| " | 26 | Cleveland vs. Detroit | Cleveland | 2 | 0 |
| " | 27 | " " | Detroit | 4 | 1 |
| " | 27 | Buffalo vs. Chicago | Chicago | 14 | 6 |
| " | 27 | Philadelphia vs. Providence | Philadelphia .. | 4 | 3 |
| " | 27 | New York vs. Boston | Boston | 2 | 1 |
| " | 29 | Chicago vs. Detroit | Chicago | 15 | 5 |
| " | 29 | Cleveland vs. Buffalo | Cleveland | 8 | 0 |
| " | 29 | Boston vs. Philadelphia | Boston | 7 | 6 |
| " | 29 | Providence vs. New York | New York | 10 | 8 |
| " | 30 | " " | Providence | 12 | 9 |
| " | 30 | " Philadelphia | " | 9 | 2 |
| " | 30 | Boston vs. Philadelphia | Boston | 11 | 2 |
| " | 30 | " New York | New York | 5 | 1 |
| " | 30 | Cleveland vs. Buffalo | Buffalo | 9 | 5 |
| " | 30 | " " | Cleveland | 7 | 3 |
| " | 30 | Chicago vs. Detroit | Chicago | 11 | 10 |
| " | 30 | " " | " | 12 | 2 |
| " | 31 | " " | Detroit | 12 | 6 |
| " | 31 | Cleveland vs. Buffalo | Buffalo | 9 | 7 |
| " | 31 | Providence vs. Philadelphia | Providence | 6 | 5 |
| " | 31 | Boston vs. New York | Boston | 8 | 4 |
| June | 2 | Providence vs. New York | Providence | 9 | 3 |

## RECORD OF CHAMPIONSHIP GAMES.—*Continued.*

| DATE 1884 | NAMES OF CONTESTANTS. | WINNING CLUB. | Runs Scored. Winning Club. | Losing Club. |
|---|---|---|---|---|
| June 2 | Boston vs. Philadelphia | Boston | 10 | 1 |
| " 2 | Detroit vs. Cleveland | Detroit | 9 | 3 |
| " 3 | " " | " | 3 | 2 |
| " 3 | Chicago vs. Buffalo | Chicago | 4 | 3 |
| " 3 | Boston vs. Philadelphia | Boston | 11 | 6 |
| " 3 | Providence vs. New York | New York | 12 | 7 |
| " 4 | Boston " | Boston | 9 | 1 |
| " 4 | Providence vs. Philadelphia | Providence | 4 | 0 |
| " 4 | Chicago vs. Buffalo | Chicago | 5 | 4 |
| " 4 | Detroit vs. Cleveland | Cleveland | 13 | 7 |
| " 5 | " " | " | 5 | 4 |
| " 5 | Chicago vs. Buffalo | Buffalo | 12 | 5 |
| " 5 | Providence vs. Philadelphia | Philadelphia | 9 | 8 |
| " 5 | Boston vs. New York | New York | 10 | 6 |
| " 6 | Detroit vs. Buffalo | Detroit | 11 | 5 |
| " 6 | New York vs. Philadelphia | New York | 7 | 6 |
| " 6 | Chicago vs. Cleveland | Chicago | 11 | 2 |
| " 7 | " " | " | 13 | 6 |
| " 7 | New York vs. Philadelphia | New York | 10 | 6 |
| " 7 | Detroit vs. Buffalo | Buffalo | 6 | 0 |
| " 7 | Boston vs. Providence | Providence | 2 | 1 |
| " 9 | Providence vs. Boston | Boston | 2 | 0 |
| " 9 | Detroit vs. Buffalo | Buffalo | 5 | 4 |
| " 9 | Philadelphia vs. New York | New York | 12 | 8 |
| " 10 | " " | " | 16 | 6 |
| " 10 | Chicago vs. Cleveland | Chicago | 2 | 0 |
| " 10 | Boston vs. Providence | Boston | 3 | 1 |
| " 11 | Providence vs. Boston | Boston | 4 | 1 |
| " 11 | Detroit vs. Chicago | Chicago | 8 | 4 |
| " 11 | New York vs. Philadelphia | Philadelphia | 11 | 7 |
| " 12 | " " | " | 1 | 0 |
| " 12 | Detroit vs. Chicago | Detroit | 9 | 7 |
| " 12 | Buffalo vs. Cleveland | Buffalo | 6 | 0 |
| " 13 | " " | " | 12 | 8 |
| " 13 | Detroit vs. Chicago | Detroit | 6 | 5 |
| " 13 | Philadelphia vs. New York | New York | 9 | 1 |
| " 13 | Providence vs. Boston | Boston | 4 | 0 |
| " 14 | Boston vs. Providence | Providence | 4 | 3 |
| " 14 | Philadelphia vs. New York | Philadelphia | 8 | 4 |
| " 14 | Detroit vs. Chicago | Chicago | 9 | 5 |
| " 14 | Buffalo vs. Cleveland | Buffalo | 8 | 5 |
| " 16 | Buffalo vs. Chicago | Buffalo | 20 | 9 |
| " 16 | Cleveland vs. Detroit | Cleveland | 2 | 0 |
| " 16 | Providence vs. Philadelphia | Providence | 13 | 1 |
| " 16 | Boston vs. New York | Boston | 6 | 1 |
| " 17 | " " A. M. | New York | 7 | 6 |
| " 17 | " Philadelphia, P. M | Philadelphia | 7 | 2 |
| " 17 | Providence vs. New York | Providence | 9 | 0 |
| " 17 | Buffalo vs. Chicago | Buffalo | 8 | 7 |
| " 17 | Cleveland vs. Detroit | Cleveland | 9 | 3 |
| " 18 | " Chicago | " | 4 | 2 |

LEAGUE CHAMPIONSHIP GAMES. 131

RECORD OF CHAMPIONSHIP GAMES.—*Continued.*

| DATE 1884 | NAMES OF CONTESTANTS. | WINNING CLUB | Runs Scored. Winning Club. | Losing Club. |
|---|---|---|---|---|
| June 18 | Buffalo vs. Detroit............................ | Buffalo............ | 16 | 3 |
| " 18 | Boston vs. Philadelphia................... | Boston............ | 11 | 2 |
| " 18 | Providence vs. New York................ | Providence...... | 15 | 0 |
| " 19 | "         Philadelphia................ | "                | 6 | 5 |
| " 19 | Buffalo vs. Detroit........................... | Detroit........... | 18 | 2 |
| " 19 | Cleveland vs. Chicago..................... | Cleveland........ | 3 | 1 |
| " 21 | "         Philadelphia................ | "                | 14 | 12 |
| " 21 | Chicago vs. Boston.......................... | Chicago........... | 11 | 7 |
| " 21 | Buffalo vs. New York...................... | Buffalo............ | 6 | 2 |
| " 21 | Detroit vs. Providence..................... | Providence...... | 10 | 0 |
| " 23 | "         "                       | "                | 4 | 3 |
| " 23 | Cleveland vs. Philadelphia............. | Cleveland........ | 5 | 1 |
| " 23 | Buffalo vs. New York...................... | New York........ | 8 | 3 |
| " 23 | Chicago vs. Boston.......................... | Boston............ | 12 | 5 |
| " 24 | "         "                       | Chicago........... | 13 | 6 |
| " 24 | Detroit vs. Providence..................... | Providence...... | 1 | 0 |
| " 24 | Buffalo vs. New York...................... | New York........ | 10 | 4 |
| " 24 | Cleveland vs. Philadelphia............. | Philadelphia.... | 6 | 2 |
| " 25 | "         "                       | Cleveland........ | 14 | 1 |
| " 25 | Detroit vs. Providence..................... | Providence...... | 3 | 0 |
| " 26 | Chicago vs. "                          | "                | 8 | 6 |
| " 26 | Buffalo vs. Philadelphia................. | Buffalo............ | 9 | 2 |
| " 26 | Detroit vs. Boston........................... | Boston............ | 21 | 4 |
| " 26 | Cleveland vs. New York.................. | Cleveland........ | 4 | 2 |
| " 27 | "         "                       | "                | 6 | 4 |
| " 27 | Detroit vs. Boston........................... | Boston............ | 15 | 4 |
| " 27 | Chicago vs. Providence................... | Chicago........... | 6 | 0 |
| " 27 | Buffalo vs. Philadelphia................. | Philadelphia.... | 8 | 7 |
| " 28 | "         "                       | Buffalo............ | 12 | 1 |
| " 28 | Chicago vs. Providence................... | Providence...... | 13 | 4 |
| " 28 | Detroit vs. Boston........................... | Boston............ | 6 | 0 |
| " 28 | Cleveland vs. New York.................. | New York........ | 10 | 5 |
| " 30 | "         "                       | "                | 6 | 2 |
| " 30 | Detroit vs. Boston........................... | Boston............ | 11 | 2 |
| " 30 | Chicago vs. Providence................... | Chicago........... | 5 | 4 |
| " 30 | Buffalo vs. Philadelphia................. | Buffalo............ | 10 | 7 |
| July 1 | Chicago vs. "                         | Chicago........... | 14 | 0 |
| " 1 | Cleveland vs. Providence................ | Providence...... | 10 | 3 |
| " 1 | Detroit vs. New York....................... | New York........ | 12 | 5 |
| " 1 | Buffalo vs. Boston........................... | Boston............ | 2 | 1 |
| " 2 | "         "                       | "                | 4 | 1 |
| " 2 | Cleveland vs. Providence................ | Cleveland........ | 4 | 2 |
| " 2 | Detroit vs. New York....................... | New York........ | 7 | 2 |
| " 3 | Chicago vs. Philadelphia................ | Philadelphia.... | 15 | 13 |
| " 4 | "    A. M................. | Chicago........... | 3 | 1 |
| " 4 | "    P. M................. | "                | 22 | 3 |
| " 4 | Cleveland vs. Providence................ | Providence...... | 4 | 2 |
| " 4 | Detroit vs. New York....................... | New York........ | 4 | 3 |
| " 5 | Chicago vs. "                         | Chicago........... | 7 | 6 |
| " 5 | Detroit vs. Philadelphia................. | Detroit............ | 10 | 6 |
| " 5 | Buffalo vs. Providence.................... | Buffalo............ | 9 | 1 |

RECORD OF CHAMPIONSHIP GAMES.—*Continued.*

| DATE 1884 | | NAMES OF CONTESTANTS. | WINNING CLUB. | Runs Scored. Winning Club. | Losing Club. |
|---|---|---|---|---|---|
| July | 5 | Cleveland vs. Boston | Boston | 6 | 0 |
| " | 7 | " " | " | 11 | 3 |
| " | 7 | Chicago vs. New York | Chicago | 7 | 0 |
| " | 7 | Buffalo vs. Providence | Providence | 14 | 9 |
| " | 7 | Detroit vs. Philadelphia | Philadelphia | 11 | 6 |
| " | 8 | Cleveland vs. Boston | Boston | 10 | 1 |
| " | 8 | Chicago vs. New York | New York | 11 | 8 |
| " | 8 | Detroit vs. Philadelphia | Philadelphia | 11 | 4 |
| " | 8 | Buffalo vs. Providence | Providence | 6 | 5 |
| " | 9 | " " | Buffalo | 7 | 1 |
| " | 9 | Cleveland vs. Boston | Cleveland | 12 | 2 |
| " | 9 | Chicago vs. New York | Chicago | 9 | 1 |
| " | 9 | Detroit vs. Philadelphia | Detroit | 7 | 1 |
| " | 11 | New York vs. " | New York | 17 | 3 |
| " | 11 | Providence vs. Boston | Providence | 2 | 0 |
| " | 11 | Cleveland vs. Buffalo | Buffalo | 19 | 2 |
| " | 11 | Detroit vs. Chicago | Detroit | 4 | 2 |
| " | 12 | " " | Chicago | 6 | 5 |
| " | 12 | Cleveland vs. Buffalo | Buffalo | 7 | 4 |
| " | 12 | Boston vs. Providence | Boston | 7 | 1 |
| " | 12 | New York vs. Philadelphia | New York | 9 | 3 |
| " | 14 | Philadelphia vs. New York | " | 3 | 2 |
| " | 14 | Providence vs. Boston | Providence | 9 | 6 |
| " | 14 | Cleveland vs. Buffalo | Buffalo | 13 | 5 |
| " | 14 | Detroit vs. Chicago | Chicago | 6 | 3 |
| " | 15 | " " | Detroit | 14 | 0 |
| " | 15 | Cleveland vs. Buffalo | Buffalo | 2 | 1 |
| " | 15 | Boston vs. Providence | Boston | 4 | 3 |
| " | 15 | Philadelphia vs. New York | New York | 4 | 3 |
| " | 16 | Providence vs. Boston | Boston | 5 | 2 |
| " | 17 | Boston vs. Providence | Providence | 5 | 4 |
| " | 17 | Buffalo vs. Chicago | Chicago | 2 | 1 |
| " | 17 | Cleveland vs. Detroit | Detroit | 8 | 2 |
| " | 18 | Buffalo vs. Chicago | Buffalo | 12 | 7 |
| " | 18 | Cleveland vs. Detroit | Cleveland | 11 | 2 |
| " | 18 | Providence vs. New York | Providence | 5 | 2 |
| " | 19 | Boston vs. " | Boston | 12 | 1 |
| " | 19 | Providence vs. Philadelphia | Providence | 6 | 1 |
| " | 19 | Buffalo vs. Chicago | Buffalo | 7 | 5 |
| " | 19 | Cleveland vs. Detroit | Detroit | 10 | 4 |
| " | 21 | Boston vs. Philadelphia | Boston | 4 | 0 |
| " | 22 | Cleveland vs. Chicago | Chicago | 11 | 3 |
| " | 22 | Buffalo vs. Detroit | Buffalo | 11 | 7 |
| " | 22 | Providence vs. Philadelphia | Philadelphia | 10 | 6 |
| " | 23 | " New York | Providence | 11 | 5 |
| " | 23 | Boston vs. Philadelphia | Philadelphia | 5 | 1 |
| " | 23 | Cleveland vs. Chicago | Cleveland | 16 | 13 |
| " | 23 | Buffalo vs. Detroit | Buffalo | 10 | 2 |
| " | 24 | " " | Detroit | 7 | 2 |
| " | 24 | Cleveland vs. Chicago | Chicago | 9 | 5 |
| " | 24 | Boston vs. New York | New York | 5 | 3 |

## LEAGUE CHAMPIONSHIP GAMES.

### Record of Championship Games.—*Continued.*

| Date 1884 | NAMES OF CONTESTANTS. | Winning Club | Runs Scored. Winning Club | Losing Club |
|---|---|---|---|---|
| July 25 | New York vs. Boston | Boston | 10 | 4 |
| " 25 | Buffalo vs. Cleveland | Buffalo | 4 | 2 |
| " 26 | " " | " | 2 | 1 |
| " 26 | New York vs. Boston | New York | 12 | 8 |
| " 26 | Philadelphia vs. Providence | Providence | 16 | 3 |
| " 28 | " " | " | 11 | 4 |
| " 28 | New York vs. Boston | New York | 7 | 0 |
| " 28 | Buffalo vs. Cleveland | Buffalo | 9 | 3 |
| " 28 | Chicago vs. Detroit | Chicago | 5 | 3 |
| " 29 | " " | " | 16 | 8 |
| " 29 | Buffalo vs. Cleveland | Buffalo | 1 | 0 |
| " 30 | " " | " | 9 | 3 |
| " 30 | New York vs. Providence | Providence | 8 | 5 |
| " 30 | Philadelphia vs. Boston | Boston | 14 | 6 |
| " 31 | " " | " | 9 | 1 |
| " 31 | Chicago vs. Detroit | Chicago | 4 | 0 |
| Aug. 1 | " " | " | 5 | 2 |
| " 1 | New York vs. Providence | Providence | 7 | 3 |
| " 2 | Chicago vs. Cleveland | Cleveland | 10 | 8 |
| " 2 | Detroit vs. Buffalo | Buffalo | 2 | 0 |
| " 2 | New York vs. Boston | Boston | 2 | 1 |
| " 2 | Philadelphia vs. Providence | Providence | 9 | 2 |
| " 4 | Chicago vs Cleveland | Chicago | 9 | 2 |
| " 4 | Detroit vs. Buffalo | Buffalo | 18 | 0 |
| " 5 | Chicago vs. Cleveland | Cleveland | 8 | 5 |
| " 6 | " " | Chicago | 13 | 4 |
| " 6 | New York vs. Providence | New York | 2 | 1 |
| " 6 | Philadelphia vs. Boston | Boston | 4 | 1 |
| " 7 | " " | Philadelphia | 6 | 2 |
| " 7 | New York vs. Providence | Providence | 4 | 2 |
| " 7 | Chicago vs. Cleveland | Cleveland | 3 | 2 |
| " 7 | Detroit vs. Buffalo | Buffalo | 9 | 0 |
| " 8 | " " | " | 14 | 2 |
| " 8 | " " | Detroit | 1 | 0 |
| " 8 | Philadelphia vs. Providence | Providence | 6 | 0 |
| " 9 | Boston vs. Providence | " | 1 | 0 |
| " 9 | Detroit vs. Cleveland | Detroit | 5 | 4 |
| " 9 | Chicago vs. Buffalo | Chicago | 11 | 5 |
| " 11 | Providence vs. Boston | Providence | 3 | 1 |
| " 11 | Philadelphia vs. New York | Philadelphia | 8 | 3 |
| " 11 | Detroit vs. Cleveland | Cleveland | 8 | 1 |
| " 12 | Chicago vs. Buffalo | Buffalo | 11 | 9 |
| " 12 | Boston vs. Providence | Providence | 4 | 0 |
| " 12 | Philadelphia vs. New York | New York | 4 | 3 |
| " 12 | Detroit vs. Cleveland | Cleveland | 6 | 2 |
| " 13 | " | " | 1 | 0 |
| " 13 | New York vs Philadelphia | New York | 9 | 4 |
| " 13 | Chicago vs. Buffalo | Buffalo | 15 | 4 |
| " 14 | " " | Chicago | 17 | 10 |
| " 14 | New York vs. Philadelphia | Philadelphia | 8 | 2 |
| " 14 | Providence vs. Boston | Providence | 1 | 0 |

## LEAGUE CHAMPIONSHIP GAMES.

### Record of Championship Games.—*Continued.*

| DATE 1884 | NAMES OF CONTESTANTS. | WINNING CLUB. | Runs Scored. Winning Club. | Losing Club. |
|---|---|---|---|---|
| Aug. 15 | Providence vs. Cleveland. | Providence | 3 | 2 |
| " 15 | New York vs. Boston. | Boston | 3 | 1 |
| " 16 | "  Chicago | Chicago | 13 | 9 |
| " 16 | Boston vs. Cleveland. | Boston | 4 | 0 |
| " 18 | New York vs. Chicago. | New York | 5 | 3 |
| " 18 | Philadelphia vs. Cleveland. | Cleveland | 5 | 4 |
| " 19 | New York vs. Buffalo. | New York | 3 | 1 |
| " 19 | Boston vs. Chicago. | Boston | 4 | 3 |
| " 19 | Providence vs. Detroit. | Providence | 4 | 2 |
| " 20 | "  " | " | 5 | 2 |
| " 20 | New York vs. Buffalo. | New York | 14 | 6 |
| " 20 | Boston vs. Chicago. | Boston | 7 | 4 |
| " 21 | Philadelphia vs. Cleveland. | Philadelphia | 20 | 1 |
| " 21 | New York. vs Buffalo. | New York | 3 | 2 |
| " 21 | Providence vs. Chicago. | Providence | 5 | 3 |
| " 21 | Boston vs. Detroit. | Boston | 12 | 4 |
| " 22 | Philadelphia vs. Cleveland. | Philadelphia | 5 | 2 |
| " 23 | "  " | " | 5 | 4 |
| " 23 | Boston vs. Detroit. | Boston | 7 | 5 |
| " 23 | Providence vs. Chicago. | Providence | 7 | 3 |
| " 23 | New York vs. Buffalo. | Buffalo | 5 | 3 |
| " 25 | Philadelphia vs. " | " | 8 | 3 |
| " 26 | New York vs. Cleveland. | Cleveland | 9 | 4 |
| " 27 | "  " | New York | 9 | 7 |
| " 27 | Philadelphia vs. Buffalo. | Buffalo | 2 | 0 |
| " 27 | Providence vs. Chicago. | Providence | 5 | 3 |
| " 27 | Boston vs. Detroit. | Boston | 5 | 3 |
| " 28 | "  " | " | 3 | 0 |
| " 28 | New York vs. Cleveland. | New York | 10 | 2 |
| " 28 | Philadelphia vs. Buffalo. | Buffalo | 7 | 0 |
| " 28 | Providence vs. Chicago. | Providence | 6 | 4 |
| " 29 | "  Detroit. | " | 7 | 1 |
| " 30 | "  " | " | 6 | 5 |
| " 30 | Boston vs. Chicago. | Chicago | 6 | 5 |
| " 30 | Philadelphia vs. Buffalo. | Philadelphia | 5 | 3 |
| " 30 | New York vs. Cleveland. | New York | 9 | 2 |
| Sept. 1 | Philadelphia vs. Detroit. | Philadelphia | 6 | 2 |
| " 1 | Boston vs. Chicago. | Boston | 7 | 4 |
| " 2 | "  Cleveland. | " | 4 | 1 |
| " 2 | Philadelphia vs. Detroit. | Detroit | 11 | 4 |
| " 2 | Providence vs. Buffalo. | Providence | 4 | 0 |
| " 2 | New York vs. Chicago. | Chicago | 8 | 3 |
| " 3 | "  " | " | 9 | 3 |
| " 3 | Providence vs. Buffalo. | Providence | 10 | 1 |
| " 3 | Boston vs. Cleveland. | Boston | 7 | 0 |
| " 3 | Philadelphia vs. Detroit. | Philadelphia | 5 | 4 |
| " 3 | "  " | Detroit | 2 | 1 |
| " 4 | New York vs. Chicago. | Chicago | 7 | 5 |
| " 4 | Providence vs. Cleveland. | Providence | 3 | 1 |
| " 4 | Boston vs. Buffalo. | Boston | 7 | 2 |
| " 5 | Philadelphia vs. Detroit. | Philadelphia | 5 | 2 |

## LEAGUE CHAMPIONSHIP GAMES.  135

### RECORD OF CHAMPIONSHIP GAMES.—*Continued.*

| DATE 1884 | NAMES OF CONTESTANTS | WINNING CLUB | Runs Scored. Winning Club. | Losing Club. |
|---|---|---|---|---|
| Sept. 5 | Providence vs. Cleveland | Providence | 5 | 4 |
| " 6 | " " | " | 3 | 0 |
| " 6 | Boston vs. Buffalo | Buffalo | 2 | 1 |
| " 6 | New York vs. Chicago | Chicago | 3 | 2 |
| " 6 | Philadelphia vs. Detroit | Philadelphia | 6 | 4 |
| " 8 | " Chicago | Chicago | 15 | 10 |
| " 9 | New York vs. Detroit | New York | 11 | 3 |
| " 9 | Providence vs. Buffalo | Buffalo | 2 | 0 |
| " 9 | Boston vs. Cleveland | Boston | 10 | 8 |
| " 10 | " Buffalo | " | 8 | 0 |
| " 10 | Philadelphia vs. Chicago | Chicago | 16 | 6 |
| " 10 | Providence vs. Cleveland | Providence | 5 | 3 |
| " 10 | New York vs. Detroit | New York | 13 | 3 |
| " 11 | " " | " | 2 | 1 |
| " 11 | Philadelphia vs. Chicago | Chicago | 19 | 2 |
| " 11 | Boston vs. Buffalo | Buffalo | 1 | 0 |
| " 11 | Providence vs. Cleveland | Providence | 9 | 1 |
| " 12 | " Buffalo | " | 8 | 2 |
| " 13 | " " | " | 6 | 1 |
| " 13 | Boston vs. Cleveland | Boston | 11 | 2 |
| " 13 | Philadelphia vs. Chicago | Chicago | 5 | 2 |
| " 13 | New York vs. Detroit | New York | 13 | 2 |
| " 15 | Cleveland vs. Providence | Providence | 10 | 2 |
| " 16 | " New York | Cleveland | 12 | 3 |
| " 16 | Chicago vs. Boston | Chicago | 17 | 0 |
| " 16 | Buffalo vs. Philadelphia | Buffalo | 7 | 4 |
| " 16 | Detroit vs. Providence | Providence | 4 | 2 |
| " 17 | Cleveland vs. New York | New York | 9 | 1 |
| " 17 | Chicago vs. Boston | Chicago | 18 | 9 |
| " 17 | Detroit vs. Providence | Providence | 9 | 5 |
| " 17 | Buffalo vs. Philadelphia | Buffalo | 22 | 8 |
| " 18 | Chicago vs. Boston | Boston | 5 | 3 |
| " 18 | Buffalo vs. Philadelphia | Buffalo | 6 | 2 |
| " 18 | Cleveland vs. New York | New York | 9 | 3 |
| " 18 | Detroit vs. Providence | Providence | 9 | 6 |
| " 19 | Chicago vs. Boston | Boston | 7 | 4 |
| " 20 | " " | Chicago | 7 | 2 |
| " 20 | Buffalo vs. Philadelphia | Philadelphia | 3 | 0 |
| " 20 | Cleveland vs. New York | Cleveland | 6 | 1 |
| " 20 | Detroit vs. Providence | Detroit | 7 | 1 |
| " 22 | Cleveland vs. Philadelphia | Philadelphia | 7 | 6 |
| " 23 | Buffalo vs. New York | Buffalo | 4 | 3 |
| " 24 | " " | " | 6 | 0 |
| " 24 | Chicago vs. Providence | Chicago | 5 | 3 |
| " 25 | " " | Providence | 6 | 5 |
| " 25 | Cleveland vs. Philadelphia | Philadelphia | 7 | 3 |
| " 25 | Buffalo vs. New York | New York | 14 | 2 |
| " 25 | Detroit vs. Boston | Detroit | 5 | 3 |
| " 26 | " " | " | 9 | 5 |
| " 26 | Cleveland vs. Philadelphia | Philadelphia | 10 | 2 |
| " 26 | Chicago vs. Providence | Providence | 8 | 3 |

## RECORD OF CHAMPIONSHIP GAMES.—*Continued*.

| Date 1884 | NAMES OF CONTESTANTS. | Winning Club. | Runs Scored Winning Club | Runs Scored Losing Club |
|---|---|---|---|---|
| Sept. 27 | Chicago vs. Providence | Chicago | 15 | 10 |
| " 27 | Cleveland vs. Philadelphia | Philadelphia | 11 | 9 |
| " 27 | Detroit vs. Boston | Detroit | 6 | 5 |
| " 27 | Buffalo vs. New York | New York | 12 | 10 |
| " 29 | " " | " | 10 | 5 |
| " 29 | Detroit vs. Boston | Boston | 5 | 0 |
| " 30 | " Philadelphia | Philadelphia | 3 | 1 |
| " 30 | Chicago vs. New York | Chicago | 17 | 2 |
| " 30 | Cleveland vs. Boston | Cleveland | 3 | 0 |
| Oct. 1 | " " | Boston | 10 | 3 |
| " 1 | Detroit vs. Philadelphia | Detroit | 1 | 0 |
| " 1 | Buffalo vs. Providence | Buffalo | 2 | 0 |
| " 2 | Cleveland vs. Boston | Boston | 6 | 2 |
| " 2 | Chicago vs. New York | Chicago | 9 | 5 |
| " 3 | " " | " | 13 | 5 |
| " 3 | Cleveland vs. Boston | Boston | 7 | 6 |
| " 3 | Detroit vs. Philadelphia | Philadelphia | 5 | 4 |
| " 3 | Buffalo vs. Providence | Buffalo | 11 | 2 |
| " 4 | " " | Providence | 4 | 1 |
| " 4 | Detroit vs. Philadelphia | Philadelphia | 4 | 3 |
| " 4 | Chicago vs. New York | Chicago | 7 | 5 |
| " 6 | Buffalo vs. Providence | Buffalo | 13 | 7 |
| " 7 | " Boston | Boston | 7 | 3 |
| " 7 | Cleveland vs. Providence | Providence | 9 | 7 |
| " 7 | Detroit vs. New York | Detroit | 5 | 1 |
| " 8 | Chicago vs. Philadelphia | Chicago | 9 | 2 |
| " 9 | " " | " | 19 | 7 |
| " 9 | Detroit vs. New York | New York | 9 | 5 |
| " 9 | Cleveland vs. Providence | Cleveland | 11 | 3 |
| " 10 | " " | Providence | 11 | 2 |
| " 10 | Buffalo vs. Boston | Boston | 25 | 7 |
| " 10 | Chicago vs. Philadelphia | Chicago | 4 | 3 |
| " 11 | " " | " | 12 | 3 |
| " 11 | Cleveland vs. Providence | Providence | 8 | 1 |
| " 11 | Buffalo vs. Boston | Buffalo | 14 | 5 |
| " 11 | Detroit vs. New York | Detroit | 9 | 2 |
| " 13 | " " | New York | 4 | 3 |
| " 14 | " " | " | 4 | 3 |
| " 14 | Buffalo vs. Boston | Buffalo | 14 | 3 |
| " 15 | " " | " | 9 | 8 |
| " 15 | Philadelphia vs. Providence | Providence | 8 | 0 |
| Total | | | 3578 | 1362 |

### Total Number of Runs Scored, 4940.

**RUNS SCORED BY CLUBS.**

Providence......662 Opponents 394 | Philadelphia.....541 Opponents 815
Boston .........661  "        446 | Cleveland.......449  "        707
Buffalo.........683  "        610 | Detroit.........438  "        729
Chicago ........828  "        642 |
New York .......678  "        607 | Total........4940             4940

Average number of runs scored per game by winning clubs..........8.02
Average number of runs scored per game by losing clubs..........3.05

LEAGUE CHAEPIONSHIP GAMES.

# BATTING RECORD

Of Players who have taken part in fifteen or more championship games.

## SEASON 1884.

| Rank. | NAME. | CLUB. | Games Played. | Times at Bat. | Runs Scored. | Ave. per Game. | First Base Hits. | Percentage. | Total Bases. | Ave. per Game. |
|---|---|---|---|---|---|---|---|---|---|---|
| 1 | O'Rourke..... | Buffalo......... | 104 | 4 8 | 112 | 1 07 | 157 | .341 | 214 | 2.05 |
| 2 | Sutton...... | Boston......... | 106 | 447 | 97 | .91 | 156 | .349 | 203 | 1.91 |
| 3 | Kelly........ | Chicago........ | 107 | 448 | 120 | 1.1 | 15 | .341 | 231 | 2.16 |
| 4 | Anson...... | " ......... | 111 | 471 | 108 | .97 | 159 | .337 | 258 | 2.32 |
| 5 | { White....... | Buffalo......... | 106 | 436 | 80 | 0.7 | 112 | .325 | 195 | 1.84 |
|   | { Brouthers..... | " ......... | 90 | 381 | 80 | 0.88 | 124 | .325 | 217 | 2 41 |
| 6 | { Gore ....... | Chicago......... | 101 | 417 | 103 | 1.02 | 132 | .316 | 175 | 1.73 |
|   | { Connor........ | New York...... | 112 | 462 | 93 | 0.83 | 146 | .316 | 193 | 1.72 |
| 7 | { Rowe ....... | Buffalo......... | 91 | 393 | 81 | 0.89 | 122 | .310 | 168 | 1.84 |
|   | { Dalrymple..... | Chicago......... | 110 | 516 | 110 | 1.00 | 160 | .310 | 258 | 2.34 |
| 8 | Pinkney . .. | Cleveland...... | 85 | 139 | 17 | 0.48 | 43 | .309 | 51 | 1.45 |
| 9 | Hines....... | Providence...... | 112 | 480 | 92 | 0.82 | 146 | .304 | 205 | 1.83 |
| 10 | Sweeny........ | " ...... | 40 | 162 | 24 | 0.60 | 49 | .302 | 61 | 1.52 |
| 11 | Richardson... | Buffalo........ | 98 | 421 | 85 | 0.86 | 127 | .301 | 184 | 1.87 |
| 12 | Pfeffer...... | Chicago........ | 111 | 463 | 104 | 0.93 | 134 | .289 | 287 | 2.13 |
| 13 | { Williamson.... | " ......... | 106 | 413 | 82 | 0.77 | 115 | .278 | 228 | 2.15 |
|   | { Ewing......... | New York...... | 88 | 374 | 87 | 0.98 | 10 | .278 | 162 | 1.84 |
| 14 | Dorgan ....... | " ......... | 79 | 333 | 60 | 0.76 | 92 | .276 | 116 | 1.46 |
| 15 | McKinnon..... | " ......... | 112 | 454 | 66 | 0.59 | 125 | .275 | 178 | 1.59 |
| 16 | Start ........ | Providence...... | 90 | 377 | 80 | 0.88 | 103 | .273 | 123 | 1.36 |
| 17 | { Phillips ...... | Cleveland...... | 110 | 459 | 57 | 0.51 | 125 | .272 | 180 | 1.63 |
|   | { Manning...... | Philadelphia..... | 103 | 418 | 70 | 0.68 | 114 | .272 | 164 | 1 59 |
| 18 | Hanlon....... | Detroit......... | 112 | 443 | 8 | 0.76 | 119 | .268 | 164 | 1 46 |
| 19 | Burdock....... | Boston ........ | 84 | 351 | 64 | 0.76 | 94 | .267 | 134 | 1 59 |
| 20 | Hornung .. | " ........ | 110 | 492 | 115 | 1.04 | 131 | .266 | 194 | 1 76 |
| 21 | { Crowley .... | " ........ | 103 | 384 | 49 | 0.47 | 102 | .265 | 146 | 1.41 |
|   | { Morrill ....... | " ........ | 106 | 418 | 76 | 0.73 | 111 | .265 | 153 | 1.44 |
| 22 | Bennett...... | Detroit ......... | 88 | 336 | 36 | 0.40 | 89 | .264 | 126 | 1 43 |
| 23 | Gillespie...... | New York...... | 97 | 401 | 71 | 0.73 | 106 | .264 | 127 | 1 31 |
|   | McCormick.... | Cleveland ...... | 48 | 190 | 15 | 0.31 | 50 | .263 | 63 | 1.31 |
| 24 | { Buffinton ..... | Boston......... | 84 | 338 | 47 | 0.56 | 89 | .2 3 | 115 | 1.37 |
|   | { Clarkson..... | Chicago........ | 20 | 84 | 16 | 0.80 | 22 | .261 | 41 | 2.05 |
|   | { Carroll ...... | Providence...... | 112 | 447 | 90 | 0.80 | 117 | .261 | 151 | 1.34 |
| 25 | Whitney....... | Boston......... | 62 | 250 | 39 | 0.63 | 65 | .260 | 98 | 1.58 |
| 26 | Richardson .... | New York...... | 70 | 262 | 34 | 0.48 | 68 | .259 | 81 | 1.15 |
| 27 | { Smith .. ..... | Cleveland...... | 71 | 286 | 31 | 0.43 | 74 | .258 | 109 | 1.53 |
|   | { Evans......... | " ...... | 80 | 313 | 32 | 0.40 | 81 | .258 | 105 | 1.31 |
| 28 | { Welch ....... | New York...... | 67 | 234 | 45 | 0.67 | 60 | .256 | 87 | 1.29 |
|   | { McClellan..... | Philadelphia..... | 110 | 444 | 70 | 0.63 | 114 | .256 | 138 | 1.25 |
| 29 | { Denny ....... | Providence...... | 108 | 430 | 57 | 0.52 | 108 | .251 | 165 | 1.50 |
|   | { Ferguson ..... | Philadelphia..... | 51 | 199 | 25 | 0.49 | 50 | .251 | 61 | 1.19 |
|   | { Wood......... | Detroit ........ | 112 | 465 | 78 | 0.69 | 117 | .251 | 180 | 1.60 |

## BATTING RECORD.—Continued.

| Rank | NAME. | CLUB. | Games Played. | Times at Bat. | Runs Scored. | Ave. per Game. | First Base Hits. | Percentage. | Total Bases. | Ave. per Game. |
|---|---|---|---|---|---|---|---|---|---|---|
|    | Glasscock | Cleveland    | 72  | 281 | 45 | 0.62 | 70  | .249 | 85  | 1.20 |
| 30 | Ward      | New York     | 109 | 466 | 99 | 0.90 | 116 | .249 | 154 | 1.41 |
|    | Scott     | Detroit      | 108 | 429 | 29 | 0.26 | 107 | .249 | 143 | 1.32 |
| 31 | Farrar    | Philadelphia | 110 | 422 | 61 | 0.55 | 104 | .246 | 131 | 1.19 |
|    | Irwin     | Providence   | 99  | 395 | 73 | 0.73 | 97  | .245 | 122 | 1.23 |
| 32 | Coleman   | Philadelphia | 43  | 171 | 16 | 0.37 | 42  | .245 | 51  | 1.18 |
|    | Burns     | Chicago      | 82  | 359 | 54 | 0.65 | 88  | .245 | 124 | 1.51 |
|    | Gilligan  | Providence   | 80  | 286 | 47 | 0.58 | 70  | .244 | 90  | 1.12 |
| 33 | Crowley   | Philadelphia | 44  | 168 | 26 | 0.59 | 41  | .244 | 55  | 1.25 |
|    | Purcell   | "            | 102 | 422 | 64 | 0.62 | 103 | .244 | 131 | 1.28 |
| 34 | Hotaling  | Cleveland    | 101 | 404 | 66 | 0.65 | 98  | .242 | 134 | 1.32 |
| 35 | Manning   | Boston       | 84  | 323 | 50 | 0.59 | 78  | .241 | 102 | 1.21 |
| 36 | Muldoon   | Cleveland    | 109 | 417 | 45 | 0.41 | 100 | .239 | 134 | 1.23 |
| 37 | Hankinson | New York     | 101 | 374 | 43 | 0.42 | 88  | .235 | 134 | 1.22 |
| 38 | Radbourn  | Providence   | 85  | 352 | 48 | 0.56 | 82  | .233 | 95  | 1.11 |
| 39 | Caskin    | New York     | 97  | 344 | 50 | 0.51 | 80  | .232 | 95  | 0.97 |
| 40 | Bushong   | Cleveland    | 60  | 199 | 23 | 0.38 | 46  | .231 | 54  | 0.90 |
| 41 | Corcoran  | Chicago      | 63  | 247 | 41 | 0.65 | 57  | .230 | 70  | 1.11 |
| 42 | Mulvey    | Philadelphia | 99  | 401 | 47 | 0.47 | 92  | .229 | 111 | 1.12 |
| 43 | Murphy    | Cleveland    | 42  | 168 | 18 | 0.43 | 38  | .226 | 50  | 1.19 |
| 44 | Farrell   | Detroit      | 108 | 453 | 57 | 0.52 | 102 | .225 | 133 | 1.23 |
| 45 | Sunday    | Chicago      | 43  | 176 | 25 | 0.58 | 39  | .221 | 57  | 1.32 |
|    | Andrews   | Philadelphia | 108 | 415 | 76 | 0.70 | 92  | .221 | 119 | 1.10 |
|    | Farrell   | Providence   | 109 | 459 | 70 | 0.64 | 101 | .220 | 125 | 1.14 |
| 46 | Wise      | Boston       | 109 | 406 | 57 | 0.52 | 90  | .220 | 135 | 1.23 |
| 47 | Lillie    | Buffalo      | 110 | 453 | 65 | 0.58 | 100 | .219 | 131 | 1.19 |
| 48 | Brown     | Chicago      | 15  | 61  | 6  | 0.40 | 13  | .213 | 14  | 0.93 |
| 49 | Fogarty   | Philadelphia | 95  | 374 | 43 | 0.45 | 79  | .211 | 102 | 1.07 |
|    | Kearns    | Detroit      | 18  | 71  | 9  | 0.50 | 15  | .211 | 17  | 0.94 |
| 50 | Jones     | "            | 34  | 129 | 23 | 0.67 | 27  | .209 | 31  | 0.91 |
| 51 | Force     | Buffalo      | 102 | 389 | 45 | 0.44 | 81  | .208 | 100 | 0.98 |
| 52 | Flint     | Chicago      | 71  | 275 | 35 | 0.49 | 57  | .207 | 93  | 1.31 |
| 53 | Harkins   | Cleveland    | 60  | 224 | 24 | 0.40 | 46  | .205 | 56  | 0.93 |
| 54 | Hackett   | Boston       | 68  | 260 | 27 | 0.39 | 53  | .203 | 72  | 1.05 |
| 55 | Radford   | Providence   | 96  | 346 | 55 | 0.57 | 70  | .202 | 89  | 0.92 |
| 56 | Burch     | Cleveland    | 31  | 119 | 8  | 0.26 | 24  | .201 | 28  | 0.90 |
| 57 | Eggler    | Buffalo      | 58  | 227 | 25 | 0.43 | 45  | .198 | 50  | 0.86 |
| 58 | Shaw      | Detroit      | 36  | 136 | 16 | 0.44 | 26  | .191 | 3   | 0.97 |
| 59 | Myers     | Buffalo      | 76  | 316 | 34 | 0.44 | 59  | .186 | 74  | 0.97 |
| 60 | Annis     | Boston       | 26  | 92  | 16 | 0.61 | 17  | .184 | 19  | 0.73 |
| 61 | Galvin    | Buffalo      | 68  | 258 | 34 | 0.50 | 47  | .182 | 57  | 0.83 |
| 62 | Hines     | Boston       | 34  | 127 | 16 | 0.47 | 23  | .181 | 26  | 0.76 |
|    | Bagley    | New York     | 32  | 121 | 13 | 0.40 | 22  | .181 | 26  | 0.81 |
| 63 | Moffett   | Cleveland    | 66  | 251 | 25 | 0.38 | 45  | .179 | 61  | 0.92 |
| 64 | Collins   | Buffalo      | 45  | 169 | 24 | 0.53 | 30  | .177 | 34  | 0.75 |
| 65 | Geiss     | Detroit      | 75  | 283 | 22 | 0.29 | 50  | .176 | 74  | 0.98 |
| 66 | Serad     | Buffalo      | 37  | 137 | 12 | 0.32 | 24  | .175 | 28  | 0.75 |
| 67 | Ardner    | Cleveland    | 26  | 92  | 6  | 0.23 | 16  | .174 | 19  | 0.73 |
| 68 | Briody    | "            | 43  | 148 | 17 | 0.39 | 25  | .169 | 34  | 0.79 |
| 69 | Meinke    | Detroit      | 90  | 334 | 28 | 0.31 | 56  | .167 | 93  | 1.03 |
| 70 | Weidman   | "            | 79  | 295 | 23 | 0.29 | 48  | .162 | 54  | 0.68 |

## Batting Record.—*Continued.*

| Rank. | NAME. | CLUB. | Games Played. | Times at Bat. | Runs Scored. | Ave. per Game. | First Base Hits. | Percentage. | Total Bases. | Ave. per Game. |
|---|---|---|---|---|---|---|---|---|---|---|
| 71 | Kinzie | Chicago | 19 | 82 | 4 | 0.21 | 13 | .158 | 22 | 1.15 |
| 72 | Bassett | Providence | 21 | 76 | 9 | 0.43 | 11 | .144 | 15 | 0.71 |
| 73 | Buker | Detroit | 30 | 110 | 5 | 0.16 | 15 | .136 | 16 | 0.53 |
| 74 | Goldsmith | Chicago | 22 | 81 | 11 | 0.50 | 11 | .135 | 19 | 0.86 |
| 75 | Ringo | Philadelphia | 25 | 91 | 4 | 0.16 | 12 | .132 | 14 | 0 56 |
| 76 | Cox | Detroit | 27 | 102 | 6 | 0.22 | 13 | .127 | 18 | 0.66 |
| 77 | Vinton | Philadelphia | 21 | 78 | 9 | 0.43 | 9 | .115 | 9 | 0.43 |
| 78 | Get/ein | Detroit | 17 | 55 | 4 | 0.23 | 6 | .109 | 6 | 0.35 |
| 79 | Humphries | New York | 19 | 64 | 6 | 0.31 | 6 | .093 | 6 | 0.33 |
| 80 | Nava | Providence | 32 | 112 | 10 | 0.31 | 10 | .089 | 10 | 0.31 |
| 81 | Gastfield | Detroit | 22 | 79 | 5 | 0.22 | 5 | .063 | 6 | 0.27 |

## FIELDING AVERAGES

Of Players who have taken part in fifteen or more Championship Games,
SEASON OF 1884.

### FIRST BASEMEN.

| Rank | NAME. | CLUB. | Games Played. | Number Put Out. | Times Assisting. | Fielding Errors. | Total Chances. | Percentage Accepted. |
|---|---|---|---|---|---|---|---|---|
| 1 | Start | Providence | 90 | 923 | 21 | 20 | 964 | .974 |
| 2 | Morrill | Boston | 88 | 917 | 33 | 29 | 979 | .976 |
| 3 | Scott | Detroit | 108 | 1102 | 26 | 38 | 1166 | .969 |
| 4 | Farrar | Philadelphia | 110 | 1132 | 42 | 42 | 1216 | .967 |
| 5 | Brouthers | Buffalo | 89 | 908 | 29 | 35 | 972 | .960 |
| 6 | Phillips | Cleveland | 110 | 1095 | 30 | 46 | 1171 | .965 |
| 7 | Anson | Chicago | 108 | 1203 | 39 | 58 | 1300 | .954 |
| 8 | McKinnon | New York | 112 | 1059 | 31 | 52 | 1142 | .950 |
| 9 | O'Rourke | Buffalo | 18 | 206 | 1 | 14 | 221 | .935 |

### SECOND BASEMEN.

| 1 | Burdock | Boston | 84 | 177 | 269 | 36 | 482 | .925 |
|---|---|---|---|---|---|---|---|---|
| 2 | Farrell | Providence | 106 | 246 | 342 | 50 | 638 | .921 |
| 3 | Morrill | Boston | 15 | 42 | 37 | 7 | 86 | .918 |
| 4 | Collins | Buffalo | 42 | 108 | 137 | 23 | 268 | .914 |
| 5 | Pfeffer | Chicago | 111 | 393 | 419 | 87 | 899 | .903 |
| 6 | Jones | Detroit | 16 | 41 | 46 | 10 | 97 | .897 |
| 7 | Richardson | Buffalo | 67 | 180 | 224 | 47 | 451 | .895 |
| 8 | Ward | New York | 43 | 83 | 167 | 30 | 280 | .892 |
| 9 | Andrews | Philadelphia | 108 | 230 | 320 | 68 | 618 | .889 |
| 10 | Smith | Cleveland | 41 | 111 | 131 | 34 | 276 | .876 |
| 11 | Ardner | Cleveland | 25 | 54 | 74 | 20 | 148 | .865 |
| 12 | Geiss | Detroit | 72 | 190 | 217 | 65 | 472 | .862 |
| 13 | Connor | New York | 67 | 230 | 205 | 71 | 506 | .859 |
| 14 | Pinkney | Cleveland | 25 | 56 | 67 | 22 | 145 | .848 |
| 15 | Kearns | Detroit | 18 | 42 | 44 | 23 | 109 | .789 |

### THIRD BASEMEN.

| 1 | Sutton | Boston | 106 | 115 | 174 | 30 | 319 | .906 |
|---|---|---|---|---|---|---|---|---|
| 2 | Denny | Providence | 96 | 140 | 164 | 43 | 347 | .876 |
| 3 | Hankinson | New York | 101 | 131 | 178 | 47 | 356 | .868 |
| 4 | Williamson | Chicago | 98 | 119 | 248 | 60 | 427 | .859 |
| 5 | Farrell | Detroit | 108 | 124 | 192 | 59 | 375 | .842 |
| 6 | Mulvey | Philadelphia | 99 | 151 | 216 | 73 | 440 | .834 |
| 6 | Muldoon | Cleveland | 108 | 125 | 203 | 65 | 393 | .834 |
| 7 | White | Buffalo | 104 | 110 | 194 | 66 | 370 | .821 |

## LEAGUE FIELDING AVERAGES—CONTINUED.

### SHORT STOPS.

| Rank. | NAME. | CLUB. | Games Played. | Number Put Out. | Times Assisting. | Fielding Errors. | Total Chances. | Percentage Accepted. |
|---|---|---|---|---|---|---|---|---|
| 1 | Smith | Cleveland | 30 | 44 | 107 | 16 | 167 | .904 |
| 2 | Force | Buffalo | 101 | 107 | 294 | 44 | 445 | .901 |
| 3 | Glasscock | Cleveland | 68 | 118 | 267 | 46 | 431 | .893 |
| 4 | Wise | Boston | 103 | 149 | 290 | 56 | 495 | .886 |
| 5 | Caskin | New York | 92 | 118 | 274 | 52 | 444 | .882 |
| 6 | Irwin | Providence | 99 | 95 | 297 | 54 | 446 | .878 |
| 7 | Buker | Detroit | 19 | 22 | 6 | 13 | 98 | .867 |
| 8 | McClellan | Philadelphia | 109 | 164 | 311 | 83 | 558 | .851 |
| 9 | Meinke | Detroit | 47 | 57 | 143 | 38 | 238 | .840 |
| 10 | Burns | Chicago | 79 | 97 | 254 | 68 | 419 | .837 |
| 11 | Kinzie | Chicago | 17 | 18 | 46 | 13 | 77 | .831 |
| 12 | Richardson | New York | 17 | 32 | 30 | 13 | 75 | .826 |
| 13 | Cox | Detroit | 27 | 28 | 80 | 25 | 133 | .812 |

### FIELDERS.

| Rank. | NAME. | CLUB. | Games Played. | Number Put Out. | Times Assisting. | Fielding Errors. | Total Chances. | Percentage Accepted. |
|---|---|---|---|---|---|---|---|---|
| 1 | Richardson | Buffalo | 24 | 44 | 5 | 3 | 52 | .942 |
| 2 | Fogarty | Philadelphia | 75 | 193 | 12 | 19 | 224 | .915 |
| 3 | Hornung | Boston | 106 | 176 | 13 | 18 | 207 | .913 |
| 4 | Evans | Cleveland | 76 | 136 | 19 | 14 | 169 | .911 |
| 5 | Carroll | Providence | 112 | 204 | 11 | 23 | 238 | .903 |
| 6 | Richardson | New York | 53 | 72 | 19 | 10 | 101 | .901 |
| 7 | Annis | Boston | 26 | 21 | 5 | 3 | 29 | .896 |
| 8 | Hines | Providence | 107 | 202 | 20 | 26 | 248 | .895 |
| 9 | O'Rourke | Buffalo | 81 | 112 | 6 | 14 | 132 | .894 |
| 10 | Wood | Detroit | 111 | 185 | 17 | 24 | 226 | .893 |
| 11 | Burch | Cleveland | 31 | 48 | 9 | 7 | 64 | .890 |
| 11 | Gillespie | New York | 97 | 155 | 8 | 20 | 183 | .890 |
| 12 | Radford | Providence | 94 | 143 | 26 | 22 | 191 | .884 |
| 13 | Eggler | Buffalo | 58 | 98 | 13 | 15 | 126 | .881 |
| 14 | Dalrymple | Chicago | 110 | 174 | 18 | 26 | 218 | .880 |
| 15 | Purcell | Philadelphia | 102 | 182 | 12 | 28 | 222 | .874 |
| 16 | Hanlon | Detroit | 112 | 239 | 30 | 39 | 308 | .873 |
| 17 | Manning | Boston | 68 | 109 | 14 | 18 | 141 | .872 |
| 18 | Gore | Chicago | 101 | 184 | 25 | 32 | 241 | .867 |
| 19 | Crowley | Boston | 103 | 115 | 22 | 22 | 159 | .861 |
| 20 | Lillie | Buffalo | 110 | 183 | 40 | 37 | 260 | .857 |
| 21 | Dorgan | New York | 59 | 97 | 12 | 19 | 128 | .851 |
| 22 | Connor | New York | 34 | 54 | 7 | 11 | 72 | .847 |
| 22 | Hotaling | Cleveland | 101 | 172 | 23 | 35 | 230 | .847 |
| 23 | Ward | New York | 59 | 103 | 13 | 21 | 137 | .846 |
| 23 | Weidman | Detroit | 54 | 76 | 12 | 16 | 104 | .846 |
| 24 | Manning | Philadelphia | 103 | 137 | 24 | 30 | 191 | .842 |
| 25 | Coleman | Philadelphia | 22 | 47 | 6 | 10 | 63 | .841 |
| 26 | Rowe | Buffalo | 25 | 34 | 1 | 7 | 42 | .833 |
| 27 | Harkins | Cleveland | 15 | 26 | 2 | 6 | 34 | .823 |
| 28 | Moffett | Cleveland | 40 | 65 | 6 | 17 | 88 | .807 |
| 29 | Kelly | Chicago | 61 | 68 | 30 | 26 | 124 | .790 |
| 30 | Myers | Buffalo | 31 | 47 | 3 | 14 | 64 | .781 |
| 31 | Murphy | Cleveland | 42 | 60 | 7 | 26 | 93 | .720 |
| 32 | Sunday | Chicago | 43 | 45 | 8 | 27 | 80 | .662 |

## BATTING RECORD.

### CATCHERS' AVERAGES.

| Rank | NAME. | CLUB. | Games Played. | Number Put Out. | Times Assisting. | Fielding Errors. | Passed Balls. | Total Chances. | Percentage Accepted. |
|---|---|---|---|---|---|---|---|---|---|
| 1 | Hackett | Boston | 67 | 502 | 101 | 48 | 35 | 686 | .879 |
| 2 | Ewing | New York | 74 | 431 | 125 | 41 | 38 | 635 | .875 |
| 3 | Gilligan | Providence | 79 | 584 | 91 | 51 | 46 | 772 | .874 |
| 4 | Briody | Cleveland | 43 | 243 | 74 | 27 | 24 | 368 | .861 |
| 5 | Rowe | Buffalo | 60 | 373 | 60 | 26 | 45 | 504 | .859 |
| 6 | Bennett | Detroit | 77 | 444 | 97 | 49 | 49 | 639 | .846 |
| 7 | Nava | Providence | 26 | 162 | 39 | 27 | 16 | 244 | .823 |
| 8 | Hines | Boston | 34 | 241 | 60 | 26 | 40 | 367 | .820 |
| 9 | Humphries | New York | 19 | 138 | 35 | 20 | 21 | 214 | .808 |
| 10 | Gastfield | Detroit | 18 | 112 | 49 | 33 | 15 | 209 | .770 |
| 11 | Flint | Chicago | 71 | 346 | 110 | 61 | 82 | 599 | .761 |
| 12 | Bushong | Cleveland | 60 | 250 | 98 | 58 | 95 | 601 | 745 |
| 13 | Myers | Buffalo | 45 | 261 | 55 | 62 | 51 | 429 | .736 |
| 14 | Kelly | Chicago | 25 | 105 | 55 | 32 | 32 | 224 | .714 |
| 15 | Crowley | Philadelphia | 44 | 198 | 49 | 50 | 66 | 363 | .680 |
| 16 | Ringo | Philadelphia | 25 | 107 | 16 | 34 | 32 | 189 | .650 |

## LEAGUE PITCHERS' RECORD.

## PITCHERS' RECORD IN ALPHABETICAL ORDER.

| NAME. | CLUB. | Games Played. | Times at Bat of Opponents | Runs Scored by Opponents | Average per game. | Runs Earned by Opponents | Average per Game. | First Base Hits Made by Opponents. | Percentage. | Number Put Out. | Times Assisting. | Fielding Errors. | Wild Pitches. | Total Chances. | Percentage Accepted. |
|---|---|---|---|---|---|---|---|---|---|---|---|---|---|---|---|
| Bagley | New York | 81 | 1134 | 208 | 6.71 | 56 | 1.80 | 299 | .263 | 16 | 93 | 111 | 27 | 247 | .411 |
| Buffinton | Boston | 65 | 2259 | 228 | 3.51 | 109 | 1.67 | 496 | .219 | 34 | 404 | 83 | 22 | 548 | .799 |
| Coleman | Philadelphia | 19 | 725 | 150 | 1.89 | 78 | 4.10 | 217 | .299 | 14 | 49 | 25 | 9 | 97 | .649 |
| Corcoran | Chicago | 59 | 2072 | 288 | 4.58 | 123 | 2.08 | 484 | .233 | 47 | 332 | 152 | 29 | 560 | .676 |
| Ferguson | Philadelphia | 46 | 1681 | 287 | 6.24 | 103 | 2.24 | 433 | .257 | 27 | 98 | 8:8 | 38 | 323 | .579 |
| Galvin | Buffalo | 68 | 2344 | 238 | 3.50 | 104 | 1.53 | 525 | .234 | 30 | 160 | 63 | 29 | 493 | .843 |
| Getzein | Detroit | 17 | 580 | 70 | 4.11 | 23 | 1.35 | 120 | .207 | 3 | 29 | 28 | 14 | 69 | .463 |
| Goldsmith | Chicago | 21 | 852 | 153 | 7.28 | 69 | 3.28 | 255 | .299 | 6 | 386 | 63 | 9 | 560 | .560 |
| Harkins | Cleveland | 45 | 1588 | 297 | 6.60 | 105 | 2.33 | 396 | .249 | 14 | 64 | 42 | 13 | 398 | .603 |
| Meinke | Detroit | 33 | 1210 | 266 | 7.15 | 97 | 2.94 | 350 | .289 | 11 | 226 | 107 | 51 | 209 | .615 |
| Moffett | Cleveland | 22 | 815 | 164 | 7.45 | 58 | 2.63 | 234 | .287 | 10 | 112 | 70 | 10 | 208 | .528 |
| McCormick | Cleveland | 40 | 1423 | 286 | 5.20 | 85 | 2.12 | 357 | .250 | 19 | 94 | 65 | 30 | 197 | .711 |
| Radbourn | Providence | 72 | 24!0 | 217 | 3.01 | 83 | 1.15 | 334 | .211 | 21 | 220 | 108 | 35 | 356 | .528 |
| Shaw | Detroit | 26 | 933 | 152 | 5.84 | 57 | 2.19 | 224 | .240 | 9 | 227 | 73 | 8 | 391 | .634 |
| Serad | Buffalo | 36 | 1330 | 265 | 7.94 | 104 | 2.80 | 268 | .276 | 4 | 139 | 121 | 14 | 229 | .646 |
| Sweeney | Providence | 25 | 831 | 89 | 3.28 | 25 | 1.00 | 153 | .184 | 10 | 170 | 40 | 11 | 338 | .514 |
| Vinton | Philadelphia | 21 | 766 | 132 | 6.28 | 58 | 2.76 | 178 | .232 | 8 | 68 | 31 | 22 | 120 | .650 |
| Welch | New York | 60 | 2101 | 268 | 4.46 | 110 | 1.83 | 513 | .244 | 21 | 60 | 40 | 34 | 386 | .506 |
| Whitney | Boston | 36 | 1220 | 130 | 3.61 | 49 | 1.36 | 254 | .238 | 16 | 246 | 132 | 19 | 352 | .869 |
| Weidman | Detroit | 23 | 850 | 182 | 7.91 | 64 | 2.78 | 249 | .279 | 11 | 65 | 54 | 10 | 140 | .542 |

## BATTING AND FIELDING.

### Record of Clubs, Members of the National League of Professional B. B. Clubs.

### SEASON OF 1884.

| Rank. | NAME OF CLUB. | Games Played. | Games Won. | BATTING | | | | | | | | FIELDING | | | | | |
|---|---|---|---|---|---|---|---|---|---|---|---|---|---|---|---|---|---|
| | | | | Times at Bat. | Runs Scored. | Average per Game. | Runs Earned. | Average per Game. | First Bases. | Percentage. | Total Bases. | Average per Game. | Number Put Out. | Times Assisting. | Fielding Errors. | Passed Balls and Wild Pitches. | Total Chances. | Percentage Accepted. |
| 1 | Providence | 112 | 84 | 4008 | 662 | 5.91 | 217 | 1.93 | 975 | .243 | 1262 | 11.26 | 3026 | 1463 | 552 | 150 | 5191 | .864 |
| 2 | Boston | 111 | 73 | 3996 | 661 | 5.95 | 244 | 2.10 | 1016 | .255 | 1404 | 12.65 | 2859 | 1847 | 496 | 146 | 5448 | .882 |
| 3 | Buffalo | 110 | 63 | 4054 | 683 | 6.21 | 284 | 2.58 | 1062 | .262 | 1459 | 13.26 | 2890 | 1685 | 621 | 160 | 5356 | .854 |
| 4 | Chicago | 111 | 62 | 4147 | 828 | 7.46 | 389 | 3.50 | 1163 | .280 | 1817 | 16.64 | 2965 | 1979 | 836 | 208 | 5968 | .825 |
| 5 | New York | 112 | 62 | 3984 | 678 | 6.04 | 267 | 2.38 | 1025 | .257 | 1866 | 12.19 | 2921 | 1489 | 800 | 191 | 5401 | .816 |
| 6 | Philadelphia | 112 | 39 | 3951 | 541 | 4.83 | 162 | 1.44 | 921 | .233 | 1178 | 10.51 | 2895 | 1463 | 788 | 342 | 5488 | .794 |
| 7 | Cleveland | 112 | 35 | 3891 | 449 | 4.01 | 195 | 1.74 | 920 | .236 | 1208 | 10.78 | 2935 | 1807 | 765 | 241 | 5748 | .825 |
| 8 | Detroit | 112 | 28 | 3902 | 438 | 3.91 | 155 | 1.38 | 814 | .208 | 1116 | 9.96 | 2922 | 1529 | 776 | 153 | 5380 | .827 |
| | Total | 892 | 446 | 31923 | 4940 | 5.53 | 1913 | 2.14 | 7896 | .247 | 10840 | 12.15 | 23513 | 13262 | 5634 | 1591 | 44000 | .896 |

## LEAGUE CHAMPIONSHIP GAMES FOR 1884.

|  | Providence. | Boston. | Buffalo. | Chicago. | New York. | Philadelphia. | Cleveland. | Detroit. | Games Won. |
|---|---|---|---|---|---|---|---|---|---|
| Providence........................ | — | 9 | 10 | 11 | 13 | 13 | 13 | 15 | 84 |
| Boston............................. | 7 | — | 9 | 10 | 8 | 13 | 14 | 12 | 73 |
| Buffalo............................ | 6 | 6 | — | 10 | 5 | 11 | 14 | 12 | 64 |
| Chicago............................ | 5 | 6 | 6 | — | 12 | 14 | 8 | 11 | 62 |
| New York......................... | 3 | 8 | 11 | 4 | — | 11 | 11 | 14 | 62 |
| Philadelphia..................... | 3 | 3 | 5 | 2 | 5 | — | 10 | 11 | 39 |
| Cleveland......................... | 3 | 2 | 2 | 8 | 5 | 6 | — | 9 | 35 |
| Detroit............................. | 1 | 4 | 4 | 5 | 2 | 5 | 7 | — | 28 |
| Games lost..................... | 28 | 38 | 47 | 50 | 50 | 73 | 77 | 84 | 447 |

One game forfeited by Chicago to the Buffalo Club.

## SCHEDULE OF LEAGUE GAMES FOR 1885.

| CLUBS. | At Chicago. | At Detroit. | At St. Louis. | At Buffalo. | At Boston. | At Providence. | At New York. | At Phila. |
|---|---|---|---|---|---|---|---|---|
| Chicago | | June 1<br>" 2<br>" 3<br>" 4<br>Aug. 12<br>" 13<br>" 14<br>" 15 | April 30<br>May 1<br>" 2<br>" 4<br>Sept. 8<br>" 9<br>" 10<br>" 12 | May 6<br>" 7<br>" 8<br>" 9<br>July 13<br>" 14<br>" 15<br>" 16 | May 23<br>" 26<br>" 28<br>" †30<br>July 18<br>" 20<br>" 23<br>" 28 | May 21<br>" 22<br>" 27<br>" *30<br>July 21<br>" 22<br>" 25<br>" 27 | May 11<br>" 12<br>" 15<br>" 16<br>Aug. 1<br>" 3<br>" 6<br>" 8 | May 13<br>" 14<br>" 18<br>" 19<br>July 30<br>" 31<br>Aug. 4<br>" 5 |
| Detroit | June 12<br>" 13<br>" 15<br>" 16<br>Aug. 25<br>" 26<br>" 27<br>" 29 | | June 17<br>" 18<br>" 19<br>" 20<br>Sept. 1<br>" 2<br>" 3<br>" 5 | June 6<br>" 8<br>" 9<br>" 10<br>Sept. 8<br>" 9<br>" 10<br>" 12 | May 21<br>" 22<br>" 27<br>" *30<br>July 30<br>" 31<br>Aug. 4<br>" 5 | May 23<br>" 26<br>" 28<br>" †30<br>Aug. 1<br>" 3<br>" 6<br>" 8 | May 13<br>" 14<br>" 18<br>" 19<br>July 21<br>" 22<br>" 27<br>" 28 | May 11<br>" 12<br>" 15<br>" 18<br>July 18<br>" 20<br>" 23<br>" 25 |
| St. Louis | June 6<br>" 8<br>" 9<br>" 10<br>Aug. 18<br>" 19<br>" 20<br>" 22 | May 6<br>" 7<br>" 8<br>" 9<br>July 13<br>" 14<br>" 15<br>" 16 | | June 1<br>" 2<br>" 3<br>" 4<br>Aug. 12<br>" 13<br>" 14<br>" 15 | May 11<br>" 12<br>" 15<br>" 16<br>Aug. 1<br>" 3<br>" 6<br>" 8 | May 13<br>" 14<br>" 18<br>" 19<br>July 30<br>" 31<br>Aug. 4<br>" 5 | May 23<br>" 26<br>" *30<br>" †30<br>July 18<br>" 20<br>" 23<br>" 25 | May 21<br>" 22<br>" 27<br>" 28<br>July 21<br>" 22<br>" 27<br>" 28 |
| Buffalo | June 17<br>" 18<br>" 19<br>" 20<br>Sept. 1<br>" 2<br>" 3<br>" 5 | April 30<br>May 1<br>" 2<br>" 4<br>Aug. 18<br>" 19<br>" 20<br>" 22 | June 12<br>" 13<br>" 15<br>" 16<br>Aug. 25<br>" 26<br>" 27<br>" 29 | | May 13<br>" 14<br>" 18<br>" 19<br>July 21<br>" 22<br>" 25<br>" 27 | May 11<br>" 12<br>" 15<br>" 16<br>July 18<br>" 20<br>" 23<br>" 28 | May 21<br>" 22<br>" 27<br>" 28<br>July 30<br>" 31<br>Aug. 4<br>" 5 | May 23<br>" 25<br>" *30<br>" †30<br>Aug. 1<br>" 3<br>" 6<br>" 8 |

|  | | | | | | | |
|---|---|---|---|---|---|---|---|
| Boston......... | June 27, 29, 30, July 15, Sept 16, 17, 19 | July 3, *4, †4, 6, Oct 6, 7, 8, 10 | June 23, 24, 25, 26, Sept 22, 23, 24 | July 8, 9, 10, 11, Sept 29, 30, Oct 1, 3 | | June 2, 4, Aug 19, 18, 20, Sept 1, 3, 7 | May 1, 2, 6, 7, July 16, 17, Aug 27, 29 | May 4, 5, 8, 9, July 14, 15, Aug 24, 25 |
| Providence...... | July 8, 9, 10, 11, Sept 22, 23, 24, 26 | June 23, 24, 25, 26, Sept 29, 30, Oct 1, 3 | July 3, *4, †4, 6, Sept 15, 16, 17, 19 | June 27, 29, 30, July 1, Oct 6, 7, 8, 10 | June 3, 6, Aug 20, 19, 22, 31, Sept 2, 5 | | May 4, 5, 8, 9, July 14, 15, Aug 25, 26 | May 1, 2, 6, 7, July 16, 17, Aug 27, 29 |
| New York........ | July 3, *4, †4, 6, Sept 29, 30, Oct 1, 3 | June 27, 29, 30, July 1, Sept 29, 30, Oct 1, 3 | July 8, 9, 10, 11, Oct 6, 7, 8, 10 | June 23, 24, 25, 26, Sept 22, 23, 24, 26 | June 8, 9, 13, †17, Aug 11, 12, Sept 8, 9 | June 10, 11, 15, 16, Aug 13, 15, Sept 10, 12 | | June 3, 5, Aug 19, 20, 21, Sept 1, 5, 7 |
| Philadelphia.... | June 23, 24, 25, 26, Oct 6, 7, 8, 10 | June 27, 29, 30, July 1, Sept 29, 30, Oct 1, 3 | July 3, *4, †4, 6, Sept 15, 16, 17, 19 | | June 10, 11, 15, †17, Aug 13, 15, Sept 10, 12 | June 8, 9, 13, †17, Aug 11, 12, Sept 8, 9 | June 2, 6, 17, 18, 21, 22, Sept 3, 4 | |

*A. M.    †P. M.

## AMERICAN ASSOCIATION OF B. B CLUBS—SCHEDULE OF CHAMPIONSHIP GAMES SEASON OF 1885.

| CLUBS. | At St. Louis. | At Louisville. | At Cincinnati. | At Pittsburg. | At Baltimore. | At Athletic. | At Metrop'n. | At Brooklyn. |
|---|---|---|---|---|---|---|---|---|
| St. Louis...... | | May 3<br>" 5<br>June 30<br>July 1<br>" 2<br>Aug. 27<br>" 29<br>" 30 | April 28<br>" 29<br>June 26<br>" 27<br>" 28<br>Aug. 22<br>" 23<br>" 25 | May 1<br>" 2<br>June 23<br>" 24<br>" 25<br>Aug. 18<br>" 19<br>" 20 | May 30<br>" 30<br>June 1<br>" 2<br>Sept. 8<br>" 9<br>" 10<br>" 12 | June 4<br>" 5<br>" 6<br>" 8<br>Sept. 15<br>" 16<br>" 17<br>" 19 | June 10<br>" 11<br>" 12<br>" 13<br>Sept. 22<br>" 23<br>" 28<br>" 29 | June 17<br>" 18<br>" 20<br>" 21<br>Sept. 24<br>" 26<br>" 30<br>Oct. 1 |
| Louisville...... | April 24<br>" 25<br>Aug. 4<br>" 5<br>" 6<br>Sept. 2<br>" 3<br>" 5 | | April 18<br>" 26<br>June 23<br>" 24<br>" 25<br>Aug. 8<br>" 9<br>" 11 | April 27<br>" 28<br>June 26<br>" 27<br>" 29<br>Aug. 22<br>" 24<br>" 25 | June 16<br>" 17<br>" 18<br>" 20<br>Sept. 28<br>" 29<br>" 30<br>Oct. 1 | June 10<br>" 11<br>" 13<br>" 15<br>Sept. 21<br>" 23<br>" 24<br>" 26 | June 3<br>" 4<br>" 5<br>" 8<br>Sept. 10<br>" 12<br>" 17<br>" 19 | May 30<br>" 30<br>" 31<br>June 2<br>Sept. 8<br>" 9<br>" 15<br>" 16 |
| Cincinnati..... | April 21<br>" 23<br>July 31<br>Aug. 1<br>" 2<br>" 13<br>" 15<br>" 16 | April 19<br>May 2<br>July 26<br>" 28<br>" 29<br>Aug. 18<br>" 19<br>" 20 | | May 4<br>" 5<br>June 30<br>July 1<br>" 2<br>Sept. 2<br>" 3<br>" 5 | June 4<br>" 5<br>" 6<br>" 8<br>Sept. 15<br>" 16<br>" 17<br>" 19 | May 20<br>" 30<br>June 1<br>" 2<br>Sept. 8<br>" 9<br>" 10<br>" 12 | June 16<br>" 17<br>" 18<br>" 20<br>Sept. 24<br>" 26<br>" 30<br>Oct. 1 | June 10<br>" 11<br>" 13<br>" 14<br>Sept. 20<br>" 22<br>" 27<br>" 29 |
| Pittsburg...... | April 18<br>" 19<br>July 26<br>" 28<br>" 29<br>Aug. 8<br>" 9<br>" 11 | April 21<br>" 22<br>July 31<br>Aug. 1<br>" 2<br>" 13<br>" 15<br>" 16 | April 24<br>" 25<br>Aug. 4<br>" 5<br>" 6<br>" 27<br>" 29<br>" 30 | | June 10<br>" 11<br>" 12<br>" 13<br>Sept. 22<br>" 23<br>" 24<br>" 26 | June 16<br>" 17<br>" 18<br>" 20<br>Sept. 26<br>" 29<br>" 30<br>Oct. 1 | June 9<br>Sept. 9<br>" 15<br>" 16<br>" 18 | June 4<br>" 5<br>" 6<br>" 7<br>Sept. 12<br>" 13<br>" 17<br>" 19 |

|  | | | | | | | | |
|---|---|---|---|---|---|---|---|---|
| Baltimore | May 12<br>" 13<br>" 14<br>" 16<br>July 4<br>" 4<br>" 5<br>" 7 | May 7<br>" 8<br>" 9<br>" 10<br>July 9<br>" 10<br>" 11<br>" 12 | May 17<br>" 19<br>" 20<br>" 21<br>July 19<br>" 21<br>" 22<br>" 23 | May 23<br>" 25<br>" 26<br>" 27<br>July 14<br>" 15<br>" 16<br>" 18 | | June 27<br>" 29<br>Aug. 11<br>" 12<br>" 24<br>Sept. 2<br>" 3<br>" 4 | April 27<br>" 28<br>June 25<br>" 26<br>Aug. 13<br>" 15<br>" 25<br>" 26 | April 24<br>" 25<br>" 28<br>" 29<br>" 30<br>Aug. 16<br>" 18<br>" 22<br>" 23 |
| Athletic | May 7<br>" 8<br>" 9<br>" 10<br>July 9<br>" 10<br>" 11<br>" 12 | May 12<br>" 13<br>" 14<br>" 16<br>July 19<br>" 21<br>" 22<br>" 23 | May 23<br>" 24<br>" 26<br>" 27<br>July 9<br>" 10<br>" 11<br>" 12 | May 18<br>" 19<br>" 20<br>" 21<br>July 4<br>" 4<br>" 6<br>" 7 | May 1<br>" 2<br>June 23<br>" 24<br>July 27<br>" 28<br>Aug. 3<br>" 4 | | | April 24<br>" 25<br>" 29<br>" 30<br>Aug. 19<br>" 20<br>" 28<br>" 31 | May 4<br>" 5<br>June 25<br>" 26<br>July 30<br>" 31<br>Aug. 8<br>" 9 |
| Metropolitan | May 17<br>" 19<br>" 20<br>" 21<br>July 19<br>" 21<br>" 22<br>" 23 | May 23<br>" 24<br>" 26<br>" 27<br>July 4<br>" 4<br>" 5<br>" 7 | May 12<br>" 13<br>" 14<br>" 16<br>July 14<br>" 15<br>" 16<br>" 18 | May 7<br>" 8<br>" 9<br>July 11<br>" 30<br>" 30<br>Aug. 9<br>" 10<br>" 11<br>" 13 | April 22<br>" 23<br>May 4<br>" 5<br>July 30<br>" 31<br>Aug. 7<br>" 8 | April 18<br>" 20<br>June 30<br>July 1<br>Aug. 17<br>" 18<br>" 21<br>" 22 | | | May 1<br>" 2<br>June 24<br>" 28<br>July 28<br>Aug. 1<br>" 2<br>" 30 |
| Brooklyn | May 23<br>" 24<br>" 26<br>" 27<br>July 9<br>" 10<br>" 11<br>" 12 | May 17<br>" 19<br>" 20<br>" 21<br>July 14<br>" 15<br>" 16<br>" 18 | May 7<br>" 8<br>" 9<br>" 10<br>July 4<br>" 4<br>" 5<br>" 7 | May 12<br>" 13<br>" 14<br>" 16<br>" 20<br>July 21<br>" 22<br>" 23 | April 20<br>" 21<br>June 30<br>July 19<br>Aug. 20<br>" 27<br>" 29 | April 22<br>" 23<br>" 27<br>" 28<br>Aug. 13<br>" 15<br>" 25<br>" 26 | June 23<br>" 27<br>Aug. 11<br>" 12<br>Sept. 1<br>" 2<br>" 5<br>" 7 | | |

# The New York Clipper

Founded in 1853, by FRANK QUEEN.

THE OLDEST AMERICAN SPORTING AND THEATRICAL NEWSPAPER.

THE STANDARD AUTHORITY IN

**Baseball,**
**Cricket,**
**Athletics,**
**Billiards,**
**Chess,**
**Checkers,**

AND OTHER

Sports and Pastimes of the Day.

Publishes the Latest and Most Reliable News. Special Correspondence from all Sections.

**SINGLE COPIES 10 CENTS EACH.**

Order through your Newsdealer. Subscription—One year, $4.00; six months, $2.00; three months, $1.00.

The New York Clipper Annual for 1885.

An unusually interesting number. Is replete with Theatrical and Sporting Chronologies, Fast-Time Records, Remarkable Performances, Biographical Sketches of Actors and Actresses, etc.

**PRICE 15 CENTS.**

Address all communications to

**THE FRANK QUEEN PUBLISHING CO. (Limited),**

P. O. Box 3,578. Clipper Building, 88 and 90 Center St., NEW YORK.

# THE CHICAGO TRIBUNE.

## The Western Sporting Authority.

THE SUNDAY EDITION OF THE CHICAGO TRIBUNE, and the Daily Edition throughout the playing season of 1885, will be found, as heretofore, indispensable to those who desire accurate, reliable, and comprehensive base ball records and reports.

Every club and club-room should keep THE SUNDAY TRIBUNE on file.

## THE TURF DEPARTMENT

of THE TRIBUNE is universally admitted to be without an equal, and during 1885 it will be still further improved. Special telegraphic reports of the principal running and trotting meetings will be furnished, and particular attention be given to the performances of the American horses in England.

In other departments of sport THE TRIBUNE will maintain the superiority it has so long enjoyed.

### TERMS:

**SUNDAY EDITION, 16 Pages, per year,** - $ 2.00
**DAILY TRIBUNE, including Sunday,** - - 14.00

Address,

## THE TRIBUNE,
### CHICAGO, ILL.

# THE
# Sporting Life.

The Best and Cheapest Sporting Paper in America.

## CONTAINS

*All the News for Five Cents.*

Its Base Ball Department is the Best Published.

All--the--Sporting--News--Chronicled.

Subscription per Annum, $2.25.

Single Copies, 5 cents.

## The Sporting Life Publishing Co.,
### Proprietors,
No. 202 SOUTH NINTH STREET,

PHILADELPHIA, PA.

FRANCIS C. RICHTER, Editor.

**FOR SALE BY ALL NEWSDEALERS.**
**SAMPLE COPIES FREE—SEND FOR THEM.**

# The Chicago Herald

Has the LARGEST MORNING CIRCULATION in Chicago because it gives *all the News* for

## 2 Cents

## The Sunday Herald

Is LARGELY DEVOTED TO SPORTS AND THE DRAMA, and is the Favorite Sunday Paper of Chicago.

### BY MAIL, ONE YEAR, $2.

Address—

### THE CHICAGO HERALD,
#### 120 and 122 FIFTH AVE.,
### CHICAGO, ILL.

**JAMES W. SCOTT, Publisher.**

# "TAKE TIME BY THE FORELOCK."

## INCREASE IN PRICE OF
# The Mirror of American * Sports.

Beginning with Friday, May 1, 1885, this paper will be increased in size improved in appearance, and price increased as follows:

## SUBSCRIPTION PRICE,
### IN ADVANCE.

| | |
|---|---:|
| One Year. - - - - - - - | $3.00 |
| Six Months, - - - - - - | 1 75 |
| Three or more Yearly Subscriptions, Club Rates. - - - | each, 2.50 |
| Three or more Six-Months Subscriptions, Club Rates, - - | each, 1.50 |
| Foreign Postage, extra, per year, - - - | 1.56 |
| Sample Copies, from office of publication, - | each, .10 |

For sale at retail by all newsdealers.
For Sale at wholesale by the Western News Company, Chicago.

## The Mirror of American Sports

- **IS THE** Leading Cycle publication of the West, and the Official Organ of the Illinois Division of the League of American Wheelmen.
- **IS THE** Leading Rink Paper, and Authority in the West on Roller Skating, with strong probability of its being appointed to officiate as the organ of the proposed United States Roller Skating Organization.
- **IS THE** Leading Base Ball Authority of the West.
- **IS THE** Leading Authority on Billiards and best Billiard Paper in America.
- **IS THE** Leading Chess Authority of America, ranking among the chief Chess publications of the world.
- **IS THE** Best Hunting and Fishing Paper not exclusively devoted to that sport.
- **IS THE** Best Rink Polo Paper and Official Organ of the Western Polo League.

### DO NOT FORGET

That from now until May 1st, 1885, you have the privilege of subscribing for one year at the rate of **Two Dollars**. On and after that date no deviation will be made from increase in rates as above.

Address all communications to

**THE MIRROR OF AMERICAN SPORTS,**

Correspondents wanted.      157 Dearborn Street, Chicago.

# MICHIGAN
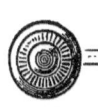 # CENTRAL

## "The Niagara Falls Route."

### THE WAY THE LEAGUE CLUBS TRAVEL.

The cities that have representative clubs contesting for the championship pennant this year are—Chicago, Boston, New York, Providence, Buffalo, Detroit, St. Louis and Philadelphia. All of these cities are joined together by the Michigan Central Railroad. This road has enjoyed almost a monopoly of Base Ball travel in former years, by reason of its quick time and first-class accommodations, first-class implying all possible comfort and elegance in Sleeping Cars, Day Coaches and Smoking Cars, and particularly its sumptuous Dining Cars. It is luxury to eat and fly, which must be experienced in order to be appreciated.

The trains of the Michigan Central pass through Detroit, and run in full view of Niagara Falls. It is the only road that does this, and the only road that runs trains to Niagara Falls, N. Y., and Niagara Falls, Ont. It is the only road under a single management from Chicago to Niagara Falls and Buffalo, and runs Palace Cars through without change between Chicago and Toronto, Buffalo, Syracuse, Albany, Boston and New York. It is not only "**THE NIAGARA FALLS ROUTE**" and the Great East and West Highway, but also the route that insures the greatest degree of comfort and safety, and possesses **THE MOST COMPLETE AND PERFECT THROUGH CAR SERVICE BETWEEN CHICAGO AND THE EAST.**

Information in regard to Rates, Routes, Accommodations, etc., will be furnished by any of the Company's Agents on application.

**O. W. RUGGLES,**
*Gen'l Passenger and Ticket Agent, Chicago.*

**F. I. WHITNEY,**
*Asst. Gen'l Passenger and Ticket Agent, Chicago.*

# CLIFTON HOUSE,

## CHICAGO.

The Proprietors of the CLIFTON would respectfully solicit the patronage of the League and other traveling Base Ball Clubs for the season of 1885. We offer a special rate of

## $2.00 Per Day,

And refer to all the League Clubs for the past three seasons, who have made their home with us, also to Messrs. A. G. SPALDING & BROS., 108 Madison St.

## WOODCOCK & LORING,

PROPRIETORS.

**MIXTURES FOR PIPE OR CIGARETTE.**

THREE KINGS, Turkish, Perique and Virginia.
MELLOW MIXTURE, Turkish and Perique.
TURKISH AND VIRGINIA.
PERIQUE and VIRGINIA.
GENUINE TURKISH.

**FLAKE CUTS, Especially Adapted for the Pipe.**
VANITY FAIR,
——OLD GOLD,——
BLACK AND TAN.

Fragrant Vanity Fair and Cloth of Gold Cigarettes.

*AWARDED 13 FIRST PRIZE MEDALS.*

# WM. S. KIMBALL & CO.,

## SPORTSMEN'S WEAR.

No. A 1 Barnard Canvas Shooting Coat.......................$5.00
No. 1 Barnard Canvas Shooting Coat........................... 4.00
No. 2 Barnard Canvas Shooting Coat........................... 2.50
No 3 Barnard Canvas Shooting Coat........................... 1 75

For sale by all Gun and Sporting Goods Dealers. Ask for them. See that our trade-mark is on the lining. They are the best. Take no other. We also manufacture

**Hats, Caps Leggings, Pants. Vests, Waterproof Horsehide Boots and Shoes, Carryall Bags, Gun Cases, Cartridge Bags, Shell Boxes,**

And every description of Goods used by Sportsmen, made from Canvas, Corduroy and Waterproof Leather. Illustrated Catalogue, Samples and Measurement Blanks sent free upon application.

## GEO. BARNARD & CO.,
### 108 Madison St., CHICAGO, ILL.
Eastern Agency—241 Broadway, NEW YORK.
**F. N. WHITE, Manager.**

―THE LARGEST―

# General Sporting Goods House in the World.

# A. G. Spalding & Bros.,

Manufacturers, Importers, and Wholesale and Retail Dealers in

# General Sporting Goods.

### A FULL LINE OF ALL STANDARD MAKES OF

## Guns, Rifles and Revolvers,

### AMMUNITION, HUNTING CLOTHING,

AND EVERYTHING NECESSARY FOR A

### SPORTSMAN'S COMPLETE OUTFIT.

―ALSO―

## Fishing Tackle of Every Variety.

**Rods, Reels, Lines, Hooks, Baits,**

### AND ALL ARTICLES NECESSARY IN ANGLING.

OUR PRICES GUARANTEED AS LOW AS ANY OTHER REPUTABLE HOUSE IN THE TRADE.

Send for 32-page Illustrated Gun Catalogue, FREE.
Send for 20-page Illustrated Fish Tackle Catalogue, FREE.

### A. G. SPALDING & BROS.,

108 Madison Street,          241 Broadway,
CHICAGO.                     NEW YORK.

# TO BASE BALL PLAYERS.

Nine years ago, the first of March, we issued a notice to Base Ball Players, announcing that we had engaged in the business of furnishing Base Ball Supplies, and soliciting their patronage. That our efforts to furnish satisfactory implements and paraphernalia have met with success, is evidenced by the remarkable increase in our business since that time. Having been for ten years prior to that date intimately identified with the game, we had acquired a practical knowledge of the wants of ball players; and it has always been our aim, instead of flooding the market with cheap, worthless goods that would please the trade, to manufacture and sell articles of genuine merit only, and such as would give the most perfect satisfaction to players. With our practical experience in the game, and being the largest manufacturers of everything that is necessary in the base ball player's outfit, we are now in a position to anticipate the wants of players, and furnish a better grade of goods than any other house in the trade.

Manufacturers who have no reputation to sustain are continually offering inferior goods, which are readily sought after by the average dealers in base ball supplies, who, not being acquainted with the practical wants of players, are apt to regard only the low prices, and not the quality of the goods. It is our constant endeavor to manufacture only the very best goods, and to sell them at fair prices. To illustrate, take one article, Catcher's Masks. We have seen some made by other manufacturers, which, while cheaper than ours in price, were yet so utterly worthless as protectors, that no ball player could afford to take the chance of being disfigured by using them.

As our business is largely by mail, we would urge upon our patrons the importance of writing plainly the names of their town, county and State; and in order to save return express charges on money, to accompany their orders with draft, post-office order, express money order, or currency for the amount due. In all cases where the goods are not satisfactory and exactly as represented by us, they may be returned, and the money will be refunded. We desire to sell all the goods we can, but we wish also to do more than this, and that is to please our customers in every instance. The established reputation of our goods, and the record we have made by the fair and liberal treatment of our customers, is the best guarantee that can be offered for the future.

Our patrons will no doubt be pleased to note that we have established in New York a store fully as large as our Chicago house. We shall carry duplicate and complete lines of Base Ball and all Sporting Goods in either house, and our Eastern customers can now order direct from the New York establishment.

## A. G. SPALDING & BROS.,

108 Madison St.,        241 Broadway,
CHICAGO.        NEW YORK.

# COMPLETE UNIFORMS.

Our facilities for manufacturing Base Ball, Cricket, Lawn Tennis, and all kinds of athletic uniforms are the very best. This department is under the supervision of a practical tailor and shirt cutter, who is an expert in designing and cutting base ball and athletic uniforms. We would urge clubs not to make the mistake of intrusting the making of their uniforms to local dealers, whose experience in this kind of work is necessarily small, but send direct to us, and get a good, cheap, and satisfactory outfit. We make complete base ball uniforms at prices ranging from $5.00 to $30.00 per man. Measurement blanks sent free upon application. Send ten cents for samples of flannel and belt webbing, and receive a handsome engraved fashion plate, showing the different styles and prices. At the following very low prices it is economy to order complete uniforms:

## Prices of Complete Uniforms.

No. 0. League Club outfit consisting of Pants and Shirt of extra heavy flannel, made expressly for our trade. Extra quality Stockings, Cap, Belt, Chicago Club Shoe, Steel Shoe Plates, and Necktie to match trimmings. Price complete, each...................$15.00

No. 1. Outfit, first quality twilled flannel for Pants and Shirts, first quality Cap, best English Web Belt, first quality Stockings, Amateur Shoe, Steel Shoe Plates. Price complete, each............................ 11.00

No. 2. Outfit, second quality twilled flannel (same as most dealers put into their first quality uniform), second quality Cap, English Web Belt, second quality Stockings, Amateur Shoes, malleable iron Shoe Plates. Price complete, each.......................... 9.00

No. 3. Outfit, third quality flannel, third quality Cap, American Web Belt, third quality Stockings, Amateur Shoes, malleable iron Shoe Plates. Price complete, each................................... 7.00

No. 4. Boy's uniform, fourth quality material, consisting of Shirt, Pants, Cap, Belt, Shoes and Shoe Plates complete, each..................................... 5.00

Measurement blanks and Lithographic Fashion Plate showing different styles of uniforms, furnished upon application.

## A. G. SPALDING & BROS.,

108 Madison Street,     241 Broadway,
CHICAGO.     NEW YORK.

# *——SEASON OF 1885——*

# BASE BALL POSTERS,

## WINDOW HANGERS,

## *Colored Score Cards,*

### Again Adopted by the National League and all Principal Associations.

My COLORED SCORE CARDS introduced last season were a great success, and I am making for the coming season EIGHT NEW DESIGNS, which will make a set of twenty-four.

*Inclose 35 Cents in Stamps for Sample Set,*

## JOHN B. SAGE,
### BUFFALO, N. Y.

## SPALDING'S HAND BOOKS.

**The Art of Base Ball Batting,** Containing special chapters on Scientific Batting, Facing for Position, Placing the Ball, Sacrifice Hitting, Waiting for Balls, The Batsman's Position, Standing in Good Form, Fungo Batting, Home Run Hitting, Base Hits and Earned Runs, the New Batting Rules, etc., etc. By HENRY CHADWICK, Base Ball Editor New York Clipper, Author of Routledge's Book of American Sports, and of Hand Books of Games, etc. Chicago and New York: Published by SPALDING BROS., 108 Madison Street Chicago; 241 Broadway, New York.

**The Art of Pitching.** A work containing instructive chapters on all the Latest Points of Play in Base Ball Pitching, including Special Methods of Delivery, the Philosophy of the Curve, the Tactics of a Strategist, Headwork in Pitching, the Effects of Speed, Throwing to Bases, Balking under the New Rules, the New Rules for Pitching and the Application, Battery Work, etc., etc. By HENRY CHADWICK, Base Ball Editor The New York Clipper, Author of Routledge's Book of American Sports, and of Hand Books of Games, etc. PRICE 10 CENTS. Will be ready April 1. A. G. SPALDING & BROS., 241 Broadway, NEW YORK; 108 Madison St., CHICAGO. (Copyright.)

## BASE BALL SHIRTS.

FANCY SHIELD SHIRT.   LACED SHIRT FRONT.

No.
0. Extra quality Shirt, of extra heavy flannel, made expressly for our League Club trade, any style, White, Blue or Gray........... Each. $5 00  Per Doz. $54 00
1. First quality twilled flannel, White, Blue or Red  4 00   42 00
2. Second quality twilled flannel, White, Blue or Gray..............................  3 25   36 00
3. Third quality, Shaker flannel, White only....  2 25   24 00
4. Boys' size only, of fourth quality............  1 50   18 00

TO MEASURE FOR SHIRT.—Size Collar worn. Length of Sleeve, bent, from center of back. Size around Chest. Length of Yoke from shoulder to shoulder.

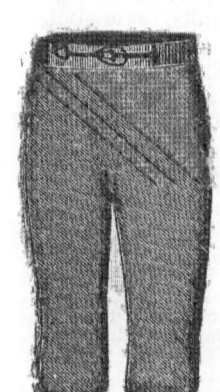

### BASE BALL PANTS.
No.                                         Each.   Dozen.
0. Extra quality flannel Pants, White, Blue or Gray.......$5 00  $54 00
1. First quality twilled flannel, White, Blue or Red.......  4 00   42 00
2. Second quality twilled flannel, White, Blue or Gray........  3 25   36 00
3. Third quality, Shaker flannel, White only..............  2 25   24 00

TO MEASURE FOR PANTS.—Size around waist. Length of outside seam from waist to eight inches below the knee (for full length pants measure to the foot). Length of inside seam. Size around hips.

## A. G. SPALDING & BROS.,

108 Madison Street,            241 Broadway,
CHICAGO.                       NEW YORK.

# Base Ball Shoes.

No. 1.                                    No. 2.

No. 1. **League Club Shoe.** Same as used by League Clubs. Made Horsehide in the best manner. Price per pair............ $6.00
No. 2. **Chicago Club Shoe.** Extra quality canvas, foxed with French calf. The Standard Screw Fastener is used. Price per pair. 4.00

No. 3.                                    No. 4.

No. 3. **Amateur, or Practice Shoe.** Good quality canvas, strap over instep. Price per pair.................... ......... $2 00
No. 3X. **Amateur Base Ball Shoe for Boys.** Second quality canvas. Price per pair.................................. ............ 1 50
No. 4. **Oxford Tie Base Ball Shoe.** Low cut, canvas. Price per pair 2 00

## SPALDING'S SHOE PLATES.

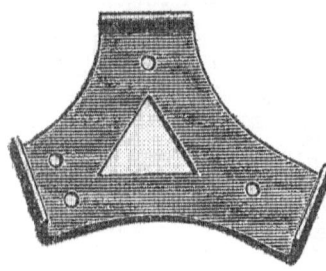

Our new design League Steel Shoe Plate has become the favorite plate among League players during the past season, and we have this year added it to our regular line of shoe plates. It is made by hand of the best quality English steel, and so tempered that it will not bend or break. The peculiar shape of the plate is shown in the adjoining cut. The majority of League players use this plate on the toe, and our No. 1, or Professional Plate, on the heel. Each pair of plates—right and left—are put up with screws.

                                        Per    Per
                                          Pair. Doz.

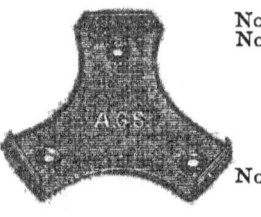

No. 0. Spalding's League Shoe Plate, $ 50 $5 00
No. 1. **Spalding's Professional Shoe Plate,** as shown in the adjoining cut, is made of first quality steel. It is lighter and smaller than the No. 0 plate, but will render good service. Each pair put up with screws, complete.................  25  2 50
No. 2. **Spalding's Malleable Iron Shoe Plate,** light and durable, with screws........................ 15  1 50

Any of the above Shoe Plates mailed upon receipt of price. Address

## A. G. SPALDING & BROS.,

108 Madison Street,                    241 Broadway,
     CHICAGO.                                   NEW YORK.

## BASE BALL CAPS AND HATS.

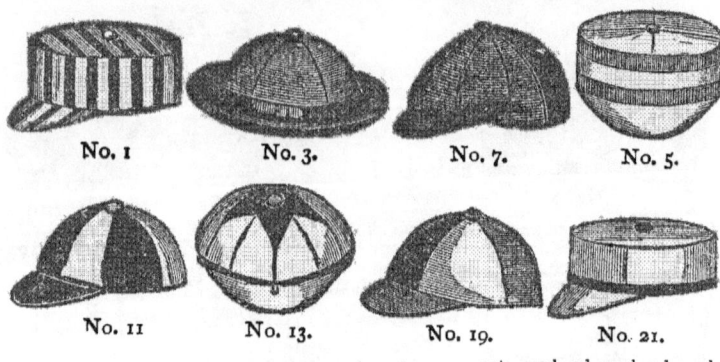

No. 1  No. 3  No. 7  No. 5
No. 11  No. 13  No. 19  No. 21

|  |  | 1st. qual. | 2d qual. | 3d qual. |
|---|---|---|---|---|
| No. 1. | League Parti-colored Cap | $12 00 | .... | .... |
| No. 3. | Base Ball Hat, any color | 18 00 | 15 00 | .... |
| No. 5. | Base Ball Cap, Chicago style, any color, with or without stripes | 9 00 | .... | .... |
| No. 7. | Base Ball Cap, Boston shape, without star, any colors | 9 00 | 7 50 | 6 00 |
| No. 7. | Ditto, all white only | 9 00 | 7 50 | 6 00 |
| No. 11. | Base Ball Cap, Jockey shape, any color | 9 00 | 7 50 | 6 00 |
| No. 11. | Ditto, all white only | 9 00 | 7 50 | 6 00 |
| No. 13. | Base Ball Cap, Boston shape, with star | 9 00 | 7 50 | 6 00 |
| No. 19. | Base Ball Skull Cap, any color | 9 00 | 7 50 | 6 00 |
| No. 19. | Ditto, white only | 9 00 | 7 50 | 6 00 |
| No. 21. | College Base Ball Cap, any color | 9 00 | 7 50 | 6 00 |
| No. 21. | Ditto, white only | 9 00 | 7 50 | 6 00 |

Boys' Flannel Caps, per dozen................................. $4 00
" Cotton Caps, Red, White, or Blue...................... 3 00

In addition to the styles above mentioned, we are prepared to make any style of Cap known, and will furnish at prices corresponding to above.

## BAT BAGS.

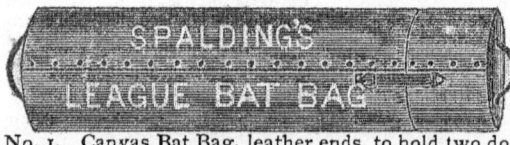

No. 0. League Club Bat Bag, made of sole leather, with name outside, to hold two dozen bats. Each .............. $15 00
No. 1. Canvas Bat Bag, leather ends, to hold two dozen bats......... $5 00
No. 2. Canvas Bat Bag, leather ends, to hold one dozen bats......... 4 00
No. 01. Spalding's new design, individual, sole leather Bat Bag for two bats, as used by the players of the Chicago club.....each, 4 00
No. 02. Same size and style as above, made of strong canvas... " 1 50

## BASES.

No. 0. League Club Bases, made of extra canvas, stuffed and quilted complete, with straps and spikes, without home plate....Per set of three $7 50
No. 1. Canvas Bases, with straps and spikes, complete without home plate................................. 5 00
Marble Home plate................................. 3 00
Iron " " ............................ 1 00

## A. G. SPALDING & BROS.,

108 Madison Street,     241 Broadway,
CHICAGO.     NEW YORK.

## SPALDING'S BASE BALL BELTS—Worsted Web Belts.

Our No. 0, or League Club Belt is made of best Worsted Webbing, 2¼ inches wide, mounted in best manner, with large nickel plated buckle, the finest belt made. Our No. 1 belt is made of same webbing, leather mounted. We use the following colors of webbing. In ordering, please state the color wanted, and size around waist.

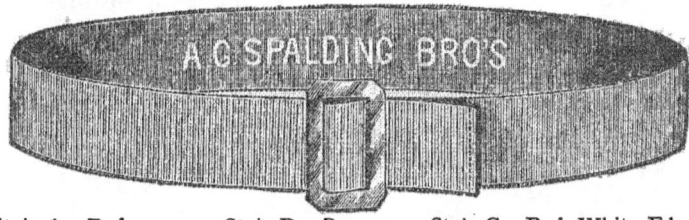

Style A. Red.           Style D. Brown.        Style G. Red, White Edge.
"     B. Blue.          "     E. Black.        "     H. Blue,    "
"     C. Navy Blue.     "     F. White.

No. 0.  League Club Belt, of any of the above colors, nickel plated buckle as shown in above cut. Per Dozen.................. $6.00

No. 1. Worsted Web Belt, same colors as above, mounted in leather, with two broad straps and buckles as shown in above cut.
Per doz................................................................. $4.50

### SPALDING'S COTTON WEB BELTS.

Our Cotton Web Belts are made of best quality Cotton Webbing, in the following fast colors. In ordering please state color, and size around waist.

Style L. Red.          Style O. Blue, White    Style R. Red and White,
                                Edge.                   Narrow Stripe.
"     M. Blue.         "     P. Red, White     "     S. Blue and White,
                                and Blue.               Narrow Stripe.
"     N. Red, White    "     Q. White.         "     T. Yellow & Black,
         Edge.                                          Wide Stripe.

No. 3. Cotton Web Belts, any of above colors, large patent nickel. plated buckle. Per dozen................................................ $4.00
No. 4. Cotton Web, Leather Mounted........................Per doz.$2.50

### SPALDING'S BASE BALL STOCKINGS.   PER DOZ.

No. 0. League Regulation, made of the finest worsted yarn. The following colors can be obtained: White, Light Blue, Navy Blue, Scarlet, Gray, Green, Old Gold, Brown...................$18.00
No. 1. Fine Quality Woolen Stockings, Scarlet, Blue or Brown.... 12.00
No. 2. Good      "      "      "      "      "      "     .... 9.00
No. 3. Second   "      "      "      "      or Blue, with White or drab cotton feet............................................. 6.00

## A. G. SPALDING & BROS.,
### 108 Madison Street,            241 Broadway,
### CHICAGO.                        NEW YORK.

## Spalding's Trade-Marked Catcher's Mask.

The first Catcher's Mask brought out in 1875, was a very heavy, clumsy affair, and it was not until we invented our open-eyed mask in 1877 that it came into general use. Now it would be considered unsafe and even dangerous for a catcher to face the swift underhand throwing of the present day unless protected by a reliable mask. The increased demand for these goods has brought manufacturers into the field who, having no reputation to sustain, have vied with each other to see how *cheap* they could make a so-called mask, and in consequence have ignored the essential qualification, *strength*. A cheaply made, inferior quality of mask is much worse than no protection at all, for a broken wire or one that will not stand the force of the ball without caving in, is liable to disfigure a player for life. We would warn catchers not to trust their faces behind one of these *cheap* made masks. Our trade-marked masks are made of the very best hard wire, plated to prevent rusting, and well trimmed, and every one is a thorough face protector. We shall make them in three grades as described below, and with our increased facilities for manufacturing, are enabled to improve the quality, and at the same time reduce the price.

Beware of counterfeits. *None genuine without our Trade Mark stamped on each Mask.*

| | | Each. |
|---|---|---|
| No. 0. | SPALDING'S SPECIAL LEAGUE MASK, used by all the leading professional catchers, extra heavy wire, well padded with goat hair and the padding faced with the best imported dogskin, which is impervious to perspiration and retains its pliability and softness................... | $3 00 |
| No. 2. | SPALDING'S AMATEUR MASK, made the same size and general style as the League Mask, but with lighter wire and faced with leather, (we guarantee this mask to be superior to so-called professional Masks sold by other manufacturers)............................... | 2 00 |
| No. 3. | SPALDING'S BOY'S MASK, similar to the Amateur Mask, only made smaller to fit a boy's face................................. | 1 75 |

☞ Any of these Masks mailed postpaid on receipt of price.

## Spalding's Trade-Marked Catcher's Gloves.

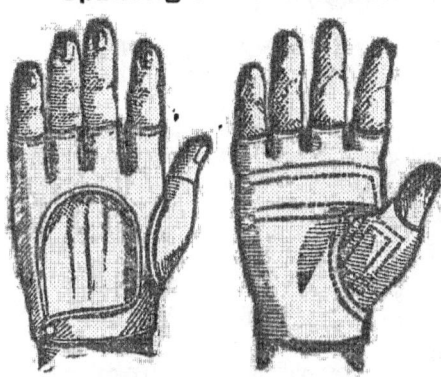

After considerable expense and many experiments we have finally perfected a Catcher's Glove that meets with general favor from professional catchers.

The old style of open backed gloves introduced by us several years ago is still adhered to, but the quality of material and workmanship has been materially improved, until now we can lay claim to having the best line of catcher's gloves on the market. These gloves do not interfere with throwing, can be easily put on and taken off, and no player subject to sore hands should be without a pair of these gloves. We make these gloves in four different grades, as follows:

Price per Pair.

No. 00. SPALDING'S FULL LEFT-HAND CATCHER'S GLOVES, made of extra heavy Indian tanned buck, with full left-hand, usual style right hand, open backs and well padded, fully warranted. Best catcher's glove made........... $3 50

No 0. SPALDING'S LEAGUE CLUB CATCHER'S GLOVES, made of extra heavy Indian tanned buck, and carefully selected with special reference to the hard service required of them, open back, well padded, and fully warranted................ 2 50

No. 1. SPALDING'S PROFESSIONAL GLOVES, made of Indian tanned buckskin, open back, well padded, but not quite as heavy material as the No. 0 .................................... 2 00

No. 2. SPALDING'S AMATEUR GLOVES, made of lighter buckskin, open back, well padded and adapted for amateur players ...................... 1 50

No. 3. SPALDING'S PRACTICE GLOVES, made of light material, open back, well padded............ 1 00

No. 4. SPALDING'S BOY'S GLOVES, open back, well padded, and made only in boy's sizes......... 1 00

☞ Any of the above Gloves mailed postpaid on receipt of price. In ordering, please give size of ordinary dress gloves usually worn.

## A. G. SPALDING & BROS.,

108 Madison Street,  
CHICAGO.

241 Broadway,  
NEW YORK.

# MORTON'S
# PERFECT SUPPORTER.

The best fitting, most comfortable and effective supporter yet devised. Made of best quality canton flannel, with laced front, cool and pleasant to wear. Prices each, 75 cents.

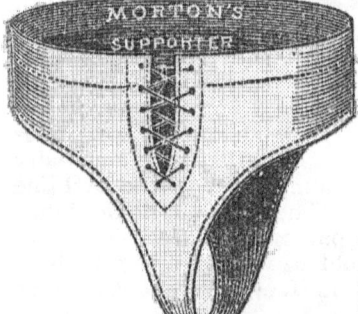

———o———

## GUTH'S
## Improved Supporter,

Well known to Professional Ball Players. Price, Chamois Skin, $1.00.

## SPALDING'S AUTOMATIC UMPIRE INDICATOR.

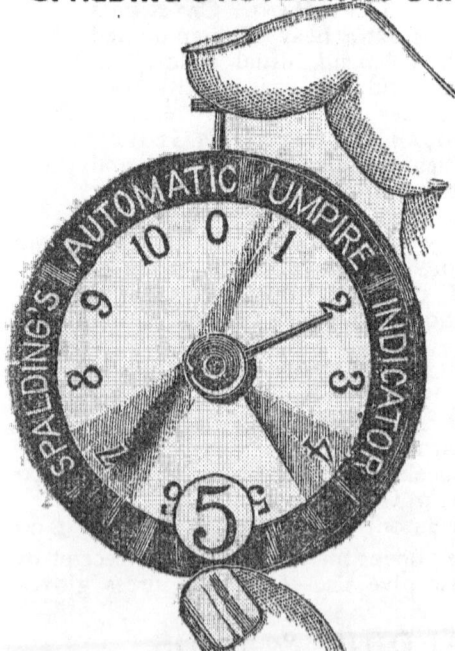

As the name implies, this little apparatus is intended for umpires of base ball matches, and is the best thing of the kind ever brought out; in fact, it is the only really practical umpire's indicator, or guide, on the market. The illustration, which represents the exact size of the indicator, gives a good idea of its construction and mode of handling. By touching the spring at the top of the indicator the number of balls called from 1 to 6 or 7 are registered, and so remain until the spring is touched again. The index hand upon the dial serves to record the number of strikes on the batter. It works automatically, and can be carried in the palm of the hand unobserved by the spectators. It is recommended and is in general use by all the prominent League and Association umpires. It is neatly packed in a pasteboard box, and will be mailed to any address upon receipt of price. **Price, 50 Cents.**

## A. G. SPALDING & BROS.,

108 Madison Street,  
CHICAGO.

241 Broadway,  
NEW YORK.

# BRIGHT'S AUTOMATIC REGISTERING TURN STILE.

Is acknowledged to be the most reliable, durable and simple Turn Stile made. It is designed especially for Base Ball and Fair Grounds, Expositions, etc., and is an almost indispensable assistant in making a correct division of receipts and avoiding all possibility of the gate-keeper's appropriating any portion of them, by accurately counting and registering each person passing through it.

The movement registers from 1 to 10,000, and can easily and almost instantly be reversed to zero by any person having the key, without the necessity of removing from the Stile to which it is securely attached and locked. It is provided with all necessary stops, etc., to prevent its getting out of order through being handled by meddlesome persons, and is shipped complete and in readiness to be placed beside a doorway or other suitable entrance to inclosure, either permanent or temporary, and used without delay.

They have been in use during the past season by the Cleveland and Philadelphia League Clubs and by all of the Clubs of the N. W. League, without an instance of failure or dissatisfaction, but have since been greatly improved by the addition of several valuable features, making it unquestionably the best adapted and most durable Turn Stile in the market.

Orders from Base Ball Clubs should be sent in as early as possible, insuring their being filled before the beginning of the season.

Price complete......................................................$50 00

## GRAND STAND CUSHIONS FOR BASE BALL GROUNDS.

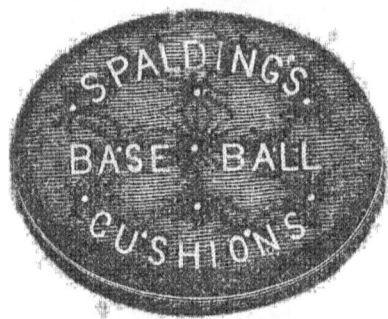

The Chicago Club have for several seasons furnished cushions to ther patrons at a nominal rental of 5 cents per game. It is a feature highly appreciated by base ball spectators. We are now manufacturing these cushions, and can supply them to clubs at 50 cents each. Special prices made when ordered in hundred lots.

### A. G. SPALDING & BROS.,

108 Madison Street,      241 Broadway,
CHICAGO.      NEW YORK.

# Gray's Patent Body Protector.

The most useful device ever invented for the protection of catchers or umpires, and renders it impossible for the catcher to be injured while playing close to the batter. Made very light and pliable, and does not interfere in any way with the movements of the wearer, either in running, stooping or throwing. No catcher should be without one of these protectors.

Price,............each, $10.00.

## The Reach Ball.

Frequent calls for the Reach Ball and the Reach Red Band Bat, during the past season, has warranted us in carrying a stock of these goods.

Players and dealers throughout the country will find a full line of these Balls and Bats, and all other standard articles required by ball players (of our own make or other manufacturers), at either the New York or Chicago stores.

## Reach's Association Ball.

Highly indorsed by professional and amateur players as a first-class ball.

Price, each,..........$1.25. | Per doz.............$13.50.

## Reach's Red Band Bats.

Made from well seasoned, straight-grained wood; well polished and finished. A professional bat of excellent quality.

Price, each,.........$ .50. | Per doz.............$5.00.

## A. G. SPALDING & BROS.,

241 Broadway,     108 Madison Street,
NEW YORK.     CHICAGO.

# SPALDING'S SCORE BOOK.

Spalding's new design Pocket and Club Score Book continues to be the popular score book, and is used by all the leading scorers and base ball reporters. They are adapted for the spectator of ball games, who scores for his own amusement, as well as the official club scorer, who records the minutest detail. By this new system, the art of scoring can be acquired in a single game.

Full instructions, with the latest League rules, accompany each book.

## WHAT AUTHORITIES SAY OF IT.

Messrs. A. G. SPALDING & BROS., Chicago, Ill.

Gentlemen:—I have carefully examined the Spalding Score Book, and, without any hesitation, I cheerfully recommend it as the most complete system of scoring of which I have any knowledge.

Respectfully,
N. E. YOUNG, Official Scorer Nat'l League P. B. B. Clubs.

---

The new system of score books just issued by A. G. Spalding & Bros. of Chicago, are the neatest thing of the kind we ever saw. Every lover of the game should have one. They are simple in their construction, and are easily understood.—*Cincinnati Enquirer.*

THE TRIBUNE has received from A. G. Spalding & Bros., 108 Madison Street, a copy of their new score book for use this year. The book or system is so far in advance of anything ever brought out in the way of simplicity, convenience and accuracy, that it seems wonderful that it was not thought of years ago. The new style will be in universal use before the season is half through.—*Chicago Tribune.*

A. G. Spalding, Captain of the Chicago White Stockings, has just brought out a new score book, which will meet with the unqualified indorsement of everybody who has ever undertaken to score a game of base ball. They are of various sizes, to meet the requirements both of the spectator who scores simply for his own satisfaction, and for official scores of clubs. The novel and commending feature of the book is the manner in which each of the squares opposite the name of the player is utilized by a division which originated with Mr. Spalding. Each of these squares is divided into five spaces by a diamond in its center, from the points of which lines extend to each of the four sides of the square. Each of these spaces is designed for the use of the scorer according to marks and signs given in the book. By thus dividing the squares into spaces he scores without the liability to make mistakes. The League rules of scoring are printed in the book.—*N. Y. Clipper.*

### PRICES:
#### POCKET.

|  |  | EACH. |
|---|---|---|
| No. 1. Paper Cover, 7 games | | $ .10 |
| No. 2. Board Cover, 22 games | | .25 |
| No. 3. Board Cover, 46 games | | .50 |
| Score Cards | | .05 |

#### CLUB BOOKS.

| No. 4. | Large Size, | 30 games | $1.00 |
| No. 5. | Large " | 60 games | 1.75 |
| No. 6. | Large " | 90 games | 2.50 |
| No. 7. | Large " | 120 games | 3.00 |

Mailed upon receipt of price.

## A. G. SPALDING & BROS.,

108 Madison Street,　　　　　　　241 Broadway,
　　CHICAGO.　　　　　　　　　　　NEW YORK.

# SPALDING'S
# Trade Marked Bats.

Probably no class of Sportsmen are more particular about their weapons than a professional ball player is about his bat, for it is a recognized fact, that no player can excel as a batsman, unless he uses a frst-class, well-proportioned, thoroughly seasoned bat. A cheap, poor bat is worthless at any price. Recognizing that ball players would appreciate a good article, and would willingly stand the slight additional expense, about six years ago we introduced "Spalding's Trade Marked Bats," and they proved so popular, and were so far ahead of anything else ever put upon the market, that for a time it seemed impossible to keep up with the demand. We have improved these bats from year to year, until now they are the bat *par excellence*, and are used by every prominent professional player in America.

We can, if desired, furnish testimonials from every one of the leading batters of the country, and as to the general merits of these bats, we can refer to any professional or amateur player in the United States.

## Beware of Cheap Imitations which Flood the Market.

### None Genuine without our Trade-Mark Plainly Stamped on Each Bat.

These Bats are used exclusively by the following champion batters, who consider them superior to any bats in use.

James O'Rourke, champion of 1884.
Dennis Brouthers, champion of 1882 and 1883.
A. C. Anson, champion of 1879 and 1881.
Geo. F. Gore, champion 1880.
A. Dalrymple, champion of 1878.
Jas. White, champion of 1877.

### *A. G. SPALDING & BROS.,*

241 Broadway,  
NEW YORK.

108 Madison Street,  
CHICAGO.

# SPALDING'S TRADE-MARKED BATS.

These celebrated bats were first introduced in 1877, and they gradually grown into popularity, until now they are used exclusively by all prominent professional and amateur. All the timber used in these bats is allowed to season for two years in the sun before being made up, and the res[t] enabled to make much lighter and stronger bats than where [it] is hastily "kiln-dried," as done by nearly all manufacturers of ch[eap] goods. Each bat is turned by hand, after the most approved and varied models, and if found to answer the requirements as to weight, size, length, etc., the *trade-mark* is stamped on each bat to insure its genuineness. We point with much pride to the handsome testimonials given these bats by the leading batters of the country, as shown by their universal and continued use.

## PRICES.

**SPALDING'S TRADE MARKED BATS.**

|  |  |  | Each. | To Clubs. Per doz. |
|---|---|---|---|---|
| No. 00. | Spalding's 2d Growth Ash, Black Band League Bat, Patent Granulated Handle.................. | | 75c | $8 00 |
| " 0. | Spalding's 2d Growth Ash, Black Band, League Bat, Plain Handle.......... | | 75c | 7 50 |
| " 1. | Spalding's Trade Marked Ash Bat..... | | 40c | 4 00 |
| " 2. | "   "   " Cherry Bat.. | | 40c | 4 00 |
| " 3. | "   "   " Bass " .. | | 30c | 3 50 |
| " 4. | "   "   " Willow " .. | | 50c | 5 00 |
| " 1B. | " Boy's " " Ash " .. | | 30c | 3 00 |
| " 3B. | "   "   " Bass " .. | | 25c | 2 50 |

**SPALDING'S TRADE MARKED FANCY BATS.**

| No. A. | Spalding's Fancy Ash, Full Polished.. | 60c | $6 00 |
|---|---|---|---|
| " AA. | "   "   "   " and Patent Granulated Handle........... | 75c | 6 50 |
| " B. | Spalding's Fancy Bass, Full Polished.. | 60c | 6 00 |
| " BB. | "   "   "   " and Patent Granulated Handle........... | 75c | 6 50 |

**PLAIN FINISHED BATS.**

| No. 6. | Men's Ash Bats, plain finish, 36 to 40 in.. | 25c | $2 50 |
|---|---|---|---|
| " 7. | " Bass " " 36 to 40 in.. | 20c | 2 00 |
| " 8. | Boy's Ash " " 28 to 34 in.. | 15c | 1 50 |
| " 9. | " Bass " " 28 to 34 in.. | 15c | 1 50 |

**FANCY BATS.**

| No. 10. | Cherry Bats, oiled, selected timber..... | 25c | $2 50 |
|---|---|---|---|
| " 11. | Ash Bats, one-half polished............. | 30c | 3 00 |
| " 12. | Bass Bats, one-half polished............ | 30c | 3 00 |
| " 13. | Ash Bats, full polished................. | 50c | 5 00 |
| " 14. | Bass Bats, full polished................ | 50c | 5 00 |
| " 15. | Ash Bats, wound handles, plain......... | 50c | 5 00 |
| No. 16. | Bass Bats, wound handles, plain........ | 50c | 5 00 |
| " 17. | Ash Bats, wound handles, highly polished...... | 60c | 6 00 |
| " 18. | Bass Bats, wound handles, highly polished..... | 60c | 6 00 |

Save express charges by sending money with order, that we may send by freight.

## A. G. SPALDING & BROS.,

241 Broadway,            108 Madison Street,
NEW YORK.                 CHICAGO.

www.ingramcontent.com/pod-product-compliance
Lightning Source LLC
Chambersburg PA
CBHW020302170426
43202CB00008B/466